The Ultimate Router Guide

Jigs, Joinery, Projects & More from *Popular Woodworking*

Edited by David Thiel

POPULAR WOODWORKING BOOKS
CINCINNATI, OHIO
www.popularwoodworking.com

22

Contents

68

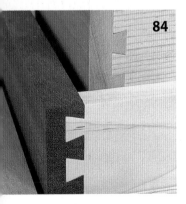

84

104

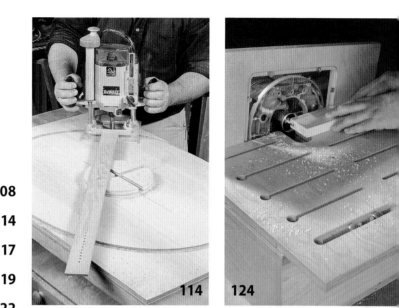

Introduction

I LOVE ROUTERS. In fact, as I'm writing this I can hear the high-pitched whine of a 2 hp router bearing into the edge of a piece of wood begging to be formed. Okay, I love most things about routers. They are a little noisy, and they do make dust, but I see those as necessary by-products of an incredibly versatile workhorse that will always have a home in my shop.

From edge treatments, to joinery, to inlay, to cleaning up rough cuts and in some cases using them as a jointer or planer, the router can do almost everything in the shop. They come in a wonderful array of styles and sizes, and I honestly feel that a shop with less than three routers is woefully handicapped.

This book is a collection of some of the best information on routers ever published in *Popular Woodworking Magazine*. Starting with a terrific primer on all things router by Nick Engler, you'll learn how to choose the right router for each specific job, then learn all about bits, maintenance, applications and, well … everything you need to know.

Then we've collected some great articles on joinery that is specifically created using a router, with pros, cons and variations that will teach and also make you think about other ways to put the router to work in your shop.

To follow that section we have router jigs to make using routers easier … and expand the useful horizons of these wonderful machines. And lest we forget what may be the best of all router attachments, we've included a section on using routers in tables. Even more variation!

To round things out we've added a few woodworking projects that put the router to work in all applications.

Whether it's a small trimmer that fits snuggly in the palm of one hand (offering terrific control) or a 3hp monster mounted in a router table creating cope-and-stick joinery for an entry door, routers are amazing tools!

If this is your first introduction to the router, I hope you'll find it as amazing a tool as I do. And if you're already familiar with routers, I hope you'll find ways to expand their use in your woodworking.

David Thiel
Editor

Fixed-base Router

by Nick Engler

The router is perhaps the most versatile tool in your shop. You can rout not only decorative shapes, but also many joints.

Reduced to its simplest form, the router is a motor and a shaft with means of holding interchangeable bits. Once you understand that, using the router becomes a much simpler task. But first, you should know what all those other parts are, and why they're there.

Types of Routers

When you look for a portable router, you will find that they can generally be classified into four categories:

The Basic Router: Sometimes called a fixed-base router, this is just a motor mounted on a base. Most offer ½- to 1½-horsepower motors, and their collets will accept router bits with ¼"

or ½" shanks. The bases are usually 6" in diameter. This is the router we will be discussing here.

The Laminate Trimmer: A scaled-down version of the basic router, this has a smaller motor and base. It has a ¼" collet and is used for trimming laminates and veneers, and is especially handy when you are balancing the tool on thin or narrow workpieces. It's also useful for chores that require finesse, as opposed to strength. Some laminate trimmers come with interchangeable bases that let you work in tight areas or will allow you to rout at an angle, which no full-size router can.

The Rotary Tool: This lets you use very small bits and accessories for

more delicate work. It's a carving or engraving tool (such as a Dremel) that can be mounted in a router base accessory. It usually has interchangeable collets for ¹⁄₁₆" or ⅛" shanks. The small size lets you rout inlays, cut mortises for small hardware, make delicate joints or do other jobs where a standard-size router would be too clumsy or difficult to balance.

The Plunge Router: This does all the things that the basic router can do, plus it makes "plunge cuts." Its motor is mounted on two spring-loaded slides above the base, which let you position the motor above the work, push the bit into the wood and begin cutting. The plunge router excels at cutting joints, such as mortises.

PRO TIP

Back-routing (climb-cutting)
Occasionally you must back-rout a piece to reduce tear-out on figured wood. This means you cut with the bit's rotation, instead of against it. It's much more difficult to control your work this way, so be sure to take shallow cuts and feed very slowly. Keep the router and the work steady, making sure you don't let the bit chatter.

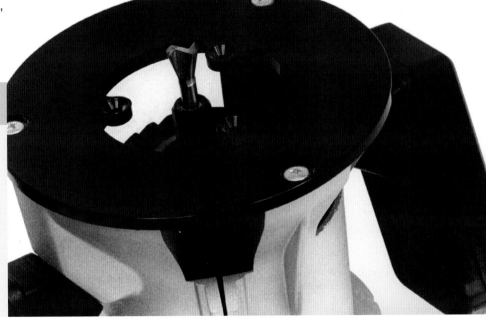

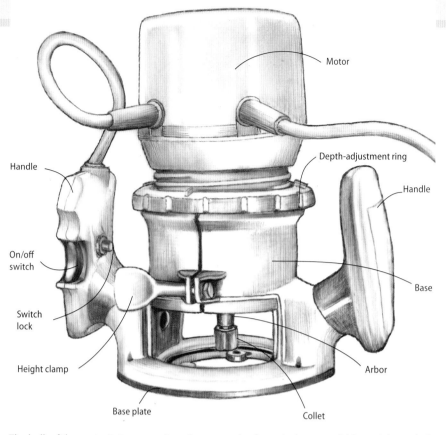

Motor

Depth-adjustment ring

Handle

Handle

Base

On/off switch

Switch lock

Height clamp

Arbor

Base plate

Collet

ILLUSTRATION BY MARY JANE FAVORITE; PHOTO COURTESY OF PATRICK WARNER, PATWARNER.COM

The bulk of the router is its **motor**. An **arbor** protrudes from the bottom of this, and the end of the arbor is fitted with a **collet** to hold a bit in place. These three pieces are mounted in a **base**, which incorporates a **depth-adjustment ring** to raise or lower the motor, and a **height clamp** to secure it in position – these clamps differ for the plunge router, as you'll see in the next chapter. A router also has **handles** so it can be guided, with a nearby **on/off switch**. This entire assembly rests on a removable plastic **base plate** or sole.

Router Features and Capabilities

No matter what kind of router you opt for, there are several features you need to understand that are important in the operation of the tool:

Collet: Although it might seem small and insignificant, the collet is crucial – a poorly designed one might let the bit slip, ruining the cut. To compensate, many woodworkers overtighten the collet, which only aggravates the problem. Overtightening makes the bits hard to mount and dismount, and can cause excessive wear on your tool.

To avoid this, make sure you get a router with a good collet. You can judge if a collet will give you problems by learning how it works. A collet is a split or segmented collar at the end of the arbor that holds the shank of the bit. Tightening a nut squeezes the collar around the shank, locking the bit.

Generally, the more segments on a collet the better, because these make the collet more flexible so it can get a better grip on the bit shank, as you can see in the drawing at right. Routers with multiple-segment collets tend to be a bit more expensive, but the potential headaches they eliminate are well worth it.

Some routers have split arbors, rather than collets. Either way, the same rule applies: the more segments, the better.

Collets come in three standard sizes – ¼", ⅜" and ½", which is the measure of the inside diameter. Most router bits have ¼" and ½" shanks. If you want to take full advantage of all

The Need for Speed

Despite a popular misconception, speed controllers will not harm universal motors (the type of motor found in all routers and most hand-held power tools). However, they can ruin induction motors. If you buy an in-line speed controller, be sure you use it for your portable power tools only.

A Better Bit Goes a Long Way

You should put as much, if not more, care and consideration into choosing bits as you would the machines that run them. After all, it's not the router that does the actual cutting – it's the bit. A mediocre router outfitted with a better-than-normal bit will cut a lot better than the world's greatest router with a mediocre bit.

Offset Baseplates Keep Your Router from Tipping Over

Even with half of the router base in contact with the wood surface, it can be difficult to keep the tool from tipping. When you must hang the router over an edge, as when routing an edge detail, make sure you attach an offset baseplate to the router's base. Keep the offset portion of the plate over a solid surface and press down on it as you work, thereby steadying the tool.

the bits available, you should look for a router with interchangeable collets.

Some routers have only ½" collets, but come with split bushing so you can adapt them to hold ¼" and ⅜" bits. This is OK, but not as desirable as interchangeable collets.

Power: The type of woodworking you want to do with the router will determine the horsepower you need. If you just want to make a few occasional mouldings and joints, a 1-horsepower router should be more than sufficient. On the other hand, if you expect to do a lot of routing or if you want to use bits with large flute diameters, you should look at 2- or 3-horsepower models.

Speed: Most single-speed routers operate between 20,000 and 30,000 rpm. This is adequate for bits with flute diameters of 2" or less. But larger bits should run at slower speeds; otherwise they'll overheat and burn the wood.

If you intend to use large bits often, it might be wise to invest in a variable-speed tool or a method of altering the speed, such as a rheostat or an electronic speed controller. Rheostats reduce the line voltage, which lowers both the speed and the available torque – the ability of your router to do serious work. Electronic speed controllers, on the other hand, have a feedback mechanism that boosts the available torque at low speeds, which means the tool is less likely to quit when the going gets tough.

Height Adjustment: Most basic routers can be raised or lowered up to 2". If you think you'll need more movement than this, you'll want to look at the plunge router. But whichever router you choose, consider the ease and accuracy with which you can change the height. Because you'll be changing the height quite often, you'll want to make it as easy as possible on yourself.

On some basic routers, the motor housings are threaded in the base so you can screw them up or down. This allows you to make minute height changes accurately. But in some respects, this arrangement is a pain in the neck. Because some on/off switches revolve with the motor, you never quite know where the switch is. And if you mount the router to a table or a stationary jig, the cord can quickly become twisted.

Switches mounted on handles or heights that adjust without spinning the motor remove this concern.

Configuration: For this, you just have to ask yourself how the router feels to you:

Is it too heavy or too light when you are holding it and working with it?

Can you reach all the controls without taking your hands off the handles?

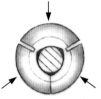

Three segments - three contact points

Multiple segments - many contact points

Collets with just 2-3 segments (left) don't squeeze router bit shanks evenly. In fact, they make contact at just a few points. Collets with multiple segments (right) are more flexible and make contact all the way around the shank, which helps keep the bit from slipping.

Router bases come in a variety of sizes and shapes. The round base found on many basic routers (left) is useful for most operations, but may be slightly inaccurate when following a straightedge. If the base isn't perfectly round or perfectly centered on the router bit, turning the base (riding against the straightedge) during operation can change the distance from the bit. The D-shaped plunge router base (middle) has one straight side so you can accurately follow both straight and curved templates without concern of changing the distance to the bit. The laminate trimmer (right) has a square base with rounded corners, so you can follow straight and curved templates no matter how you turn it. You can buy an accessory base for the fixed-base router that has a straightedge, too.

The shank of the bit must be inserted far enough into the collet for the collet to get a solid grip. If possible, the entire length of the collet should contact the shank. However, don't insert the bit so far that the collet closes around the transition fillet – the portion of the bit where the shank ends and the flutes begin. If the bit is positioned incorrectly – inserted either too far or not enough – the collet may not grip the shank securely and the bit may creep out of the collet when you rout.

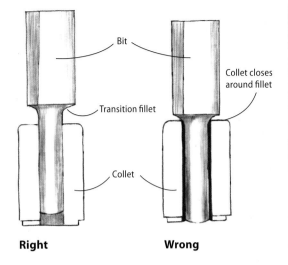

Bit

Transition fillet

Collet closes around fillet

Collet

Right   **Wrong**

Is it well-balanced or does it seem top-heavy and ready to tip?

Routing Rules

The first step in using any tool is to make sure it is properly aligned and adjusted.

For the router, there are only two things you need to check. If you're using it as a portable tool, check the depth of cut (the distance the bit protrudes beneath the sole) and the position of the guide (if there is one). If your router is mounted in a jig, check the depth of cut (the distance the bit protrudes past the mounting plate) and the position of the fence (if there is one).

Once you've adjusted your router, you'll need to keep a couple of things in mind as you work:

• Before you turn the router on, make sure the bit is properly mounted and the collet is secure. When changing the bits, know that you might have to clean dust out of the collet. A dirty collet won't grip router bit shanks as well.

• Make several test cuts to check your setup; if a job requires several different setups, make sure you have enough test pieces at each subsequent stage to carry you through the entire procedure.

• Remove only a small amount of stock with any single pass. Set your

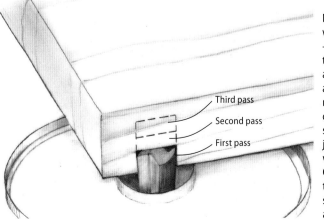

Third pass

Second pass

First pass

Never "hog" the cut when using a router – the tool is designed to remove only small amounts of stock at any one time. If you need to make a deep cut, rout your piece in several passes, cutting just ⅛" to ¼" deeper with each pass. Generally, the harder the wood, the less you should remove with any one pass.

Tear-out on
scrap wood

If your project requires you to rout across the end grain, clamp a scrap to the edge of the board where the bit will exit. This will prevent splintering and tear-out. If routing all four edges of a board, start with a cross-grain edge so the long-grain pass will remove any tear-out.

depth of cut to take shallow cuts, usually ⅛" or ¼" deep. The illustration below explains this concept in more detail.

• Keep the router moving as steadily as you can while you cut. If you pause in the middle or move too slowly, friction will cause the bit to heat up and burn the wood. However, if you feed the router too quickly, it will leave scallops or mill marks in your piece.

• Cut against the rotation of the bit whenever possible, as shown in the drawing at right. If you use a fence or a straightedge, use the rota-

tion to help keep the work (or the router) against it.

• Take note of the wood grain direction and rout with the grain as much as possible. When you must rout across the grain, back up the wood where the bit will exit. This prevents the bit from tearing and chipping the wood.

Guiding the Router

In addition to those rules, here are some extra tips on guiding the router. You can use these whether you're routing hand-held or with a jig:

• Always hold the router firmly with both hands. Be prepared for the initial jerk when you start it up – that annoying momentary wrench can be difficult to control on some of the more-powerful routers. You may want to buy a router with a "soft-start" motor to eliminate this unnerving tendency – but we think that once you start using your router more often, you'll get used to this and become more comfortable.

• A router motor, like any other spinning body, generates lots of centrifugal force, which is the force that draws a rotating body away from the center of rotation, caused by the inertia of the body. Because of this, your router will resist any effort to cut in a straight line. As you push it along, it will want to drift to one side or the other, so you have to exert some force against your guide or edge to keep it tracking correctly.

• Make sure the router base is properly supported. When used hand-held, routers are top-heavy. If the workpiece is too narrow, it may be hard to balance the router. A good tip to help you with this is to clamp a

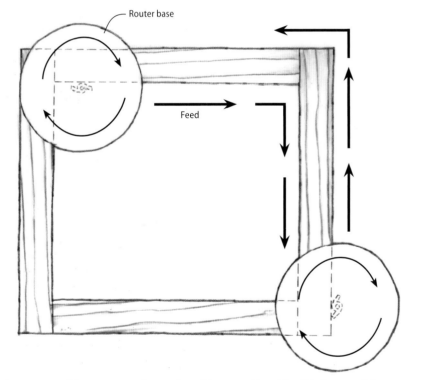

Router base

Feed

Whenever possible, cut against the rotation of the router bit – this will help control the router. If you rout with the rotation, the router or the workpiece will try to pull itself out of your hands. To make sure you're routing against the rotation, just remember that the bit rotates clockwise when the router is used right-side up. To rout the inside of a piece, move the router clockwise within the perimeter; when routing the outside, move it counterclockwise. Treat fences and straightedges as if they were the outside of a workpiece – envision yourself cutting counterclockwise around these guides.

There is one application for routing with the rotational direction. This is known as "climb-cutting" or back-routing. While this action demands better control of the router by the operator, climb-cutting can reduce tear-out when routing highly figured or irregularly grained woods. You must be very comfortable with router use before attempting this.

wide scrap piece to the work (doubling its thickness in many cases) to provide additional support.

• It's not usually a good idea to rout freehand (with the router unguided). The cuts won't be very accurate, and the router will try to pull itself all over the workpiece. There are four things you can use to help you guide the router while you cut – **a piloted bit**, which has a ball bearing guide or bushing to guide the cut; **a guide collar**, which attaches to the router's base and follows a surface with the bit protruding through it; **an edge guide**, which is really just a small fence that attaches to the router's base; or **a straightedge** clamped to your workpiece.

Using a Straightedge or Fence

The difference between a straightedge and a fence is all in how you hold the router. A straightedge guides a hand-held router over the work, while a fence guides the work over a table-mounted router.

Whether using a straightedge or a fence, keep whatever is moving pressed firmly against it. Feed the work or the router slowly and steadily – do not pause or speed up if you can help it.

Here are other things to remember:

• Make sure the straightedge or the fence is straight and flat. Otherwise, the cuts won't be accurate.

• Always read the warp or bow in a board before routing (see illustra-

TIPS & TRICKS

Loose Tenons for Easy Joints

Instead of cutting perfectly fit mortise-and-tenon joinery on your workpieces, all you have to do is rout two matching mortises – then make a loose tenon to complete the joint. A single loose tenon (easily fit to both mortises) bridges the two mortises. As long as you get a good fit, this joint will be as strong as a traditional mortise-and-tenon joint.

Keep That Piece Clamped Down Tight

Whenever you're routing something, make sure that either your workpiece or your router is stable and secure – they can't both move. If you choose to move the router across the work, clamp the work to your bench. If a clamp interferes with the operation, rout up to it and turn the router off. Then move the clamp to an area on the workpiece that you've already cut and resume routing.

Back Up Your Work When Utilizing a Miter Gauge

Tear-out when routing in end grain can be a real problem. In a router table, when using a miter gauge to rout across the wood's grain, always use a piece of scrap placed behind the work piece to prevent tear-out.

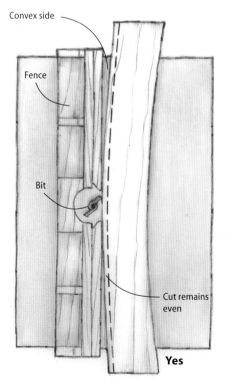

Convex side · Fence · Bit · Cut remains even · **Yes**

If your workpiece is warped or bowed – even slightly – keep the convex side of the bow against the fence or straightedge as you cut. The width of the cut will remain the same from one end of the board to the other.

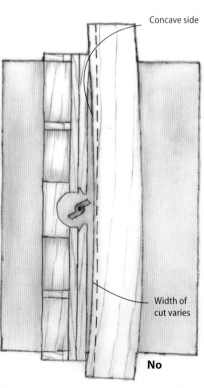

Concave side · Width of cut varies · **No**

If you turn the concave side toward the fence, the cut will be narrower toward the middle of the board than it will be at the ends.

A BIT OF ADVICE

A router bit consists of a cylindrical shank (usually ¼" or ½" in diameter) and one or more flutes or cutting wings, usually comprised of a piece of carbide brazed to the metal body of the bit. Throughout this series, we will be providing a closer look at a many of the most common (and some specialized) bits that you can use with your router.

Straight Bit

The most basic groove-forming bit will give you clean grooves and dados. Diameters range from ¹⁄₁₆" to 1¾".

Rabbet Bit

An often-used bit for edge-forming. Change the bearing size to vary the width of the rabbet. The carbide height is usually ½", with the various bearings making rabbets possible from ⁵⁄₁₆" to ½" wide.

Roundover Bit

This is a great bit for quickly changing the appearance of any project. Depending on the radius of the roundover used (³⁄₁₆", ¼" and ³⁄₈" are common), a sharp edge can be softened or almost entirely rounded over. Add a smaller bearing, and the roundover bit becomes a beading bit.

Chamfer Bit

If you prefer a less-rounded appearance but still want to soften the edges, a chamfer bit is the way to go. Commonly available in 15°, 30° and 45° bevels.

tions at right). Keep the convex surface against the fence or straightedge as you cut it.

• If the router sole is circular, paint a spot on the edge of the base plate. Keep the spot turned toward you and away from the straightedge as you rout. The bit is never perfectly centered in the base plate. If you allow the router to turn as you follow the straightedge, the cut will not be perfectly straight.

A Gauge will Help

When guiding the router with a straightedge, make a gauge to help position the straightedge when setting up the cut. To make a gauge the proper width (the distance from the router bit to the base edge), stick a thin piece of hardboard to a scrap piece with double-faced carpet tape, flushing one long edge of both pieces. Position your straightedge against the flushed edges. Mount the bit you plan to use in the router and rout along the straightedge and through the hard-

board. The strip of hardboard now functions as your gauge.

Then just lay out the cut you want to make on the work. Position the straightedge on the work parallel to the edge of the cut and offset it the width of the gauge by using your gauge piece to guide you. Secure the straightedge to the work and make the cut, keeping the router firmly against the straightedge.

Selecting Bits

There are an enormous number of router bits available, many more than can be shown here. But all these cutting accessories can be organized into four simple categories: **decorative**, used to cut molded shapes; **joinery**, used to make woodworking joints; **trimming/cutting**, used to trim or cut various materials; and **utility**, used to do all three of these tasks.

The cutting edges of the bits are called flutes. Most router bits have two symmetrical flutes, although there are some with just one.

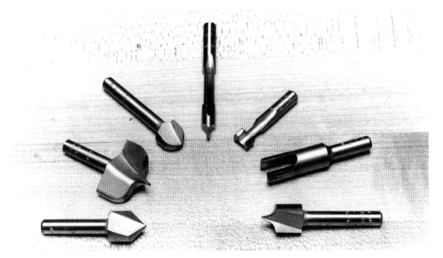

Most unpiloted router bits have either top-cut or point-cut flutes – flat or pointed cutting edges on the ends of the flutes as well as the sides. This feature lets you cut downward into the stock to make grooves, mortises and other cuts in the interior of a workpiece. For example, a point-cut beading bit (far right) lets you cut quarter-round and half-round shapes in the surface of a piece, not just on the arrises and corners.

When selecting which bit to use, know that you have a range of diameters to choose from. Router bits vary from a diameter of 1/16" up to 3 1/4". Some bits, particularly straight bits, are available with different types of flutes for cutting various materials.

When it comes to the material the bit is made from, almost all bits these days are made out of tungsten carbide. A few years back, most bits were made out of high-speed steel (HSS), which was cheaper and easier to make. But now, tungsten carbide is pretty much the only kind that's available. The flutes of most carbide cutting tools are tipped or faced with carbide, while the bulk of the tool is HSS. Carbide is brittle and won't be as sharp as HSS, but it lasts up to 15 times longer than HSS bits.

Custom Router Bits

If you find yourself looking for a specific kind of router bit and can't seem to find it anywhere in your woodworking supply store or catalogs, check this out – you can have custom router bits made to your specifications. These are a little more expensive, but if you use them continually, they could be worth the money.

Some places where custom bits are available include:

• Freeborn Tool Co.: 800-523-8988 or freeborntool.com

• Whiteside Machine Co.: 800-225-3982 or whitesiderouterbits.com

• Carbide Specialties Inc.: 800-678-3313 or carbidespecialties.com

T-SQUARE ROUTER GUIDE

When using a hand-held router to cut dados, grooves and rabbets, the part of the setup that eats most of your time is positioning the edge guide or straightedge. This T-shaped jig simplifies that chore – just use the short crossbar to instantly position the longer straightedge.

Before you can use this jig, you must cut dados in the crossbar – one on either side of the straightedge. Place the jig over a large wooden scrap and butt the crossbar against an edge. Clamp the jig to the scrap and cut the dados with a straight bit, keeping the router pressed against the straightedge. NOTE: Once you have cut these dados, you can only use the jig with that particular router and that bit. The dados won't line up with different tools.

Lay out the joints on the workpiece. Place the jig across the wood, butt the crossbar against an edge or end and line up one of the dados with the layout lines. Then clamp the jig to the workpiece and cut the joint using the straightedge to guide the router, just as you did when you made the dados in the crossbar.

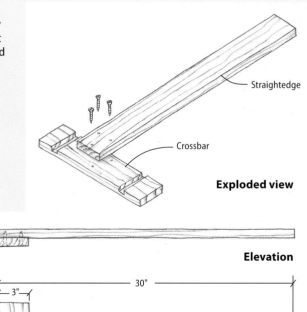

Straightedge

Crossbar

Exploded view

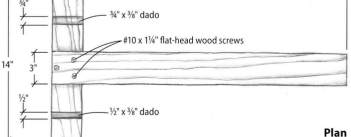

1 1/2"

3/4"

Elevation

30"

3"

3/4"

3/4" x 3/8" dado

#10 x 1 1/4" flat-head wood screws

14"

3"

1/2"

1/2" x 3/8" dado

Plan

Plunge Router

by Nick Engler

While a fixed-base router is a very versatile tool, there are still some operations that require different abilities. This is where a plunge router proves valuable.

For example, some operations require you to rout the interior of a board without cutting in from the edge. When you rout a mortise, it's best to first make a small hole in the interior of the workpiece, then enlarge it. To make this starter hole, you must lower – or "plunge" – the bit into the wood. While you don't need a plunge router to do this (woodworkers have been plunging with standard routers for years), it does make the operation safer and can be accomplished with greater precision.

The main difference between plunge and fixed-base routers (which were discussed in the previous chapter) is that plunge routers can make interior and stopped cuts much more easily. The plunge-base motor is mounted on two spring-loaded posts above the base, which let you position the motor above the work, then lower the bit straight down into the wood and begin cutting.

Similar to fixed-base routers, plunge-base routers are available in multiple sizes and power. Most will accept both ½" and ¼" collets.

Choosing the Right Size For Your First Router

Plunge routers are available in two main sizes: either a 2-horsepower (or slightly less) or a 3-hp (or slightly more) model. Most larger plunge routers have found happy homes in router tables (we will discuss router tables in the next chapter), and that's where they belong. They're honestly too large for convenient hand-held routing operations. They can be used this way, but the smaller plunge router is more likely the better choice for hand-held routing.

The smaller plunge routers are easier to use hand-held and will provide an astonishing amount of power for almost all operations. Today's plunge routers often come

PRO TIP:

How Much is Enough?
To make sure the collet is safely gripping a router bit, insert ¾" of the length of a ¼" shank bit into the collet and insert a full 1" of every ½" shank bit.

There is quite an array of router choices. At left, originally designed as a laminate trimmer, this smaller router is used very effectively for a variety of applications. Offering good power and using standard ¼"-diameter bits, it offers many of the benefits of a larger router with easier maneuverability and convenient size. Kits for the trimmers offer fixed- and beveling-base options. The standard fixed-base router in the 1½-horsepower range (middle) will accept ¼" and ½" bits and do almost everything you could need out of a router. The plunge router in the 2½-hp range (right) is able to do everything a fixed-base router can do and more, with extra torque for larger profile work such as frame-and-panel doors.

equipped with variable speed. This is good because the larger-diameter bits cut better when run at slower speeds. Also, many variable-speed routers now offer a type of turbo-boost called electronic feedback control. This feature allows the motor to maintain the revolutions per minute when the router is in use, meaning there's no slowing or stalling during a cut.

So smaller is best when the tool is used outside of a table and larger is likely better for router-table use.

Choosing the Right Size For Routing Specific Projects

As mentioned above, certain diameter bits perform better at certain speeds. While variable speed can give you a certain amount of leeway in your routing abilities, there are places where the size of your router makes a difference.

In particular, when performing any process that removes a large amount of material in a single pass, a larger plunge router will better meet

your needs. This also will indicate that the operation is best performed in a router table. These operations include rail-and-stile applications for doors, panel-raising for doors and frame-and-panel cabinetry, and large profile work, such as in crown moulding, base moulding or banisters.

In fact, the design of the tool will help you make that decision, too. Most smaller plunge routers will not have an opening in the base that is large enough to accommodate a large-profile bit. If the bit won't fit, you've probably grabbed the wrong router for the application.

Height-adjustment Features

With fixed-base routers, the depth of cut usually is set and adjusted manually by sliding the motor up and down in the base. Some motors will rotate to adjust the height, while others slide straight up and down. When the height is set, the motor is locked in the base and the work proceeds. With plunge routers, the depth of cut also is set by sliding

TIPS & TRICKS

Use Ball-bearing Guided Bits Instead of Template Guides to Protect the Wood

Metal template guides can burnish the wood, crushing the fibers. This prevents stains and finishes from penetrating the wood evenly. To prevent this, purchase a set of ball-bearing guides, available from any router-bit distributor.

Ball-bearing guide

Make Sure You Use Plenty of Protection

Always wear eye and ear protectors when routing. The need for eye protection should be obvious – the router throws wood chips everywhere. But the need for ear protection is just as necessary. A high-speed router motor generates high frequency noise, which can damage your hearing a tiny amount with each exposure. You won't notice any loss after just one routing session, but over time your hearing will grow worse.

Make Sure You Get Good Up-and-down Movement

When plunging, some routers will jam if you grasp only one handle, which is OK because you should always use two hands. But if pushing both handles does not result in a smooth glide to full extremes, you should pass on that router.

The 1½-hp router, left, has a base opening that is sized for bits appropriate to that size motor. The larger plunge router, right, has a 3-hp motor, appropriately sized for larger bits for panel raising or large profiles. This base has a larger opening to accommodate those bits.

the motor in the base, but there are a variety of ways to set, adjust and fine-tune that height.

Because the plunge router is designed to slide out of the cutting position and then return to the proper depth with a plunge, a repeatable and reliable depth stop is required. The most common and simplest repeatable depth stop on plunge routers is called a "turret stop."

A height-adjustable rod is mounted to the motor housing and aligned parallel to the direction of the plunge. Mounted to the base is a rotating dial with usually three (but this can vary) stepped-height stops. The depth rod is plunged against the

lowest position for the proper height, then locked in place. The other two stops come into play when you are making deep cuts in multiple passes to reduce the strain on the bit and the motor by taking no more than a ¼"-deep cut at one time.

There are a variety of designs for the plunge-rod/depth-stop arrangement, but turret depth stops are the most common height-adjustment system. Many newer plunge routers also offer fine adjustment to the depth setting.

This is accomplished either by adding a fine-thread screw mechanism to the depth rod or by adding a fine-thread screw adjustment to the top of one of the depth rests on the stop itself. Fine adjustment can be very helpful during the initial depth setup, as you frequently can find yourself fighting a balancing act between gravity and the tension of the plunge springs to get the setting right.

The fine-adjustment feature also makes plunge routers a good choice for edge routing and profile work, applications typical for a fixed-base router. In fact, many woodworkers when faced with using only one

router (thankfully that's not too often) will choose a plunge router, since it is more versatile.

Should You Buy Two Routers?

Considering the versatility of a plunge router, why should anyone buy a fixed-base router? Simply put, with fewer moving parts and a less-complicated depth adjustment, it's a simpler tool. A fixed-base router is best used for making edge cuttings of a single depth, while the plunge router is built for depth changes and is best for multi-depth interior cuts, such as mortises.

Turret stop with fine adjustments

The turret stop is the most common depth stop in plunge routers.

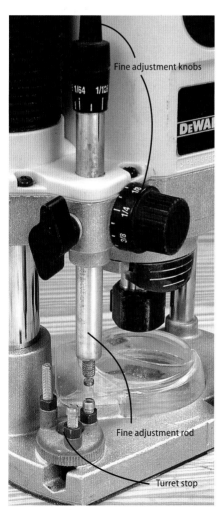

Fine adjustment knobs

Fine adjustment rod

Turret stop

The fine-adjustment knobs make the depth as accurate as possible.

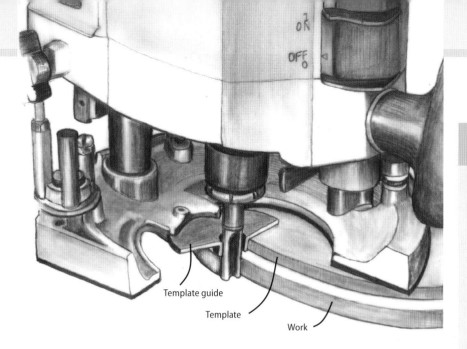

Template guide

Template

Work

Template guides are designed to follow templates. As the guide traces the shape of the template, the bit cuts a similar shape in the workpiece. The routed shape may be a little larger or smaller than the template, depending on the relative diameters of the bit and the guide.

Certainly, a plunge router can be modified or placed in a jig for nearly any cut that you'd want a fixed-base router to do, but that doesn't always make sense. When in doubt, just keep it simple and, in the best of all worlds, both a fixed-base and a plunge router should find a home in your shop.

But can't a fixed-base router be used to make plunge cuts? Sure, but it's not recommended. It's a hazardous operation because the base is supported on only one tiny edge while you tip the tool to plunge. If all you have is a fixed-base router, there are ways to get the job done, but for most people who will be making more inside cuts, it's well worth it to get that plunge router.

Base-mounted Guides and Template Guides

Base-mounted guides are available as accessories for most fixed-base and plunge routers. The guide follows the edge of the wood and you can use it rather easily. Instead of holding both router handles, grasp one handle and

hold the end of the guide with your other hand. As you cut, keep the guide pressed firmly against the edge of the workpiece. Then just feed the router slowly and easily for a smooth cut.

Template guides attach to the base or sole of the router and follow a straight or contoured edge. These round guides surround the bit and the bit protrudes out through the hole. While template guides can be

Most base-mounted guides will follow either straight or contoured edges, depending on the shape of the guide. Here, a straight guide – which looks like a small fence – rides along the edge of a board.

TIPS & TRICKS

Precise Setups with Feeler Gauges

One of the difficulties when setting up your plunge router for a cut is fine-tuning the setting in small increments. The most precise way to change your setting is to use a set of automotive feeler gauges. These thin strips of metal are marked with their precise thicknesses. When you want to adjust your bit up .005", simply place the appropriate feeler gauge between your turret depth stop and the tool's adjustment rod. Plunge the tool and lock it in place. Remove the feeler gauge and move the adjustment rod down until it contacts the turret depth stop again. Bingo. Now your cut is .005" shallower.

Use a Thick Scrap to Keep Your Router in Balance

If you're routing the thin edge of a workpiece, or if the workpiece is too narrow to balance the router easily, clamp a thick scrap to the work to provide more support.

To rout a mortise with a plunge router, clamp a straightedge or guide to the workpiece and adjust the depth stop. (You also may use a base-mounted guide attached to the router.) Position the router over the work, holding the base against the straightedge (or the guide against the work). Release the height clamp and push the bit into the wood.

used to follow along the edges of a workpiece, they were designed to follow templates.

When using template guides, make sure the bit does not rub the inside of the collar. That wear could ruin both the bit and the collar. Also, keep the guide pressed firmly against the edges of the template as you cut.

Don't forget the most simple of router guides – a straightedge clamped to the material you're cutting. This can be a simple piece of

scrap found in your shop or one of a number of commercially available guides that have built-in clamping, making their use a lot easier.

How to Rout a Mortise

Routing a mortise with a plunge router is an easy operation. First mark the location of the mortise and set up whatever guide system you choose. Your guide system can be as simple as an edge guide, as shown above, or a jig, as shown in the photo below.

Begin the mortise by making a starting hole. Just position the bit over the work, then push down. Next, enlarge (or elongate) the hole to complete the mortise by moving the router.

Cutting a mortise with the standard fixed-base router is more difficult because you must "rock" the bit into the workpiece before you can cut. You also can cut a mortise with a table-mounted fixed-base router, but the procedure requires careful layout work. You have to mark both the router table and the workpiece to know when to start and stop cutting. That's why the plunge router is perfect for this job.

Other Applications

Along with mortising, there are some other operations that plunge routers are ideally suited for:

Circles and Ellipses: Because cutting these pieces is usually a multi-stage task, the plunge router works best because it can be lowered gradually to make the cuts. You could use a

The depth stop will halt the bit at the proper depth. Secure the height clamp and rout the mortise, keeping the router against the guide.

A mortising template can be nothing more than a hole cut in a piece of plywood or particleboard. The size and shape of the hole depends on the size and shape of the mortise you wish to cut, the diameter of the template guide in your router and the diameter of the bit you are using. When you make the template, cut it large enough to support the router base. You also may want to fasten it to one or more mounting boards to help position the template and provide an easy way to clamp it to the workpiece.

fixed-base router, but it usually takes up more time, or even a band saw, which can be more efficient but won't give you the precision or finished quality of a plunge router.

Deep or Large Cuts: If you have a deep cut that is going to be more than one pass or is larger than your bit, break out the plunge router. Even if it means building up support on the outboard side of the router's base to prevent tipping, it's almost always better to use the plunge router.

With a Router Table: Plunge routers are the most popular choice with a table because there are more options in the 3-hp range than fixed-base routers. They're also relatively inexpensive, but there are some problems to be aware of. Because the router's motor is inseparable from the rest of the tool, you can't change the bit easily if the tool is fixed to the tabletop.

Router Maintenance

Like many modern portable power tools, the router is a mostly maintenance-free tool. There are, however, a few things you must do to keep it in good working order. In particular:

• Keep the motor free of dust. Use compressed air or a vacuum to clean out the housing. Otherwise, the dust will get into the bearings – even per-manently sealed bearings – and cause them wear prematurely. The dust also can damage the commutator (a part of the router's universal motor that conducts current) and field of the motor.

• Keep the collet dust-free. Dust in a collet is the most common cause of bits slipping. If you don't keep it clean, the collet also can show wear prematurely.

• Replace the collet immediately if it shows signs of wear. A worn collet changes the shanks of router bits. This may ruin the motor shaft, requiring you to replace the entire armature.

• Wax and buff the base plate and the surfaces of the tool that slide together (such as the plunge bars). This simple act will help these parts move freely and keep the router gliding smoothly across the work.

• Specifically with the plunge router, you need to make sure that the plunge bars and sleeves are correctly aligned. If the router is dropped, these parts might need to be inspected. In some routers, the return springs are inside the plunge bars; in others, the spring is fitted externally. Either way, the springs need to be seated properly and cleaned regularly.

TIPS & TRICKS

Sharpen Cutting Flutes by Using a Diamond Stone

If your cutting edges seem dull, touch up the carbide flutes on a diamond stone. Sharpen only the inside (flat) surfaces of the flutes, leaving the outside (curved) edges alone. If you try to sharpen those, you might change the diameter of the bit.

Wax That Tool; Don't Worry About Wax on Wood

There is a common misconception that if you wax a woodworking tool the wax will rub off onto the wood and interfere with a finish. This is not true, as long as you buff the wax after it dries. Once buffed, the layer of wax remaining on the tool is only a few molecules thick – enough to protect and lubricate the metal but not enough to ruin the finish.

Remove Your Plunge Springs When Routing in a Table

One of the most frustrating things about using a plunge router in a router table is that the plunge springs work against you as you try to increase the height of the bit. Many plunge routers allow you to easily remove the springs. Give it a try.

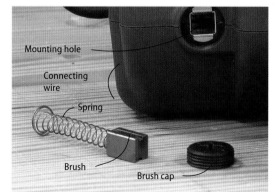

Mounting hole

Connecting wire

Spring

Brush

Brush cap

At right is the motor's brush with spring and connecting wire, the cap and the hole in the housing where the brush goes. You can see that the surface of the brush is slightly concave to form to the cylinder of the commutator. When replacing a brush that is already broken in, the shape should be properly oriented to match the motor's round commutator.

A BIT OF ADVICE

These four bits are great for making interior patterns.

Round Nose Bit

Provides a perfect radius groove and is most commonly associated with producing fluted millwork, signs and decorative designs in cabinet doors.

Beading Bit

A bead is different than a roundover in that it has a shoulder that transitions into the round. Used for decorative edges, it can be used on one side (often with a bearing guide) or two sides to make a double bead.

V-groove Bit

This decorative bit allows you to cut deep or shallow grooves by adjusting the cutting depth. Ideal for making signs and adding decorative accents to furniture and plaques.

Keyhole Bit

This is a very specialized bit that allows you to cut keyhole openings for hanging pictures and plaques. Perfect for use in plunge routers.

Cuts access hole and space for the nail or screw head

Cuts space for the shank

• Brushes are blocks of carbon that ride and wear against the commutator in all router motors as part of the motor function. Over enough time, the brushes can wear down enough to require complete replacement. Some, but not all routers, make this a simple task by making the brushes accessible from the outside of the router housing.

Sparking from the motor that is only getting worse is a good indicator that it may be time to replace the brushes. This usually is a simple task that requires removing the brush cover, removing the brush, spring and wire and inserting a new brush. Properly aligning the brushes and leaving proper "play" in the spring will ensure a good fit.

There likely will be a short period where sparking will continue as the new square brush shapes itself to the surface of the round commutator, but after that there should be no problem.

• Many switches included on routers today are sealed against dust. This makes maintenance on them unnecessary. If you happen to have an older or less-expensive router, you may want to take a look at the switch occasionally as well. After unplugging the router it's simple enough to remove the switch from the housing and use a soft toothbrush to

To remove the pitch from a router bit, soak it in lacquer thinner or spray it with oven cleaner. Give the solvent a moment or two to work, then wipe off the bit with fine steel wool.

clean any accumulated dust from the switch and the switch terminals. Compressed air is another option for cleaning out the switch. Put things back together and you're ready to go.

Bit Maintenance

Clean and maintain the router bits, not just the machine itself. After all, a bit is the most important part of your routing system. Here are some tips:

• After each use, remove dust and built-up pitch. Then polish the shaft with a piece of steel wool or 3M Scotch-Brite. This will not affect the diameter of the shaft – the tool materials are a lot harder than steel wool and Scotch-Brite.

• If there are any burrs or galling (rough spots) on the shaft of the bit, sand the entire shaft smooth with emery cloth. Carefully check the collet for dust or any signs of wear. Burrs and galling are sure signs that the bit has slipped while you were cutting.

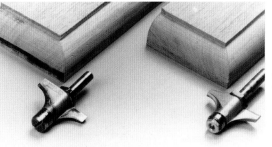

For best results, use pilot bearings, rather than bushings or pins, which turn at the same speed as the bit and rub the edge of the workpiece. The friction causes them to heat up and burn the wood. Bearings turn independently of the bit and won't rub or burn the wood.

• Lubricate pilot bushings and bearings after every one to two hours of use. Wax and buff the bushings. Apply a dry lubricant, such as powdered graphite, to the bearings – do not use oil or sprays. These mix with sawdust, forming a gummy paste that can ruin the bearing.

Using Piloted Bits

A piloted bit has either a ball bearing or a bushing to guide the cut. These pilots follow the surface of the work (or the template) and keep the width of the cut consistent, just like you do when using a base-mounted guide.

Usually they're mounted to the ends of the flutes, but some are positioned between the shank and the flutes (called "over-bearings").

When using piloted bits:

• Remember that the pilot is meant to follow the contour of the board. When you set the depth of cut, the pilot must solidly contact the wood surface.

• Anticipate the curves and corners of your work to keep the pilot pressed firmly against the board's edge.

• Treat the pilot as if it was a small straightedge or fence when trying to decide which way to move the router or feed the work. With a hand-held router right-side up, cut counterclockwise around the outside of your workpiece. (With the router mounted upside down in a table, feed the work clockwise around the bit.)

• The diameter of the pilot controls the width of the cut. Some piloted bits have interchangeable pilots for you to change the diameter, but not all do, so make sure you're prepared for this.

CIRCLE-CUTTING JIG

Many woodworkers use a router, a straight bit and a circle-cutting jig to make circles. And, naturally, there is an easy-to-build and easy-to-use jig that will help you make these perfect pieces. This jig is just an elongated router sole that you can attach to your hand-held router's base. Make the jig from plywood, hardboard or clear Lexan.

To cut a circle, drive a nail or screw into the workpiece to make a pivot – make sure you drive the pivot nail into the bottom or inside surface of the workpiece, because you don't want the hole to show on the assembled project. Then just drill a hole in the small end of the jig, place the hole over the pivot and swing the router around the pivot.

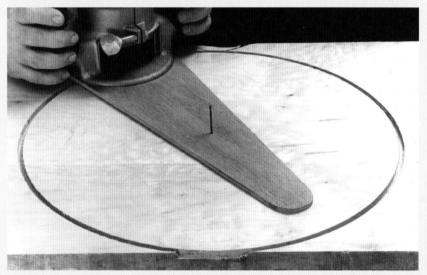

The distance from the pivot hole to the nearest edge of the router bit determines the diameter of the circle. Put a scrap of plywood under the workpiece so you don't cut into your workbench.

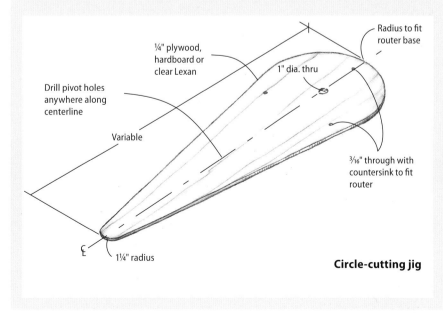

¼" plywood, hardboard or clear Lexan

Radius to fit router base

1" dia. thru

Drill pivot holes anywhere along centerline

Variable

³⁄₁₆" through with countersink to fit router

1¼" radius

Circle-cutting jig

The Router Table

by Nick Engler

After you've worked with a hand-held router for some time, you'll find that many operations are easier and safer if you pass the workpiece across the bit instead of the other way around. This is especially true when routing small pieces or when making many identical cuts. For these tasks, holding the tool stationary by mounting it in a table or a jig is a good idea.

There are two common ways to mount a router: vertically beneath the work or horizontally beside the work, as shown in the illustration on the next page. Each position offers unique advantages, and there are a number of tools and jigs available that will hold the router in each position. You can purchase or make many different router-mounting jigs and accessories, but the most versatile is the router table. This device holds the router vertically beneath

the work, with the bit protruding up through a hole in the table – all you have to do is rest your workpiece on the table's top and guide it over the bit.

There are many commercial router tables on the market, as well as several you can make from a kit. You can make your own from scratch pretty easily. A homemade router table may be a better option in the long run for a number of reasons:

PRO TIP

Rout End-grain Edges First To Avoid Any Tear-out

When routing profiles on four edges of a rectangular or square piece, start with an end-grain edge first. If the end of the cut tears out, the following pass on the long-grain edge will most likely remove the torn-out corner.

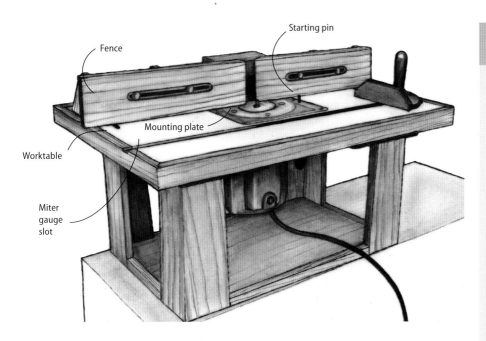

Fence

Starting pin

Mounting plate

Worktable

Miter
gauge
slot

ILLUSTRATIONS BY MARY JANE FAVORITE

• You can build it to fit whatever kind of router you already own.

• You can make it suit whatever available space you have in your shop.

• If you don't have room for a standalone table, you can customize other fixtures already in your shop to hold a router. A workbench, a table saw or a radial-arm saw all can pull double-duty as a router table.

What Router is Best with a Table?

Choosing which type of router to use in a router table has been the subject of debate for many years. When the plunge router first entered the marketplace, it quickly became the router of choice for table use, offering more precise height adjustment than fixed-base routers.

One problem that arose was when the return spring on plunge routers pushed against the height adjustment, making it a difficult process. It didn't take long for woodworkers to remove the spring from their plunge routers to make the adjustment

easier. Manufacturers recently have addressed that problem themselves by offering plunge routers that enable users to "defeat" the return spring.

Another difficulty router tables

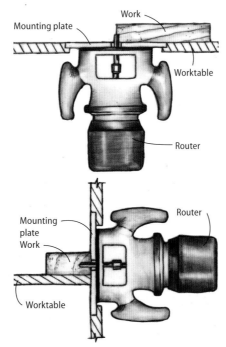

Mounting plate

Work

Worktable

Router

Mounting
plate
Work

Router

Worktable

There are two common ways to mount a portable router and hold it stationary. You can mount it vertically under the work (top) or horizontally beside the work (bottom).

TIPS & TRICKS

Titanium-coated Bits Don't Burn Wood When Sharp

Manufacturers sometimes coat the cutting edges of large, carbide-tipped router bits with a gold-colored titanium alloy and claim the bits can be used safely without reducing the routing speed. This is true to an extent. Titanium-coated carbide can be honed to a much sharper edge than the uncoated variety. While the cutting edges remain razor-sharp, the bit will cut cleanly at high speeds. But as soon as the edges dull or load up with pitch, the bit will burn the wood.

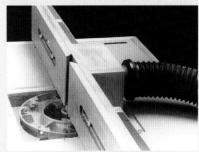

Dust Collector Keeps Table's Mess to a Minimum

If possible, make sure your router table has a dust collector to minimize airborne dust as you work. On the table seen here, the collector is part of the fence.

Mount a Power Switch Closer to Table's Front

When a router is mounted in a table, it might be hard to reach the power switch. To solve this problem, mount a combination switch/outlet near the front of the table and wire it to control the power to the outlet. Plug your router into the outlet and use the switch to turn it on and off.

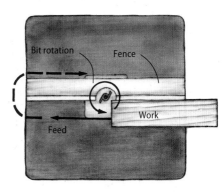

When a router is vertical under a table, the bit spins counterclockwise when viewed from above. Whether cutting the edge or interior of a workpiece, feed clockwise around the fence.

When adjusting the position of a router table fence, loosen the clamps at both ends of the fence and slide it forward or back. To make fine adjustments, tighten just one clamp and move the loose end of the fence.

presented was the need to reach under the table to make height adjustments, change bits and actually turn the router on and off. This led to removable plates in the tabletops to which the routers were attached. Rather than crawling under the table, the router and plate could be lifted free from above the table.

These plates soon became even more helpful with the addition of built-in height adjustment. The router-lift plates make it possible to fine-adjust the height of a more-affordable fixed-base router from above the table, providing the best of both worlds.

Some of the newest fixed-base and plunge routers now offer built-in, through-the-base height adjustment. This makes the router lifts obsolete, though they're still the best option for older (as well as many of the newer and less-expensive) router models.

This brings us back to the question of what router to use in your table. A 1½- to 2-horsepower router can be used successfully in a table, but it will limit you to small- or medium-diameter tables. In general,

it makes more sense to use a 2½- to 3-hp router in a table to maximize the benefits of the table.

The other strong recommendation is to outfit your router table with a variable-speed router. Because your table will support a larger-motor router, you can successfully use large-diameter bits. To get the best performance from these bits, they should be run at slower speeds, so a variable-speed router will give you optimum performance in your table, whether using smaller grooving bits or panel-raising bits for making doors.

That said, with the variety of table-friendly routers and router lifts available, it's impossible to recommend either a plunge or a fixed-base router as best for use in a table. You'll need to determine what your budget will allow and take into consideration what routers you already own. With all the choices currently avail-

able, there's no reason you shouldn't be able to buy or build a router table that allows you to adjust and operate the router from above the table surface. It's up to you to choose how you assemble the hardware.

A Closer Look at Router Lifts

Router lifts are available in a number of varying designs, ranging from a retrofit kit to replace the spring in a plunge router to heavy-duty mounting platforms that include the table plate. Prices range from $100 to $400, so you should know what you're getting into before you spend any money.

Ultimately, the router lift should adequately support the router underneath the table without any concern of deflection or slipping. Deflection will cause the bit you are using to deviate from a 90° angle to the table, ruining the cut. The lift also should adjust the height smoothly in measurable and repeatable increments, and not interfere with the table surface. Most lifts that are on the market are designed for use with fixed-base routers, which is fine, but you should choose a router with variable-speed control to take maximum advantage of the larger motor and available larger-diameter bits.

Some lifts also will allow you to change bits from above the table. These lifts raise the router high enough through the tabletop (while not running) to use both wrenches (or one wrench and a shaft lock).

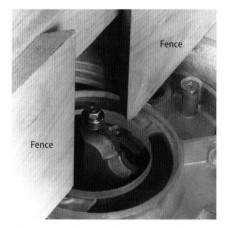

When properly used, a fence guides the work and also protects you from the bit. Even when using a bit with a bearing guide, align the fence faces even with the front edge of the bearing and adjust the fence gap as tightly against the bit as possible.

This is a great feature and highly recommended.

Using the Router Table

When using a router in a router table, you will need to pay extra attention to the tool's feed direction. When your router is mounted upside down under a table, the bit spins counterclockwise (as viewed from above). Whether you are cutting the edge or the interior of a workpiece, imagine that you are feeding it clockwise around the fence – right to left as you face the fence.

The rotation will help keep the board pressed against the fence, making it safer to make the cut. When using a fence, you also need to check that the router is properly aligned and adjusted in the table. There are two things you need to check – the depth of cut (the distance the bit protrudes past the mounting plate) and the position of the fence.

Other things to remember when using a router table with a fence include:

• Keep the workpiece pressed firmly against the fence to ensure you get as straight a cut as possible.

• Feed the work slowly and

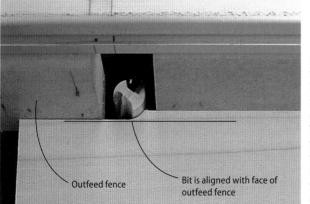

By offsetting the outfeed fence (moving it forward ¹⁄₁₆" or ⅛"), a router table can be used as an efficient edge jointer. The face of the outfeed fence is aligned with the furthest point of the straight bit and, as the wood passes the bit, the outfeed fence supports the cut.

Scrap Piece Helps when Routing Narrow Work

When routing the end of a narrow workpiece on a router table, use a large square scrap to guide it along the fence. The scrap not only holds the work perpendicular to the fence, it also backs up the wood so it won't tear out.

Keep Your Hands Away With Small Workpieces

If a workpiece is very small, your hands may come too close to the router bit as you rout it. In this case, you have two choices – you can rout the work with a portable router using a commercially available foam rubber "routing pad" to hold the work, or you can rout a portion of a larger workpiece and cut a small piece from it, as seen above.

Slide Smoothly with Wax

To help the table slide more smoothly, wax and buff the table surface, the fence faces, the miter gauge bars and the grooves for any miter fixtures.

steadily – do not pause, if you can help it.

• Let the fence surround the unused portion of the bit.

• Whenever practical, use featherboards, push sticks and push shoes to guide the work along the fence.

A router table also can be used without a fence. In these cases, a starting pin and a bit with a bearing or a template guide attached is used. This operation is similar to using a hand-held router with a similarly guided bit, but the table operation makes it safer and easier to use larger-profile bits.

The starting pin provides an extra bearing point to allow you to rest against two points while routing, adding an extra level of safety. When using the router table in this setup it's even more important to maintain proper safety and hand clearance from the exposed bit.

Doubles as a Jointer

Speaking of fences, it would be a large oversight not to mention using a router table as an edge-jointer. Some commercially available router-table fences give you the option to adjust the face of the outfeed table forward slightly (by as much as ⅛") to offset the fences.

With a straight router bit aligned tangentially to the face of the outfeed table, you can run wood across the fence and straighten or thin edges just as you would on a jointer.

If your fence assembly isn't designed to have offset fences, you can achieve the same effect by building up the face of the outfeed table with a piece of laminate or thin plywood. Adjust the outfeed face to

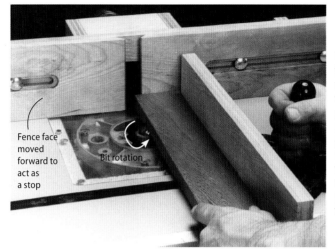

Fence face moved forward to act as a stop

Bit rotation

You also can use a fence as a stop to prevent creep. However, the fence must be precisely parallel to the miter-gauge slot and you must be feeding the workpiece with the rotation of the bit to pull the piece against the fence.

match the bit and you're ready.

Featherboards & Stop Blocks

Two useful accessories for the router table are featherboards and stop blocks.

• Featherboards are most often thought of as safety devices, and they certainly are, but they also help ensure an accurate cut from the bit. For safety, a featherboard's angled fingers allow the wood to pass the bit and then applies pressure in the same direction you are feeding your work to make it nearly impossible for the piece to kick back (which is when the material is thrown toward the user by the force of the spinning bit). A pair of featherboards used in the horizontal and vertical planes of the router table, as shown in the photograph

below, add excellent safety.

Often when using larger-diameter bits in a single pass, the tendency of the bit is to push the material away from it, causing irregular, rippled or shallow cuts. Using a pair of featherboards will keep the workpiece pushed tightly against the fence, table and bit, providing an accurate, smooth and repeatable cut.

• When using a router table, the bit is buried in the wood during the cut and you can't see when or where the cut begins or ends. When making a stopped cut of any type (groove or profile), you need to know the stopping and starting points to make an accurate cut.

One way to determine those points is to make a pencil mark on the fence identifying the infeed and

When using a fence, attach featherboards to both the fence and the table to keep the workpiece properly positioned. Featherboards provide firm, even pressure and prevent the piece from kicking back toward you. Also use push sticks and push shoes to feed the workpiece, keeping your fingers out of danger.

outfeed sides of the bit. This helps, but it isn't a positive assurance of accuracy.

That's where stop blocks come in handy. By mounting some adjustable blocks to the fence (using either integral T-tracks or a clamp on the fence) you can be sure you'll always stop and start in exactly the correct spot.

Using a Miter Gauge

A miter gauge is a simple way of to ensure you get square cuts on the ends of thin stock when using a router table. Just place the stock against the face of the gauge and feed it past the bit as if it was the blade on a table saw.

But there is an important difference – the rotation of a saw blade helps hold the work against the gauge; the rotation of the router bit pulls the wood sideways, making it "creep" across the gauge to the right as you cut.

When not using a fence, there are several things you can do to prevent this:

• Mount an extension (a long, auxiliary face) on the miter gauge and clamp the work to this.

• Clamp a stop to the miter-gauge

extension and butt the workpiece against the stop.

• Position a fence beside the miter gauge and let the end of the board ride along the fence as you cut.

• Tape #80-grit or #100-grit sandpaper to the miter gauge face with double-sided carpet tape.

It's also a good idea when cross-cutting material on the router table to use a backing board against the face of the miter gauge. This will significantly de crease tear-out on the workpiece and add some more stability.

Making a Mounting Plate

If you buy a router table, many will come with a mounting plate – a thin, flat sheet to which you attach the router base. The plate is needed to mount the router in any stationary jig, including the table.

If you're making your own table, or if the one you purchased doesn't come with a mounting plate, don't worry – making the plate is rather straightforward. All you have to do is cut the material to size, drill a few holes and screw the plate to the jig or table. However, you must make several informed decisions as you fashion this simple part.

Because router bits can range in size from 1/16" to 31/4", you should drill the plate's opening about 1/4" larger than the largest bit you own. Then you can make several inserts out of the same acrylic you used for the plate.

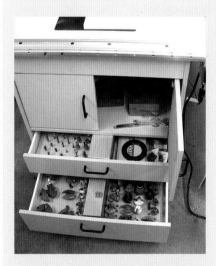

A BIT OF ADVICE

These three bits are great for use with the router table.

Crown-moulding Bit

Designed to make complicated profile shapes in one pass, a crown-moulding bit is a perfect choice for a router table because of its size and the quantity of wood likely to be run.

Table-edge Bit

Because the bit is designed to remove a lot of material in one pass (and run a lot of material at one time) a router table offers power and control for many edge profile bits. Table-edge bits are large and require more power and control.

Raised-panel Bit

Another large bit perfect for router tables is a raised-panel bit for making doors and frame-and-panel cabinetry. The one shown here is a horizontal bit, but vertical bits also are available.

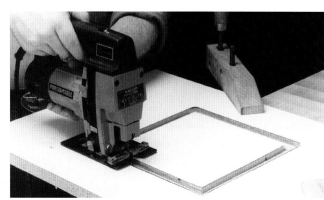

To cut the work surface for the mounting plate, first rout a square groove. Clamp a frame to the table to guide the router and cut the groove as deep as you want the thickness of the mounting plate.

Next, make the router opening by cutting the inside edges of the groove with a jigsaw. This groove will then form the ledge to hold the plate.

• The material from which you make a mounting plate must be strong enough and dense enough to absorb the vibrations of the router, but thin enough so it won't restrict the depth of cut. You should be able to cut and drill the material easily, and it should be transparent so you can see what's going on beneath it. There is really only one material that fulfills all these requirements – transparent plastic. I suggest you use ordinary acrylic plastic that's rather inexpensive. Some structural plastics are super-strong, but too flexible. Acrylic is more rigid. I suggest using a ¼"-thick sheet for routers up to 1½-hp and a ⅜"-thick sheet for more powerful routers.

• For safety and accuracy, there should be as little space as possible between the work surface and the router bit where it protrudes through the plate. However, bits can range

in size from 1/16" to 3¼". So what can you do? I suggest you drill the opening about ¼" larger than the largest bit you own, then make several inserts to fit the opening. Use the same transparent material that the mounting plate was made from and just drill a different diameter hole in

Screws work great to attach the mounting plate in the opening, but make sure you do it tightly – you don't want anything shifting while you work.

the center of each insert so you have a variety to choose from.

• Once you make these inserts, you're going to need to fashion some way to hold them in place. Some router bases have metal or plastic flanges to mount guide bushings. If your router is so equipped, you can use these flanges to support and secure the inserts. If your router doesn't have built-in flanges, attach a plastic ring under the mounting plate. The inside diameter of this ring should be ½" smaller than the diameter of the mounting plate to create a ledge to support the inserts.

• To cut an opening in the table's work surface for the mounting plate, first rout a square groove in the surface. Clamp a wooden frame to the table to guide the router and cut the groove so the depth matches the thickness of the mounting plate. (Make this groove about ⅟₃₂" smaller than the circumference of the plate; later, you can sand or file the edges of the plate to get a perfect fit.) Then make the router opening by cutting around the inside edges of the groove with a jigsaw. When the waste falls away, the groove will form a ledge to hold the mounting plate.

• You can attach the mounting plate in the opening with several screws. Don't leave it loose, because you don't want it to shift as you work.

• The work surface should be thick enough to permit you to attach the mounting plate securely – short screws may vibrate or pull loose. If the work surface is less than 1¼" thick, build up the area immediately beneath the mounting plate by gluing a hardwood frame to the table.

HEIGHT GAUGE

Sometimes you need three hands to adjust the depth of a cut on a router – one to raise or lower the motor, one to secure the height clamp and one to hold the measuring device. And if the router is in a table, you may need to be extremely flexible to scrunch down and read the rule.

This simple shop-made height gauge eliminates the need for one of those extra hands and most of the contortions. The gauge is stable enough that it does not have to be held and the scale can be read accurately from most angles. You can use the gauge with the arm facing down to measure heights of less than 3" or with the arm up for heights between 3" and 6". This gauge also can be used with a shaper, table saw, dado cutter or any other tool or accessory in which the blade or cutter protrudes through a worktable or fence.

You also can use the gauge to measure the position of a router-table fence in relation to the bit. Just set the gauge and hold it against the fence with the arm encompassing the bit. Then move the fence forward or back until the side of the bit touches the arm.

To use the gauge, set it to the desired height. Place it on the router sole or mounting plate with the arm over the bit. Raise or lower the bit until it touches the arm.

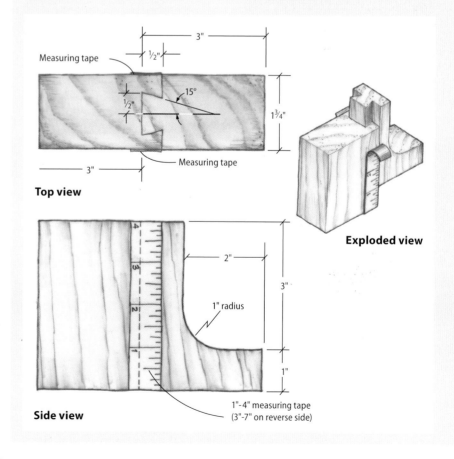

Top view

Side view

Exploded view

1"-4" measuring tape (3"-7" on reverse side)

Router Joinery

by Nick Engler

PRO TRICK

Dehumidifier Can Make Your Tenons Fit Tighter

Woodworkers who use mortise-and-tenon joints sometimes keep a dehumidifier in their shop to make it drier than the surrounding environment. Once in the shop, wood shrinks slightly. Then, when a completed project is returned to normal humidity, the tenons swell in the mortises, making the joints tighter.

Although routers were originally designed to create moulded shapes, they can be excellent joinery tools. In fact, they're better in some ways than table saws, professional-quality mortisers or dado cutters when it comes to cutting joints. There are several reasons routers have an advantage:

Simplicity: Setting up hand-held or table-mounted routers is rather straightforward. Tools dedicated to joint-making such as hollow-chisel mortisers are more complex and require more time to set up. Sure, it could be worth the effort to use a mortiser if you're planning to make dozens of duplicate joints. But if all you want to cut are a few mortises and tenons, for example, a router will save you loads of time.

Versatility: You can make a greater variety of joints with a router than with any other joinery tool. No matter if you have a fixed-base or plunge router, you can cut more types of joints than with any other kind of tool.

Accuracy: There isn't a more precise joinery tool. You may find tools just as accurate, but none that surpass the router. Because routers cut quickly, they leave a smooth surface, meaning joints fit better and bonds are stronger.

There are some disadvantages to using your router for joint-making, and I'd be remiss if I didn't mention them:

• Most routers won't stand up to continual cutting as well as heavy-duty woodworking machinery.

• Because you can't make deep cuts in a single pass on a router, it may take you longer to rout some joints than it would to use a mortiser or dado cutter.

• Depending on the joint you want to make, you may be limited by the sizes and configurations of available bits.

These shortcomings, however, are minor. Routers are indispensable joinery tools in any workshop.

Rabbets, Dados & Grooves

You can make the most basic woodworking joints – rabbets, dados and grooves – using a simple fixed-base router and an inexpensive set of straight bits.

Rabbets (and the simple tongue for a tongue-and-groove joint) are produced easily with a router. While you may need a variety of rabbet sizes, a single rabbeting bit can accomplish them all. By purchasing a rabbeting bit with interchangeable guide bearings, the width of the rabbet can be changed quickly by selecting and installing a different diameter guide-bearing on the bit.

Rabbeting can be accomplished safely using a router free-hand or in a table. For rabbeting smaller pieces (such as with frames or door mullions) I recommend using a router table. In a table, you can use a simple straight bit to cut the rabbet, or you can use a rabbeting bit with a bearing guide. Even though you may think the bearing guides make a fence unnecessary, you still should use one to limit the amount of bit exposed and to help guide the pieces. Align the fence with the outside edge of the bearing for a seamless process. For improved accuracy and safety, use a fingerboard to hold the material against the fence and table.

As mentioned earlier, a rabbet also can form the tongue for a tongue-and-groove joint. The tongue can be flush to one side of a board (for offset raised-panel doors) or the tongue can be centered on the board. Essentially, the tongue is just a long tenon. Run the groove first, then simply size the tongue to fit in that groove.

Many dados or grooves can be made with a straight bit that is sized

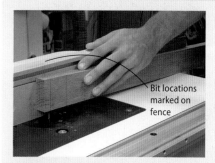

Bit locations marked on fence

TIPS & TRICKS

Tilting Pieces to Create Stopped Cuts

Stopped grooves or dados can be made safely on the router table by first marking the bit location (both sides of the bit profile) on the fence, then carefully lowering and raising the piece for the cut using the end of the board opposite the cut as a fulcrum.

No Templates Needed If You Copy an Existing Piece

To reproduce a shape quickly and precisely without making a template, just use an existing part to make copies. Adhere the shaped part to the stock with double-faced carpet tape and, using either a pattern-cutting or flush-trim bit, cut the stock while tracing the shaped part with the bearing. However, because the bit won't cut inside corners that are smaller than the bit diameter, you'll have to cut this with a band saw or scroll saw.

Mortising Bits are Worth Taking the Plunge For

Some manufacturers offer so-called mortising bits. They look like a standard straight bit with one difference: They have an additional small cutter at the end of the bit. This bit allows you to plunge directly into your work, instead of wiggling the bit as you plunge, which is typical with a straight bit.

When routing dados and grooves, the joint ordinarily will be the same width as the bit. If you need to make a joint of a larger size, first make a cut that's somewhat narrower than the joint needed (left), then move the fence or straightedge to make a second cut (below), enlarging the joint to the desired width.

Stop block

When cutting blind joints – rabbets, dados and grooves that are closed at one or both ends – use a stop block to halt the cut at the blind ends. Note that the end of the stop block is mitered. This prevents sawdust from being trapped between it and the stock, where the dust might interfere with the accuracy of the cut.

When cutting a joint in a contoured edge, use a piloted bit to follow the contour. A piloted rabbeting bit will neatly cut a rabbet in an irregular edge, while a spline cutter will likewise make a groove in an irregular edge a simple task.

to accurately make the joint with a single-width pass. To make a dado or groove that's a non-standard size, choose a cutter that's slightly smaller than the width of the joint and cut the joint in two passes, as shown in the photos on page 31.

Because most basic joints are cut parallel or perpendicular to straight edges, you must guide the router or the work in a straight line. The best way to do this is to use an edge guide, straightedge, fence or miter gauge. You also can use a shop-made

jig, such as the T-square Router Guide.

If the joint is blind (which means it stops before running through the board) at one or both ends, attach stops to the workpiece or the guides to automatically halt the cut. The location of these stops depends on where the joint is to be cut in the board. For example, to cut a blind groove that stops 6" from the ends of the board, clamp a stop to the outfeed side of the fence 6" from the router bit.

Now, if the joint is blind at both ends, you can determine the distance between the two stops by adding the length of the board to the length of the joint and subtracting the router bit diameter. (For example, if you want to cut a 4"-long double-blind groove in a 10" board with a ⅜"-diameter straight bit, position the stops 13⅝" apart.)

But what if the rabbet must follow a contour? Well, there are a couple of choices, but the only bit that makes good sense for making contoured rabbets is a bearing-piloted rabbeting bit.

For a contoured groove, a different approach will likely be necessary. The answer this time is a guide collar (also called a template guide) and a template. Because a guide collar is slightly wider than the diameter of the bit, the contour cut by the router will not be the same size as the template. For inside curves and corners, the contour will be smaller; for outside ones, it will be larger.

There always will be a small gap between the edge of the template and the nearest side of the cut because of the different diameters.

To determine the width of this space, subtract the diameter of the bit from the outside diameter of the collar and divide by two. (For example, if you cut a contoured groove with a ⅝"-diameter collar and a ½"-diameter bit, the distance between the template and the groove will be ¹⁄₁₆".)

Mortises and Tenons

To make a mortise and its matching tenon, you must combine several techniques. Although it may seem complex, a mortise-and-tenon joint is just a combination of several basic joints. After all, a mortise is simply a groove that's blind at both ends, and a tenon is made by cutting two or more rabbets in the end of a board.

The trick to cutting precise mortises and tenons is to make the cuts in the proper order. Most experienced woodworkers agree that it's easiest to cut the mortise first, then fit the tenon into it.

To make a mortise, you must bore a starter hole and expand it to the dimensions needed. There are several ways to do this using a fixed-base or a plunge router, either hand-held or in a table. However, when you make

mortises for mortise-and-tenon joints, you usually want to make several mortises in several different workpieces, all the exact same size and shape. The easiest way to accomplish this is with a simple template.

As a general rule, mortises should be about half the width of the material they're made in. So a mortise in a ¾"-wide piece of wood should be ⅜" wide, with a ³⁄₁₆" shoulder on either side of it. The depth of the mortise should be no less than ¾" to ensure a good joint, but 1" or slightly more usually is a good idea.

The simplest form of template is a piece of plywood that has a hole in it that is the exact size of the mortise you wish to rout. Just clamp the template directly onto your work and then form the mortise using a straight bit that has a bearing above the cutting flutes. There are a variety of ways to make the template, from making plunge cuts on a board with a table saw to edge-gluing four pieces of wood together and leaving a gap in the middle that is the size of the mortise. All work just fine.

When cutting the mortise, first plunge straight down in the area

Cheek — Scrap — Shoulder

To make a tenon, cut two or more rabbets in the end of the board – these rabbets will become the cheeks and shoulders of the tenon. To fit the tenon to the mortise, cut the tenon just a bit large, then slowly raise the bit, shaving away a paper-thin layer of stock on each cheek until you get the fit you're after. Guide the cuts with the miter gauge, using the fence as a stop.

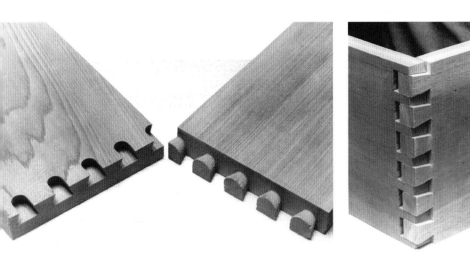

passes and two matching templates. These templates are less common than half-blind dovetail templates and, because of the precision required to make them, can be much more expensive.

Sliding dovetails require no special equipment, other than your router, router table and dovetail bit.

To make a sliding dovetail, first rout a dovetail slot the same way you would rout a dado or groove. Because of the bit shape, however, you must cut the full depth in one pass. Next, cut a dovetail tenon to fit this slot – this must be cut on a router table. The slot, on the other hand, can be cut using a hand-held router. Leave the depth of cut unchanged from the setup you used when routing the slot. Then pass a board by the bit, cutting one face. Then turn the board around and cut the other face. These two cuts form the tenon.

To assemble the joint, just slide the tenon into the slot. If necessary, adjust the fit by trimming a little

On half-blind dovetails (left), the joint is hidden from view on one side. This makes it ideal for the fronts of drawers and other applications where you don't want to see the joinery. Through dovetails (right) are visible from both sides and are often used for decoration, as well as joining.

you wish to waste away. Then, with the router fully plunged, follow the template's edge with your bearing to shape the mortise to its finished size. (See p. 33 for how to cut the tenon.)

Dovetails

There are three basic dovetail joints: half-blind dovetails, through dovetails and sliding dovetails. The router is the only power tool that can create them all, using a special dovetail bit.

Both half-blind and through dovetails are most easily made using accurate templates. These can be purchased (there are many commercially manufactured ones) or you can make your own.

Through dovetails require two

To rout a half-blind dovetail joint (right), secure both of the adjoining boards in the template. The "tail" board is held vertically, so its end is flush with the top surface of the horizontal "pin" board. Cut both the tails and the pins in one pass with a dovetail bit, using a guide collar to follow the template.

When using a fixed through-dovetail template (left) you can't change the size and position of the tails and pins. Rout the tails first, using the tail template, a guide collar and a dovetail bit. Then you can switch to the pin template and a straight bit. Fit the pins to the tails by moving the template forward or back on its holder. This will change the size, but not the location, of the pins.

stock off the tenon's cheeks, either with your router, a small plane or simply with sandpaper.

Coped Joints

Perhaps the easiest way to make a joint with a router is to cut a "coped" joint, where both adjoining surfaces are shaped. The most common example of this is on cabinet doors where the rails (the horizontal pieces) meet with the stiles (the vertical pieces). Each joint surface is a mirror image of the other, so the two surfaces mate perfectly.

This has two advantages: the shape of the joint aligns the adjoining parts so the surfaces are flush and the corners are square, and the shape increases the gluing surfaces and

strengthens the joint.

Coped joints require special router bits that can be pretty expensive. There are three types of bits, and each must be used in a different manner:

Single bit with one cutter: The male and female cutters are on the same bit, making it a long piece of tooling. You raise and lower the bit in the table to change which set of cutters are in use.

Single bit with interchangeable cutters: You switch from the male to the female cutter by disassembling the bit and changing the orientation of the cutters. There are small shims involved so you need to keep those in the right place as you assemble the bit each time.

Need a Hinge? Just Add a Hole to Finger-jointed Boards

To make a wooden hinge, roundover the ends of two boards with a roundover bit (the radius of the bit must be half the thickness of the boards). Cut finger joints in the rounded ends and assemble the joint. At the center of the rounded ends, drill a hole through the interlocking fingers and insert a wooden or metal dowel to serve as a pivot.

Two Jigs are Better than One, Especially for Dovetails

Many woodworkers keep two dovetail fixtures in their shops – one for half-blinds, one for everything else. For example, I make frequent use of two commercial dovetail routing setups. In one, I have an inexpensive half-blind dovetail jig and an old router with the necessary guide collar and dovetail bit. Because I rout more half-blind dovetails than any other dovetail joint, this saves me lots of time. Then, when I need to rout through dovetails or other special dovetail joints, I just use my other jig.

Just a Little Bit off the Top, Even when Routing Mortises

When routing deep mortises, remember to make the cut in several passes, routing no more than ⅛" with each pass. If the wood is very hard or tends to chip and splinter, it's better to rout in ¹⁄₁₆" passes. Also, use a spiral straight bit to help clear the chips from the mortise as you cut. This is especially important when you're using a hand-held router and the bit is positioned over the work because the chips tend to fall down into the mortise and clog it.

A drawer-lock joint requires only one bit and one setup. However, instead of reversing boards face for face as you cut them (like in the finger glue joint), you must cut the drawer front with the face of the workpiece against the router table, and then cut the drawer side with the face against the fence. Adjust both the depth of cut and the position of the fence so the members fit together properly.

A BIT OF ADVICE

These three bits are great when using your router for joinery.

Rabbeting Bit

This handy bit usually comes with a set of different-sized bearings that you can simply swap out to cut rabbets of different depths.

Cope-and-stick Bit

Making decorative frame-and-panel assemblies is a snap with this bit. There are three versions that have different ways of approaching the same operation. In this version, one bit cuts both the male and female pieces.

Spline-cutting Bit

Making grooves in edges is the mainstay of this bit. Newer versions allow you to adjust the size of the groove with shims or by adjusting the cutters.

Two bits: There's one bit for cutting the male part of the joint and a second for the female. This is usually the most expensive route.

There is another type of bit used for assembling boxes that routs the joinery on both edges. The drawer-lock joint – one example of these – is shown on page 35.

Loose-tenon Joints

Along with all the joints we have discussed so far that require joinery parts cut on the mating pieces, there are a number that use an extra piece to form a loose-tenon joint. The three most common are the true loose-tenon joint, the spline joint and the biscuit joint.

The true loose tenon is exactly what it sounds like. Rather than

making a mortise in one piece and a tenon on the other, both pieces have mortises. A third piece (often made in a long stock piece and cut to length) becomes a double-sided tenon, connecting the two mortises. The strength is essentially the same as it is in a mortise-and-tenon joint, but the process is perfect for use with a router, and it is quick and accurate.

The mortises are made as described earlier and can be left rounded on the ends, as created by the bit. The tenon is made from a piece of stock planed and ripped to fit the mortises. Next the four arises are rounded using a roundover bit in your router to make a perfect fit in the mortises. Then you simply cross-cut the tenon to fit the mortises.

Spline and biscuit joints are cous-

A tongue-and-groove joint requires two matching bits. Rout a groove in one edge of each of the workpieces, then change bits and rout a tongue in the other edge. You must carefully adjust the depth of cut for the second cut to match the first so the faces of the adjoining boards will be flush.

FINGER-JOINT JIG

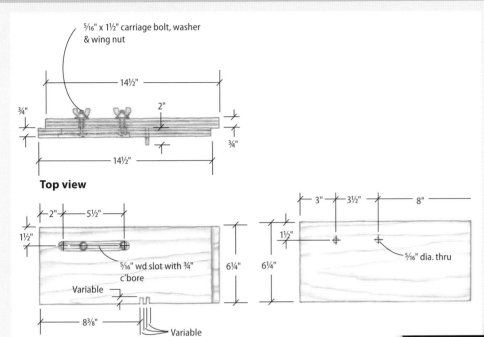

5/16" x 1½" carriage bolt, washer & wing nut

14½"
¾"
2"
¾"
14½"

Top view

2"
5½"
1½"
5/16" wd slot with ¾" c'bore
Variable
6¼"
8⅜"
Variable

Front view

3"
3½"
8"
1½"
6¼"
5/16" dia. thru

Mount layout

This jig will evenly space notches as you cut them, allowing you to make perfect finger joints. It's designed to mount on any miter gauge and will work great on your router table (or, if you're so inclined, you also can use it on your table saw).

Make the face and the mount from cabinet-grade plywood and the stop from hardwood. If you wish, you can make several different faces, each with a different-sized stop. This will enable you to cut different sizes of finger joints.

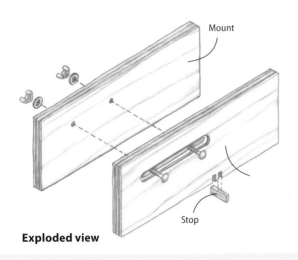

Mount

Stop

Exploded view

To use the jig, screw or bolt the mount to a miter gauge. Loosen the wing nuts that secure the face to the mount and slide the face sideways until the stop is the proper distance away from the bit. When the stop is positioned properly, tighten the wing nuts.

ins to each other. The spline joint requires a groove (usually about ¼" wide) that you run the entire length of the two pieces to join together. This can be an edge-to-edge joint or an edge-to-face joint. It doesn't matter.

A special router bit called a spline-cutting bit is used to cut the groove. As with a rabbeting bit, the spline cutter uses interchangeable bearing guides of different diameters to adjust the depth of cut. A router table's fence also can be used to adjust the depth.

With the mating grooves cut, just glue a spline in place. The spline can be made from ¼" plywood or solid wood, depending on your preference. Again, the spline should be slightly less wide (deep) than the groove to allow some room for glue squeeze-out.

Biscuits follow the same concept, except the spline cutter is used to cut shorter grooves and commercially available biscuits are used to bridge the joint. In essence you've replaced the need to buy a $150 biscuit jointer with a $20 router bit – not too bad.

Use Your Router to Build Boxes & Drawers

by Nick Engler

Woodworkers have been building boxes for at least 5,000 years. For much of that period, boxes were made using a single chunk of wood with the insides dug out to create a cavity. That's because up until about 600 or 700 years ago, turning trees into boards was an extremely expensive process – the boards had to be hand-sawn (or rived) from logs, then smoothed with planes. Consequently, only the very rich owned furniture made from boards. Most people simply found suitable logs and chopped or burned away the insides.

The invention of the water-powered sawmill in 1328 caused a revolution in woodworking, including the art of making boxes and drawers. The sawmill made it possible for everyone to own boxes made out of sawed lumber, and woodworkers

began to build storage units from more than just one board.

This multi-board box remains a rather practical and popular method of construction. While the joinery isn't much of a concern when making a one-piece box, it becomes paramount once you begin building boxes and drawers from multiple boards.

With the advent of multi-board

drawer construction, a variety of woodworking planes and saws were developed with box and drawer joinery as their sole purpose. As power tools started to replace hand tools (or at least become a serious option for many woodworkers), the router took over many of the box and drawer joinery duties. In this chapter, I'll take a look at a number of joints that

PRO TIP

Read Grain Direction To Get a Jump on Expansion

When you make a drawer with a solid-wood bottom, the grain direction should run from side-to-side so the drawer bottom will expand front-to-back. If the bottom were to expand side-to-side, it would press the drawer sides out, making the drawer bind or stick in its opening.

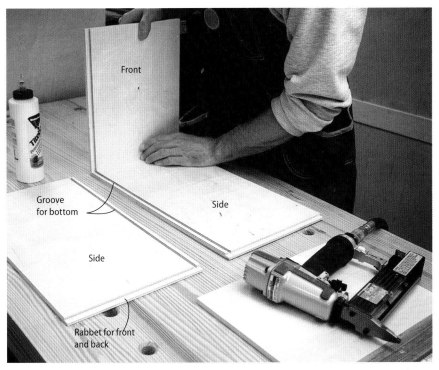

This drawer box is made pretty easily with rabbets. The front and back rest in ½"-wide x ¼"-deep rabbets in the side pieces. The bottom slides into a ¼"-wide x ¼"-deep groove in the sides and front. The back is ½" shorter than the front to allow the bottom to slide in.

can be created with a router to help you build furniture, drawers and many other boxes.

Corner Joints

A variety of joints formed by routers can be used to attach the rigid corners of boxes and drawers. The best choice of joint will depend on how the box or drawer will be used:

• Will it be a strictly utilitarian storage unit or will it be decorative as well?

• Will it see light duty or will it be subjected to heavy use?

• Will it remain stationary or will it be moved from place to place?

No matter what you decide to use your box or drawer for, we've got the joint for you. Here are some of the most common corner joints:

Butt Joints: These are usually reinforced with screws or glue blocks and work well for light-duty, utilitarian

Rabbets and grooves are pretty easy to make with a hand-held router. Here you see a router cutting a ¼"-deep groove with a ¼" straight bit and an edge guide.

TIPS & TRICKS

Drawer Sides Can Extend Past the Back

Some traditional and modern drawer designs call for the sides to extend ¼" – ½" beyond the back of the drawer. This makes the drawer simpler to build and slightly stronger than if the sides are merely flush with the back. For inset drawers, the back ends of the sides often serve as stops to keep the drawer from being pushed in too far. The sides also make more stable stops than the back. Should the back cup or warp, the drawer may protrude from its case slightly. Should the sides cup, the position of the drawer won't be affected.

Size Drawers to Holes, Then Plane Them to Fit

Make the drawers precisely the same size as the drawer openings. They'll be too big to work properly, but you can use your hand plane or belt sander to take just a little bit of stock from the outside surfaces to get a perfect fit.

It May Take some Time, but Rout Cavity in Many Passes

If you're making a one-board box with your router, make sure you rout out the cavity in several passes, cutting no more than ⅛" deeper with each pass until you reach the desired depth. Begin by routing the circumference of the cavity, keeping the pilot bearing pressed against the pattern. Then move the router back and forth to clean out the waste in the middle of the cavity. (This technique is used only for small boxes these days – usually jewelry boxes with an odd or organic shape to them.)

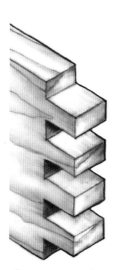

Finger joint

Through-dovetail

If the router is in a table, the fence guides the wood to quickly form the rabbets or grooves.

Miter Joints: These are a more aesthetically pleasing option, hiding the end grain on the adjoining boards so that all you see is uninterrupted face grain. However, these are comparatively weak and are best suited for light-duty projects unless reinforced with biscuits or splines (which we will discuss in greater detail next). Routers seldom are used to form miter joints, and are used instead to reinforce and decorate them.

Splined Miters: These are much stronger than regular miters and can be used for medium- or heavy-duty decorative boxes. The splines can be hidden or visible, depending on your project's style. They can be made with hand-held or table-mounted routers using a spline-cutter bit, which is essentially a tiny table saw blade with the shaft of the bit serv-

ing as an arbor. Available as many bits of different thicknesses or one bit with adjustable thicknesses, these are very versatile router accessories.

Finger Joints: Also known as "box joints," these are strong enough to qualify for heavy-duty boxes and drawers. The interlocking tenons create a vast gluing surface that holds firmly. These were once considered strictly utilitarian (many packing crates in the late 19th and early 20th centuries were made using finger joints), but in recent years they have been used in decorative applications as well. These joints are best formed with a table-mounted router using a straight bit and a miter gauge or a specially made jig.

Through-dovetails: The strongest of all common joints for boxes and drawers, these are suitable for heavy-duty projects. Similar to finger joints, through-dovetails were once thought of as utilitarian, but today they are

boxes. No routers are necessary here. It's the simplest and weakest corner joint.

Rabbets & Grooves: These look similar to butt joints when assembled, but they are strong enough to be used for medium-duty utilitarian boxes. Rabbets of many sizes are formed easily using a rabbeting bit in a hand-held or table-mounted router. Rabbets and grooves also can be made with a straight bit in a hand-held router if you use a base-mounted edge guide.

½" bottom beveled to fit in ¼"-wide groove in sides

Half-blind dovetails

The drawer bottoms in the drawers shown at above are ½" thick but are beveled to slip into a ¼" groove, a traditional drawer construction method. Also, you can see the half-blind dovetails connecting the side with the front.

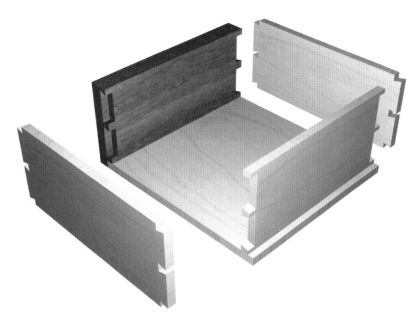

Construction of small drawers can be simple. This drawer for a spice box uses half-blind dove-tails to mate the front with the sides and through-dovetails to mate the back with the sides. The bottom is tacked to the sides and back using brads.

used just as much for decorative pieces. Routers make quick work of dovetails using specialized bits and jigs to make precise and tight joinery.

(Note: While some people will use contrasting colors or species of wood when making finger joints and dovetails to make the joinery stand out, just as many want to use the same type of wood for both parts of these joints to make them look more subtle.)

All of these joints can be used to make standard boxes or the more-common open-topped boxes we use every day – known more commonly, of course, as drawers.

Making Drawers

As mentioned earlier, a drawer is a box without a lid that slides in and out of a larger box, chest or case. Most drawers have five parts – a front, a back, two sides and a bottom.

Drawers are classified according to how the fronts and faces fit their

openings. They can be "inset" within the opening, they can "overlay" the face frame or front edges of the case, or they can be rabbeted or "lipped" so that only the lips overlap the case.

To a large degree, drawers are made the same way as the cabinets that hold them. The front, back and

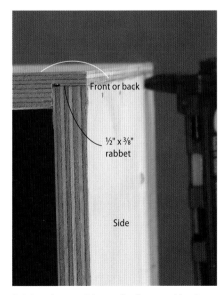

Joining drawer sides to the front and back can be as simple as cutting a rabbet. Then you can use glue and nails to complete the joint.

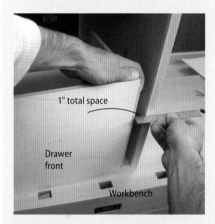

TIPS & TRICKS

Tape Helps You Fit Fabric

To fit a fabric lining in a drawer (for storing silverware, etc.), cover the bottom surface of the material with double-sided carpet tape and cut the pieces to size with scissors or a utility knife. The tape will stiffen the fabric, making it easier to cut and fit. To install the lining, just peel the paper backing off the tape and press the fabric in place.

If Your Drawer has Slides, Key Measurement is Width

When building drawers with slides, the most critical dimension is the width of the assembled box. If you're off by more than $1/32$", the slides won't work. It pays to mock up an assembled drawer to get the fit just right. Standard drawer slides usually need $1/2$" of space between the drawer and case, so shoot for a drawer that's 1" less than the total case opening.

Finishing Might Not Always be a Good Idea

Think about what you will be storing in the drawers before you decide to finish the interior surfaces. Many finishes, especially linseed oil, emit an odor long after they've cured, and they may impart chemical smells.

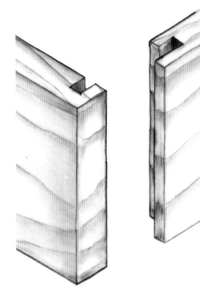

Half-blind tongue-and-rabbet

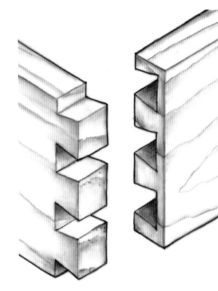

Half-blind dovetail

sides are arranged to expand and contract in the same direction and are joined rigidly at the corners. The bottom usually floats in a groove in the sides, free to move independently so its shrinking and swelling won't affect the overall drawer structure.

But there are significant differences between drawers and boxes. Typically, a drawer must withstand more punishment than a box. As you push or pull a drawer in and out, there is a good deal of stress placed on the corner joints. And because the drawer handles or pulls are attached to the front, most of this stress is concentrated on the front corners.

Consequently, drawers commonly are built with extremely strong joints at the front corners, while the back corners and the bottom are assembled with much simpler joinery.

There is another reason people opt to use different joints at the front of the drawer – traditionally, the drawer faces looked a lot like solid boards or panels in a frame. So, the front joinery had to be hidden when the drawer was closed.

The joints listed below are common router-made joints used in

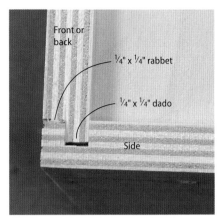

A simple and very common drawer joint in commercial furniture is the tongue-and-rabbet (or dado-and-rabbet) joint. It's made by simply running a dado in the drawer sides and then rabbets on the drawer fronts and backs. Both operations are best made with a router in a table.

drawer joinery:

Reinforced Rabbets: These are sufficient for light-duty drawers (shown below in the inset drawer). Just rabbet the drawer front, then secure the sides in these rabbets with glue, nails, screws or pegs. This joint also is frequently used to mate the drawer back and sides.

Lock Joints, or Tongue-and-rabbet Joints: These work well for light- or medium-duty drawers. Cut dados in the drawer sides, and a tongue is formed when you cut a rabbet in the drawer front and back. Then insert

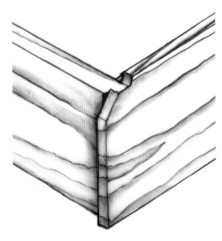

Lipped drawer

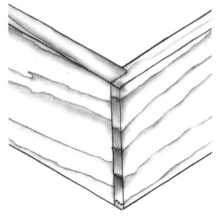

Inset drawer

Overlay drawer

Half-blind dovetail

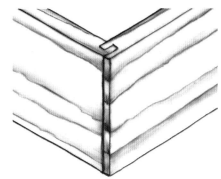

Half-blind tongue-and-rabbet

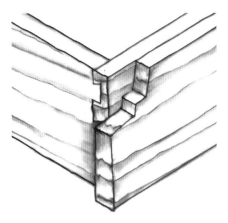

Half-blind dovetail with overlay false front

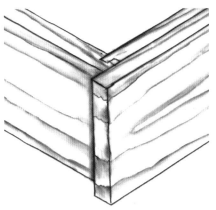

Tongue-and-rabbet with overlay false front

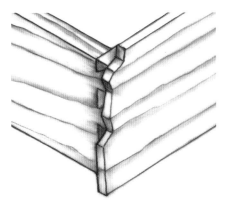

Lipped half-blind dovetail

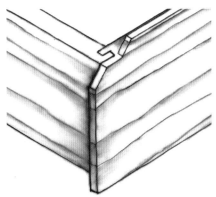

Lipped tongue-and-rabbet

the tongue in the dados. This joint (seen in the photo above left) can be used for the front and back joint in drawers, providing extra strength over a reinforced rabbet. Made using rabbeting, spline or straight router bits, these joints are a mainstay in commercial drawer joinery.

Sliding Dovetails: These are strong enough for medium- and heavy-duty

drawers. Simply cut a dovetail groove in the drawer front with a dovetail bit in your router, then cut matching tenons in the sides and slide them together. It's unlikely to be used for any drawer joinery other than attaching drawer fronts.

Half-blind Dovetails: These are the traditional choice when you need heavy-duty drawers. The interlocking tails

TIPS & TRICKS

Plunge Router is Great When Cutting Box Cavities

When selecting a straight bit for cutting box cavities, look for one designed to be used with a plunge router. On these bits, the flutes protrude below the body of the bit so it can be used for boring as well as side-cutting. This makes it easier to rout a starter hole. Then simply enlarge it to make the cavity. Some bits are intended solely for side-cutting. Their flutes are almost flush with the bottom of the bit, making it difficult to plunge the bit into the stock. Also, these bits will burn the bottom of the cavity.

Work Loose when it's Cold, Tight when it's Warm

If your doors or door frames are made from solid wood, fit them loose in winter (when the wood has shrunk) and tight in summer (when the wood has expanded).

Fake Out Your Family with False Fronts for Drawers

When making overlay or lipped drawers, fitting the drawer can be much easier if you use a false (or faux) front. After you complete the drawer box and install it, just apply a false front (either with screws or glue). Only the front needs to be fit to the cabinet opening, not the drawer. Double-sided tape makes a good temporary bond while you're fitting the fronts, and it will definitely make fitting your drawer fronts easier.

and pins offer an enormous amount of strength and they are relatively easy to make with a store-bought jig. Because they are "half-blind," they meet the requirement for being invis-

A BIT OF ADVICE

These bits are great when using your router to make boxes and drawers.

Lock-miter Bit

An excellent joint for mitered drawers, this bit provides extra gluing surfaces and locking strength. The same bit creates both joining edges by cutting one board vertically and the other horizontally with the same set-up.

Dovetail Bit

This classic drawer joint adds extra locking strength and also a decorative feature. This bit is available in a number of different angles for use in softwoods or hardwoods.

Drawer-lock Bit

This bit lets you form a stronger rabbet joint between the sides and front of a drawer. The drawer fronts are cut horizontally, while the drawer sides are cut vertically against the fence of a router table.

ible with the drawer closed.

Through-dovetails: These are a close cousin to the half-blinds. While they are easier to create, these joints will be visible from the front of the drawer. Because of this, a through-dovetail is often used for the back joinery in a drawer, while the more complicated half-blind dovetail adorns the front.

Joining the Bottom

The final piece of joinery in a drawer is finding a way to hold the bottom in place in the sides, front and back. Because the bottom usually floats, your choice of joints is more limited when looking to attach this piece.

Traditional solid-wood bottoms originally were made from ½" material and the edges were beveled or raised similar to the center section on a raised-panel door. This allowed the bottom to be captured in a relatively narrow groove (¼" or so) without losing any strength in the bottom. Raised-panel and straight router bits in a table-mounted operation make

this joinery safe and fairly easy.

With today's wood technologies, ¼" plywood often is used to create very strong drawer bottoms with no extra milling required.

On many boxes and drawers, the bottom is captured in a groove that is cut in the inside surfaces of the front, back and sides. Just slide the bottom into the grooves at the same time you assemble the box, making sure

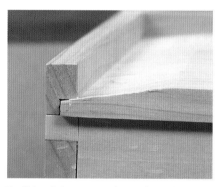

Traditional drawers used raised panels made of solid wood for the bottoms. These are easily made on a router table with a raised-panel bit, then fit into a standard groove in the drawer sides.

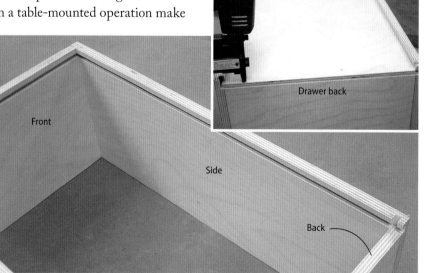

Front

Side

Drawer back

Back

A simple drawer bottom is easily made from ¼" plywood. The sides and front of the drawer are grooved with a straight router bit, ¼" up from the bottom edge. The back is held short at the top of the groove. With the bottom slipped into the groove (shown in the inset photo), you can square up the drawer, then nail the bottom in place into the drawer back.

you don't get any glue in the grooves. Once the glue has had time to dry, the bottom will be permanently locked in place.

One common variation in drawers is to cut a groove in just the drawer front and sides, cutting the back narrower to stop at the top of the bottom groove. This allows you to slide the bottom into place after the drawer is assembled. Then the bottom is tacked in place on the drawer back. With less mess and haste while the glue is drying, this method also gives you a chance to square the drawer to the bottom.

Another drawer bottom joint can be made by cutting grooves into small strips of wood, then gluing the strips to the inside surfaces of the drawer. The kind of drawer bottom that rests in grooved slips is sometimes called a "French bottom."

Or, if the drawer is particularly wide – so wide that a thin bottom might sag – you can divide the bottom into two or more sections with grooved dividers, also called "muntins."

If your project requires a removable bottom or if you must install the bottom after the rest of the parts are joined, you can rest the bottom on ledges or cleats, or you can screw it to the bottom edges of the box in some cases.

(Note: When you are fitting a solid-wood bottom in your drawer, you must remember to leave space for expansion. How much space depends on the width of the bottom. The rule of thumb is to allow ¼" for every 12" across the grain with plain-sawn wood and ⅛" with quartersawn wood.)

TENONING JIG

A tenoning jig holds a workpiece vertically to make a cut in its end. This particular jig rides along the router table fence; the workpiece rests against a quadrant and a clamp secures the workpiece to the vertical face of the jig. You can adjust the angle of the workpiece between 45° and 90° by rotating the quadrant.

Make the vertical face, leg and spacer from ¾" plywood and the quadrant from hardwood. Rout the slots in the spacer and the quadrant, then make the groove in the vertical face. Next, drill the holes needed to mount the quadrant and the clamp.

Glue and screw the spacer to the face. Secure the quadrant to the face with carriage bolts, washers and wing nuts. (Note that there are six mounting holes and the quadrant can be attached in four different positions.)

Attach the leg to the spacer with round-head wood screws and washers. Then adjust the gap between the leg and the face to fit your router table fence, then tighten the wing nuts and you're ready to go.

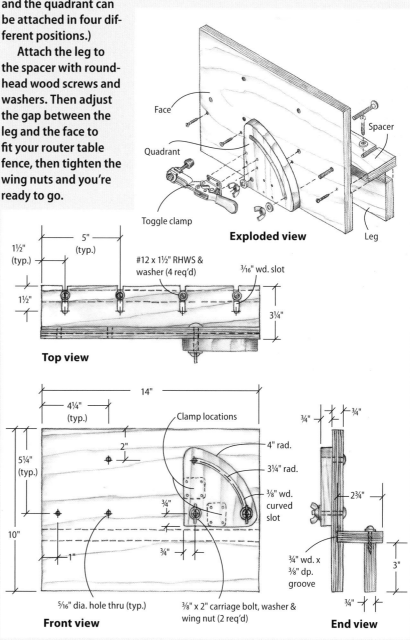

Face

Spacer

Quadrant

Toggle clamp

Exploded view

Leg

1½" (typ.)

5" (typ.)

#12 x 1½" RHWS & washer (4 req'd)

³⁄₁₆" wd. slot

1½"

3¼"

Top view

14"

4¼" (typ.)

Clamp locations

4" rad.

3¼" rad.

5¼" (typ.)

2"

¾"

¾"

¾"

10"

¾"

³⁄₈" wd. curved slot

2¾"

1"

¾"

3"

⁵⁄₁₆" dia. hole thru (typ.)

Front view

³⁄₈" x 2" carriage bolt, washer & wing nut (2 req'd)

¾" wd. x ³⁄₈" dp. groove

¾"

End view

Edge & Surface Treatments

by Nick Engler

Routers were developed to cut moulded shapes in wood. Although their workshop role has expanded (greatly) during the last century to include joinery and other operations, moulding is still what they do best. They remain the chief woodworking tools for edge and surface "treatments" – cutting decorative shapes.

Before we get into the techniques for making decorative moulded shapes, let's review these shapes and how they're combined. In many woodworkers' minds, this is muddy water. Open any tool catalog to the router bit section and you'll find whole pages of shapes, all in a jumble. But don't worry. There is some order to this chaos.

Despite the profusion of mould-ing bits, there are really only three shapes in decorative woodworking:
- Bead (convex curve)
- Cove (concave curve)
- Flat (straight line)

Every moulding, no matter how complex, is comprised of beads, coves and flats. If you had only three router bits – one for cutting beads, one for cutting coves, one for cutting flats – you could still produce any shape of moulding, no matter how intricate the shape.

PRO TIP

Safe Small Profiles
Small (½" wide or less) profiles and edge treatments can be dangerous to run. To avoid this, use a two-step process. By preparing a slab of wood the appropriate thickness of your profile (let's call it a ½" x 10" x 24" piece of cherry) you can safely run the profile on one long edge, then head to the table saw to safely cut off the thin edge piece. Then head back to the router table and repeat the process. It adds a couple of steps, but it also adds a lot of safety.

Basic moulded shapes

Fillet or listel
Use straight bit

Chamfer
Use chamfering bit
or V-bit

Bevel
Use chamfering bit
or V-bit

Flat-bottom groove
Use straight bit

V-groove
Use V-bit

Flute
Use fluting bit

Round-bottom
Use fluting bit

Cove or cavetto
Use cove bit

Quarter-round bead
Use roundover bit

Half-round bead or astragal
Use beading bit for small beads, nosing or roundover bit for large beads

Cyma recta
Use ogee bit (centers of curves are aligned horizontally)

Cyma reversa
Use ogee bit (centers of curves are aligned vertically)

Basic Moulded Shapes

Of course, there's a little more to it. Each of these three main categories is subdivided into a few basic moulded shapes that can be cut with a common bit. All mouldings are variations or combinations of these basic shapes, shown in the illustrations above.

There are no hard and fast rules dictating how you combine these shapes or how you use them. However, you may find these guidelines useful:

• Consider where people will stand when viewing the shapes and present these features at an angle that makes them easy to be seen and enjoyed.

• Vary the shapes in a complex moulding – don't just repeat the same shapes over and over. The clas-

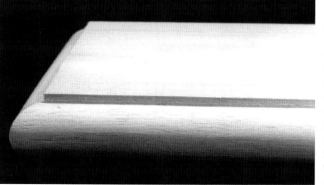

This tabletop will see a lot of use, so the woodworker who made it cut a thumbnail moulding in the edge. This relatively simple shape preserves the strength of the edge, while a more complex shape would weaken it and the edge would soon show the wear.

Two Sides of Grooves Make Pretty Decorative Panels

Cut a set of grooves in a board that are parallel to each other. Make each groove a little more than half as deep as the board is thick. Then turn the board upside down and cut another set of grooves at an angle to the first set. Where the grooves intersect, they will create openings. The size, shape and spacing of these openings depends on the size, shape and spacing of the grooves.

Simple Cock Beading

Cock beading is a simple edge detail that can dress up doors, drawers and much more. But cutting this detail on a door panel can be a lot of work. The simple option is to run a quantity of ⅛" hardwood through your router table adding a bullnose detail to one edge. Then, simply glue this edging to your panel. Presto – simple cock beading.

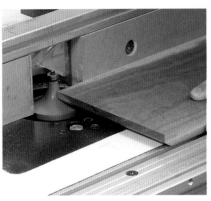

When you're ready to shape your workpiece, first cut the end grain along the ends …

… then cut the long grain along the edges.

To make an applied moulding or picture frame stock, cut the shape you want in the edge of a wide board, then rip it to the proper thickness, which I'm doing here on my table saw. Don't try to rout a shape in narrow stock – it may chip, splinter or kick back at you.

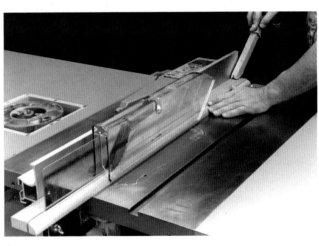

This safety consideration also applies to making curved mouldings, such as a classic "gooseneck" moulding. Cut the inside curve in the wide moulding stock, sand it so the curves are fair, then rout the shape in the edge.

When you've shaped the inside edge of the stock, you can cut the outside edge to free the moulding from the piece, as I'm doing here with my band saw.

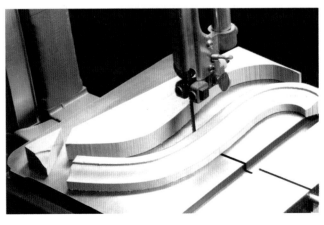

sic bead moulding, which incorporates a cove and a bead, has been a favorite of cabinetmakers for hundreds of years – you hardly ever see a moulding with a double cove or a double bead.

• To make mouldings more dramatic, use sharp, crisp transitions between the shapes. Make the curves and flats meet at distinct angles, or you can use fillets to separate shapes.

• If the structural strength of the piece is important, use simpler shapes.

Once you have designed a moulding, you need to plan how you'll make it – what bits to use, how many passes you'll need to make, etc.

Then, consider how to incorporate the moulded shapes in the project you're building. You have two choices: You can cut the shapes into the surfaces of the structural parts, or you can make separately shaped parts (mouldings) and apply them to the piece.

Each of these choices has trade-offs. If you make applied mouldings, you may not be able to match the wood grain and color of the larger piece, but you can use moulding to disguise seams and joints. If you cut the shapes in a large structural piece, you don't have to worry about matching the wood, but you do have to worry if the shape will weaken the piece. Choose whichever moulding design works best for the piece.

Cutting with the Router

Woodworkers usually shape the edges of a piece. The reasons for this are both aesthetic and practical. Because the edges often trace the outline of the project, shaping the edges emphasizes and enhances the design. Also, the edges are easier to cut than the faces.

The technique for routing moulded edges is simple and straightforward; there's little here that hasn't already been explained in previous chapters. However, a few additional considerations are worth mentioning.

Before you rout a shape in a straight edge, make sure that the edge is as smooth and even as possible. Joint it and remove all the mill marks. If the edge is contoured, make sure all the curves are "fair" – smooth and even. Because one of the purposes of a moulded shape is to emphasize the edge, the shape also will emphasize any imperfections in the edge.

When you're ready to shape the piece, cut the ends (end grain) first, then cut the edges (long grain).

Cut the large parts with a hand-held router, and cut the smaller parts on a router table. With very small parts, leave them attached to a larger board, rout the edge of the board, then cut the parts free. This last technique is particularly important when making mouldings. Most mouldings, when ripped to their final dimensions, are too slender to rout safely. The cutting action of the router may actually tear the thin stock apart.

If you use a large bit such as a panel-raising bit, slow down the speed of the router. The larger the bit, the slower you should run the router – otherwise the bit may burn

TIPS & TRICKS

Subtle Refinement
Edge treatments don't have to be complicated to be effective. A simple roundover bit or chamfering bit in the right locations can soften the look and feel of a piece of furniture, adding an extra level of elegance. And either of these bits work well with a bearing guide in an easy-to-manage trim router.

When cutting straight grooves, you can use a variety of jigs to get a decorative effect. Here, a tapering jig produces a pattern of angled grooves in a table leg. The grooves create the impression of a tapered leg, even though it's straight.

Keep That Piece Clamped Down Tight
Whenever you're routing something, make sure that either your workpiece or your router is stable and secure – they can't both move. If you choose to move the router across the work, clamp the work to your bench. If a clamp interferes with the operation, rout up to it and turn the router off. Then move the clamp to an area on the workpiece that you've already cut and resume routing.

Back-routing (Also Known as Climb-cutting) Can be Tough
Occasionally you must back-rout a piece to reduce tear-out. This means you are cutting with the bit's rotation, rather than against it. It's much more difficult to control your work this way, so be sure to take shallow cuts and feed very slowly. Keep the router and the work steady, making sure the bit doesn't chatter.

TIPS & TRICKS

Layers Can Help if You Want Complex Mouldings

Instead of making multiple passes to create a complex moulding, just glue up several simpler shapes. The easiest way to do this is to "laminate" the shapes – or build them up in layers. But you can also "join" the shapes by cutting dados, rabbets or grooves in the moulding stock, then glue smaller strips of wood in these joints. The strips that you glue together don't have to be the same species – you can use contrasting wood, if you want.

How Much is Enough?

To make sure the collet is safely gripping a router bit, insert ¾" of the length of a ¼" shank bit into the collet and insert a full 1" of every ½" shank bit.

Bits Pull Double Duty

Most edge-profile router bits are designed to be run in a specific orientation to the edge. However, if you're looking for an unusual alternative, don't hesitate to think in a different dimension. By running the wood past the bit in a vertical rather than horizontal attitude, the profile is changed subtly. And you get two profiles out of one bit.

the wood. If you can't vary the speed of the router, you shouldn't use bits larger than 2" in diameter. Even bits larger than 1½" can be troublesome.

Surface Treatments

In addition to cutting edges, you can create a variety of decorative shapes in the face of your workpiece. Surface treatments can be cut pretty

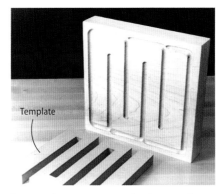

Some surface grooves are simultaneously decorative and practical, such as the groove around the perimeter of this cutting board. Not only does it collect liquids, but the groove also adds visual interest to an otherwise uninspiring piece. To make this groove, cut a template from hardboard and secure it to the cutting board with double-sided tape. Then you can cut the groove using a guide collar and core-box bit, keeping the collar firmly pressed against the template.

easily with either a hand-held or a table-mounted router fitted with either an unpiloted or a point-cut bit.

The most common surface decoration is a simple groove – flat-bottom, round-bottom or V-bottom. If the groove is straight, use a straightedge, fence or miter gauge to guide the cut. If the groove is irregular, you'll want to use a guide collar and a template.

For decorative grooves with a more-complex geometry, you can make multiple passes – or use a more-complex bit. For example, by making multiple parallel passes with a point-cut roundover bit (sometimes called a "beading" bit), you can form cock beads and reeds. Or, you can make cuts with a veining bit or a round-nose bit to create flutes. Also, a point-cut ogee bit will rout a wide groove with a double-ogee shape.

Making Complex Mouldings

When you produce complex mouldings, you often make multiple cuts, combining edge and surface treatments. It isn't difficult, but there are

Make multiple passes with a beading bit to create decorative reeds and beads in the surface of a board. Because the beading bit is actually a small point-cut quarter-round bit, each pass cuts a 90° arc – one-quarter of a circle. Half-round beads require two passes. The corner bead or reed on this table leg requires three passes because it is three-quarters round.

Point-cut bits with a complex shape, such as this pilotless ogee bit, cut a broad groove with an interesting shape. The sides of the grooves are mirror images of each other.

A flute is just a half-round groove – the opposite of a half-round bead. Often, it's blind at one or both ends. Use a veining bit to cut the flute and a straightedge to guide your router. If the flute is blind, it helps to have a plunge router. Attach stops to the straightedge to halt the cut when the flute is the correct length.

tricks to help you.

• First, you will need to decide which router bits to use to cut the different shapes. Often this is more of an art than a science. There may be three or four bits in your selection that will produce a single shape. Knowing which one will work best is a matter of experience.

• Second, when you know which bits you're using, carefully plan the cuts. Each cut should leave enough stock to adequately support the workpiece during the next cut. If possible, make small cuts before large ones, and remove stock from the interior or middle of the surface before taking it from the sides.

• Third, when you make each cut, use constant, even pressure to feed the work (or move the router) and keep it firmly against the guides. If the pressure isn't constant or if the work wanders slightly, the cut may not be even. If the problem continues over several passes, there may be considerable variation in the moulded shape along the length of the board.

• Fourth, make more moulding than you think you'll actually need, because if you run short, it will be difficult to reproduce the exact same setups you went through.

Inlaying Banding

You can decorate wooden surfaces by cutting shallow mortises and filling them with inlaid strips of veneer, patches of marquetry and parquetry, slabs of mother-of-pearl, strands of wire and so on.

Because these inlaid objects often are small and intricately shaped, cutting mortises to fit them requires precision. Not only must the shape be correct, the depth must be accurate and absolutely uniform. That's why one of the best tools for making these small cuts is the router.

Perhaps the simplest type of decorative inlay is the inset wood

A BIT OF ADVICE

These bits are great when using your router to make edge & surface treatments.

Panel-raising Bit

This bit combines two small wings (which cut downward to shear the top edge) with two large wings (which shear upward for a smooth finish). It's ideal for creating decorative tops and should be used in a router table.

Beading Bit

These bits add an attractive profile to furniture and millwork. They can be used to cut all kinds of material – plywood, hardwood and softwood. They're also available with steel pilots or bearings for similar designs.

Table Top Bit

This bit, designed with sharp curves, helps you generate a strong, uplifting edge, creating a bold effect on all kinds of furniture.

banding. These simply are ribbons of wood sliced from a board or a sheet of veneer.

They also may be made up of several contrasting colors of wood, forming long strips of marquetry (designs that are made with multiple pieces of wood arranged with the long grain showing) or parquetry (multiple-piece designs with the end grain showing). They are usually straight, but they also may be curved.

To inlay straight banding, first measure its width and thickness. Then rout a shallow rabbet, dado or groove to fit it, using either a hand-held or a table-mounted router. After cutting the recess, just glue the banding in place. For more details,

Cut recesses for banding with the same setup you would use to cut simple rabbets, dados and grooves. If the workpiece is small, cut it on your router table using a fence to guide the board. If the workpiece is too large to handle on the table, use a hand-held router and clamp a straightedge to guide the router. Either way, a straight bit is the best choice.

check out the photos at right.

If the inlaid materials are fairly thick, you'll want to rout a recess that is slightly shallower than the inlay is thick. This will make the inlay "proud" when you glue it in place – meaning it will protrude slightly above the surface of the wood. After the glue dries, scrape or sand the inlay flush with the surface.

If the inlaid materials are thin, you risk sanding through them if you mount them proud, as explained above. Instead, you will need to rout the recess to precisely the right depth. Use dial calipers to measure the thickness of the inlay, then carefully adjust the router's depth of cut to match.

Next, test-fit the banding in its recess. When you're satisfied with the fit, spread glue in the recess and press the banding in place. Wipe away any excess glue, place a piece of wax paper or plastic wrap over the banding and clamp a straight, thick board to the piece over the covering. The board helps distribute clamping pressure evenly, and the covering keeps it from sticking.

When the glue is dry, remove the board and the covering, then scrape away any glue that remains on the surface. But be careful you don't scrape too deeply – you don't want to scrape through the banding.

Some banding inlays simply are thin pieces of wood ripped from boards or cut from sheets of veneer. You can make these simple bandings in your workshop, using a saw or a knife. Other inlays can be intricate pieces of marquetry. These are made by arranging different colors of wood in geometric patterns, gluing them together and slicing them into long ribbons. You can make these yourself, too, if you have the patience, but there are many ready-made marquetry bandings available from mail-order suppliers.

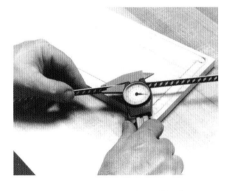

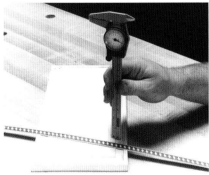

When inlay materials are thick, you can rout a recess to make the inlay "proud," then sand it flush. When inlay materials are thin, you risk sanding through them if you mount them proud. Instead, use calipers to measure the inlay thickness, then adjust the depth of cut to match.

DADO & RABBET JIG

This jig simplifies the set-up and the operation necessary to make repetitive cuts. Just lock the board between the base and clamping bar, then guide the router along the bar. The stock doesn't move, so you don't have to worry about controlling a large piece of wood, and the straightedge doubles as the clamp, so the set-up is very simple.

The jig is just two pieces of wood (a base and a clamping bar) with the sizes determined by your needs. Make the base from ¾" plywood and the clamping bar from a hard, dense wood such as oak or maple. The bar should be fairly thick so it doesn't bow when tightened. I crowned the top and bottom surfaces of my clamping bar, making it 1/32" to 1/16" thicker in the center than at the ends. Even though the bar flexes, the clamping pressure remains even.

To use the jig, position the stock on the base under the clamping bar. To do this quickly and accurately, it helps to make a positioning gauge from a scrap of thin plywood or hardboard. Lock the bar down on the base and place the scrap so that one edge rests against the side of the bar. Rout all the way through the scrap, creating a strip about as long as the bar. The width of this strip is the distance from the edge of the router to the bit's cutting edge.

Use the positioning gauge to align the stock underneath the clamping bar. The edge of the gauge indicates the inside edge of the cut.

This jig also is a timesaver for making identical cuts in multiple parts. To make multiple identical cuts, such as the cheeks and shoulders of tenons, clamp a short fence to the base to position the parts.

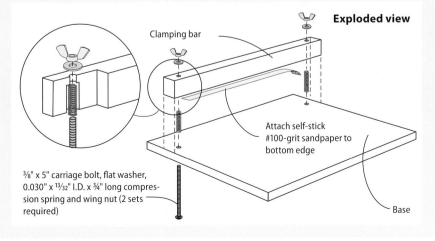

Exploded view

Clamping bar

Attach self-stick #100-grit sandpaper to bottom edge

Base

⅜" x 5" carriage bolt, flat washer, 0.030" x 13/32" I.D. x ¾" long compression spring and wing nut (2 sets required)

Advanced Techniques For the Router

by Nick Engler

The router is an amazing tool that can mimic many of the other tools in your shop, including the table saw, the shaper, the jointer and even the planer. But it's also capable of amazingly delicate profile work, complicated joinery for any type of furniture you can imagine and shaping perfect circles and ovals. For the truly creative woodworker, the router is an excellent tool for making intricate inlay work normally performed by skilled hands alone.

Two things make these and other advanced router techniques possible: jigs and specialty bits. I've devoted more space than normal in this chapter to some of my favorite router jigs because of this. Spending the time to make one (or all) of these fixtures will open up a new world of opportunities for you. I'm sure you can quickly think of many other ways to use these jigs for your woodworking than just the techniques I've mentioned here.

The specialty bits are a different story. In many cases they can be expensive, such as with a rail-and-stile set for making raised-panel doors. Each set often creates only one style of door profile. But if you think about the effort involved to create those profiles in a way other than with a router, you'll quickly see the benefit to purchasing this pricey bit set.

There are other specialty bits that can create multiple profiles with a single bit, and I've listed some to consider in the "A Bit of Advice" section. These also will be able to adapt to your specific woodworking applications.

But please – feel free to try new ideas. If you combine the tilting router table shown with any of the specialty bits, you've made it easier to change the bits, and added a new dimension to your woodworking.

PRO TIP

Rattle-free Doors

With a solid-wood raised-panel door such as the one shown here, it's important to leave a little room in the grooved frame to allow for panel expansion because of changes in humidity. That's smart, but the extra space can make the door rattle. By adding a strip of rubber tubing or weather-stripping foam in the groove prior to glue-up, the panel won't shift unnecessarily, but the tubing will compress, allowing the panel to expand.

Rule Joint

A rule joint is not so much a joint as it is two decorated, mated edges between a tabletop and a drop leaf. Cut a bead and a fillet in the table-top, then cut a matching step and cove in the drop leaf.

When the table is assembled, the bead will show when the leaf is down. When it's up, the joint will close and the surfaces will be flush.

The trick to making a rule joint is not as much in shaping the edges as it is in installing the drop-leaf hinges. Each hinge must be mortised into the wood so that its pin is at the center of the arc described by the mating cove and bead. Just fasten

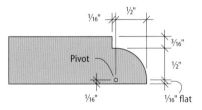

You can rout a rule joint using a simple cove bit. The bit height should leave a flat to match the mating profile's bead.

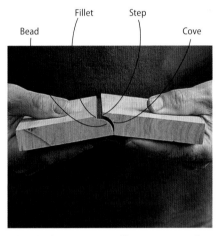

Bead   Fillet   Step   Cove

When both rule joint profiles are correct, the pieces should nest together with the top surfaces flush and a very small gap between the profiles.

Top detail

1/16"   1/2"   3/16"   1/2"   Pivot   1/16"   1/16" flat

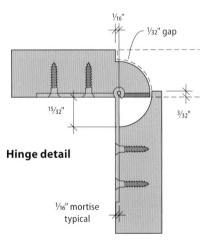

Hinge detail

1/16"   1/32" gap   15/32"   3/32"   1/16" mortise typical

1/16" flat   1/2"   5/32"   1/2"   5/32" flat

Drop-leaf detail

TIPS & TRICKS

Use a Push Block When Routing Smaller Pieces

When cutting small pieces on a router table, be careful to keep your hands and fingers clear of the bit. You may wish to secure the stock to a push block or a large scrap with double-faced carpet tape to rout it safely.

Use Bearings to Get Perfect Fence Alignment

When setting up a bearing-guided bit in a router table during an operation that uses the fences, the bearing isn't a necessary part of the procedure, but it's still useful to help you set the fence. After adjusting the proper height of the bit for your cut, use a straightedge held against the bit's bearing to align the fences perfectly. In fact, if you don't align the fences correctly, the bearing can protrude past the fence faces, causing your work to ride away from the bit in the middle of your cut.

A great application for the rule joint is to install drop-leaf table hinges. You just need to make sure you think before you act. What seems normal – just placing the hinge barrel where the leaf and top meet, like a door to a stile – is totally wrong. Also, you need to make sure that you don't make the hinges flush with the underside surface. You need a bit of depth there. As with all hinges, the location of the pivot point is the ultimate concern. With the drop-leaf hinge, the pivot point (the center of the pin) must be centered on the radius of the matching profiles.

the long leaf of the hinge to the drop leaf, then fasten the short leaf to the tabletop and you're done.

Rail-and-stile Joint

Rail-and-stile joints require two matched router bits and are normally used to join the shaped surfaces of frame members. Rout the sticking portion of the joint – the portion with the shape that you want to see – in the inside edges of the stiles and rails. Use a fence to guide the stock when routing straight edges, and rely

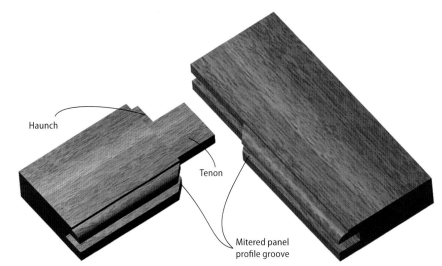

Haunch

Tenon

Mitered panel profile groove

This door shows a complex version of a rail-and-stile joint. The haunch fills the groove left by the bit. Also, the decorative moulding is mitered at the corner for a classy finish.

A BIT OF ADVICE

The bits shown here are great when using your router for some of the more advanced applications.

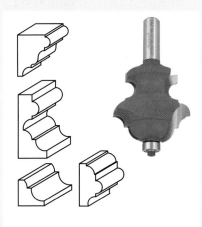

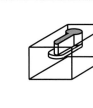

End of rail

The tandem cutters remove material on either side of what will be the tenon on the end of the rail. This bit doesn't leave a decorative profile – just a mortise for the profile.

Keyhole Bit

For hanging a project flush to the wall, a keyhole bit is the answer. It plunges into the wood, then plows a channel, perfectly sized to slip over a screw head.

Multi-profile Bit

One bit does it all. By adjusting the height and the distance to the fence, this one bit cuts a variety of profiles. Mix and match the shapes. The options are limited only by your imagination and the jigs you can use.

Upspiral Bit

At first you may say this bit just plows grooves. Not true. The spiraling flutes of this bit also remove the waste from the groove, keeping the cut clean and keeping the bit from overheating and working harder than necessary.

Rail or stile

This bit cuts the decorative profile on the inside edges of the rails and stiles, and mills the mortise for the rails and the groove for the door's panel.

on the pilot bearing only when routing contoured edges.

Rout the coped portion of the rail-and-stile joint in the ends of the rails only. Use a miter gauge to help feed the stock past the bit. To keep the board from chipping out as you finish the cut, back it up with a scrap piece.

Routing Ovals

While circles have a constant radius, ovals don't. The radius of an oval or an ellipse is greatest along the major axis (the length of the oval) and smallest along the minor axis (the width of the oval). Ovals also have two pivot points, each of which is called a focus. See the drawing below

Small Inlay? Sticky Solution
To inlay a shape, first trace the outline on the wood surface. This can be a difficult task, particularly if the design includes several small shapes. To keep wooden shapes from shifting as you trace around them, stick them to the surface with double-sided carpet tape. To keep hard, dense materials in place, glue them to the wood surface with white (polyvinyl resin) glue. The adhesive won't hold the inlays in place permanently, but it will secure them long enough to trace the outline.

Precision in a Small Package
Rout the inlay recesses with a straight bit and a hand-held router. It's easier to work with small bits rather than large ones. Not only can you cut intricate details with small bits, but they also are easier to control. You may want to work with a small router rather than a large one, because small routers give you better visibility and are easier to control. However, even with a small bit and a small router you may find it difficult to rout a line freehand. For this reason, stop cutting just short of the outline and finish the job with carving tools.

Common Multiple-cut Mouldings

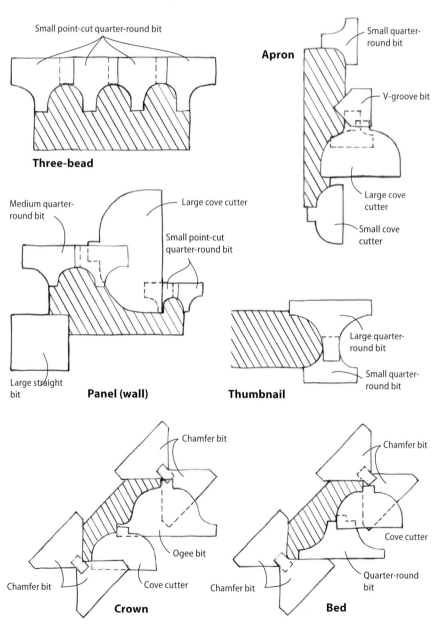

Small point-cut quarter-round bit

Three-bead

Medium quarter-round bit
Large cove cutter
Small point-cut quarter-round bit
Large straight bit
Panel (wall)

Apron
Small quarter-round bit
V-groove bit
Large cove cutter
Small cove cutter

Large quarter-round bit
Small quarter-round bit
Thumbnail

Chamfer bit
Ogee bit
Chamfer bit
Cove cutter
Crown

Chamfer bit
Cove cutter
Chamfer bit
Quarter-round bit
Bed

ILLUSTRATIONS AT LEFT AND RIGHT BY MARY JANE FAVORITE; ILLUSTRATION AT TOP BY JOHN HUTCHINSON

for more details.

The technique for routing an oval relies on the same principle as routing a circle, but you must swing the router around both pivots or foci. To do this, make a double trammel – a beam compass with two moving pivots – on which to mount the router. This jig works in the same fashion as a folk toy you might have come across that has a crank handle that describes an ellipse as you turn it. By substituting a router for the handle, you can rout perfect ovals.

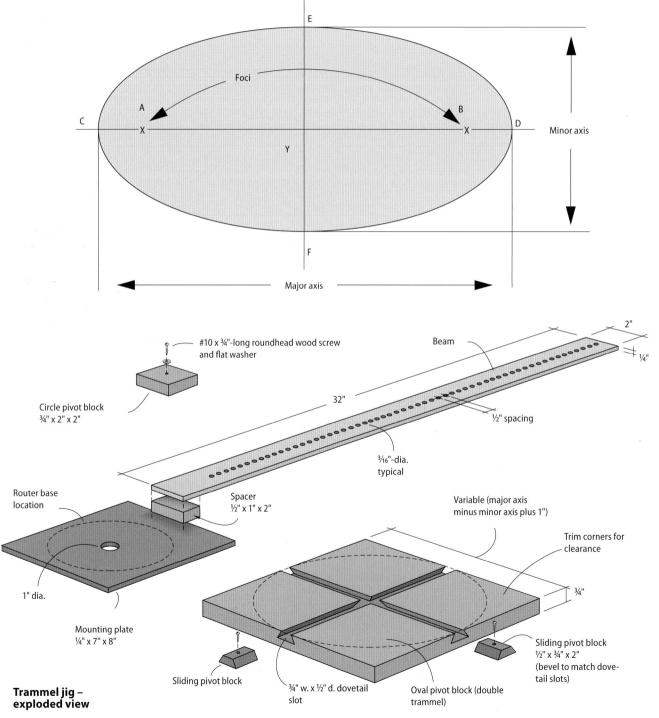

Foci

A
B
C X Y X D
E
F

Minor axis

Major axis

#10 x ¾"-long roundhead wood screw and flat washer

Beam

2"

¼"

Circle pivot block
¾" x 2" x 2"

32"

½" spacing

³⁄₁₆"-dia.
typical

Router base
location

Spacer
½" x 1" x 2"

Variable (major axis
minus minor axis plus 1")

Trim corners for
clearance

¾"

1" dia.

Mounting plate
¼" x 7" x 8"

Sliding pivot block

¾" w. x ½" d. dovetail
slot

Oval pivot block (double
trammel)

Sliding pivot block
½" x ¾" x 2"
(bevel to match dove-
tail slots)

**Trammel jig –
exploded view**

ILLUSTRATIONS BY MARY JANE FAVORITE

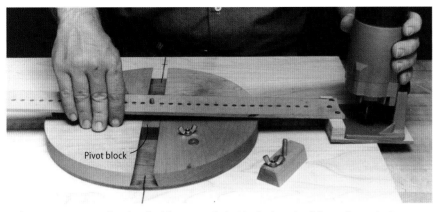

Pivot block

Before you rout an oval with a double trammel, decide the length of the major and minor axes, then mark them on the workpiece. Center the double trammel pivot block over the point where the major and minor axes cross (Y), aligning one sliding pivot with the major axis and the other with the minor axis. Stick the pivot block to the workpiece with double-faced carpet tape. Mount the router on the beam, align it with the major axis and position the router so the bit is at one end of the axis. Center the minor pivot (the pivot that moves along the minor axis) over point Y and fasten the beam to it.

TIPS & TRICKS

Hand Tools for a Crisp Look

After using a power tool to do much of the inlay work, trim up to the line with carving chisels. Use gouges to cut the curved portions of the shape, and use a skew chisel to cut straight edges and corners. Then clean out the waste with dogleg chisels and a small router plane.

Slow Sand to Smooth Finish

After gluing the inlays in, let the glue dry completely before you scrape away the excess. If the inlay is proud, hand-sand it flush with the surface. Don't use a power sander because inlays tend to be very thin and you might sand right through them.

Swing the beam 90°, aligning it with the minor axis, and position the router so the bit is at the end of that axis. Center the major pivot over point Y and fasten the beam to it. The beam should now be fastened to both pivots. To check the setup, swing the router once around the pivots with the power off. The bit should pass over the ends of the major and minor axes.

To cut the oval with this double-trammel jig, swing the router around the pivots, pulling gently outward. This slight tension will take any play out of the mechanical system as the pivots slide back and forth in their grooves. Make the cut in several passes.

Mitered Half-lap Joinery

by Glen D. Huey

One of the strongest joints in woodworking is a properly fit mortise-and-tenon and the opposite in strength is a simple butt joint. For years I built base frames with mortise-and-tenon joints at the rear and mitered corners at the front. The miters were joined with biscuits. The rear joints were much stronger, so I wanted to add strength to those mitered front corners, but how?

Not with mechanical fasteners; screws were out. I needed something quick to create and when assembled, I wanted the joint to retain a mitered look. The answer was a mitered half-lap joint. With a half-lap, there is plenty of flat-grain glue surface, and that increases the holding power, big time.

Tools for the Task

Quick means simple in my book, so if a bunch of tools are needed, forget it. Goodbye, handtools. The process I came up with works with a router, a straight bit and a piece of plywood that's a couple inches wider than your workpiece and long enough so it's easy to add clamps. Trim one end of the plywood to a 45° angle to make things easier.

With this technique, the router sits on top of the workpiece and kisses the fence on the final pass. It's best to have a straight edge on your router's base plate, or make sure you have accurately adjusted a round

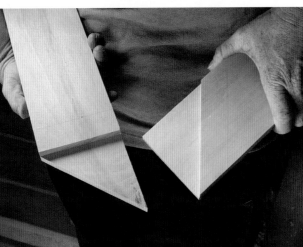

Not often considered. Mitered joints are a common woodworking joint. Most are splined or joined with biscuits and lack real strength. With a quick setup that uses your router, you can master the mitered half-lap. When assembled, this joint rivals a tightly fit mortise-and-tenon.

base plate so the bit is centered. An off-center base plate, depending on how you hold the router each time it's picked up, allows the possibility that you'll miss the layout line as you plow out the waste.

The straight bit can be any straight bit that you have in your arsenal. You're only going to use the end of the bit, so even a top-mount bearing-guided bit works. A smaller-diameter bit is a bit easier to use, but because the cut is most often ⅜" in depth (half the thickness), a larger diameter bit is no problem.

Keep the Players Straight

To begin, cut your pieces to their finished length. For a base frame, miter the ends of the front rail at 45° – the adjoining returns are left square.

Chuck a straight bit into the router and set the depth of cut very shallow.

Grab a couple pieces of scrap and position one on top of the other leaving a few inches to the right of the top piece, as shown above right. This makeshift fence allows you to find the exact offset from the edge of your base plate to the edge of the straight bit. Make one pass with the base riding along the fence then measure the distance from the fence to the dado. This is the offset measurement. Remember it.

Layout is key. Form the half-lap on the wrong face of the pieces and you'll lose the mitered look, so mark the faces to remove the bottom half of the miter-cut end and the upper half of the square-cut ends.

Draw an angled line (45°) on the squared ends beginning at the corner then square a line across the mitered

Get it exact. The key to this technique is accuracy. Find the precise offset measurement through a sample cut to ensure you'll have a perfect fit.

Offset and go. Whether it's an angled line on a square end or a square line on an angled end, the offset line is king. Plus it's where to position your fence.

Nibble away. If you're comfortable with your router abilities, remove waste using a climb-cut, as well as in the traditional left-to-right manner.

It's a keeper. With accurate layout and routing, the completed portion is perfectly cut to accept its half-lap mate.

Oh the pressure. It's easy to allow the router to tip into the cut portion as you work. Keep downward pressure on the base plate with one hand while steering the router with other.

ends beginning at the edge of the cut. Draw a second line, offset by the earlier measurement (the one I told you to remember), that's parallel to the first lines.

Position your plywood fence at the second layout line with the angled end toward the mitered end of your workpiece. Hold the fence flush with the bottom edge of the workpiece then clamp the fence in place.

After you adjust the bit to remove half the thickness of your workpiece, nibble away the waste beginning at the end of the workpiece and working toward the plywood fence.

On your last pass, hold the router base tight to the plywood. At the end of the cut, the router base plate hangs mostly off the edge of the workpiece, so maintain pressure to keep the plate tight on the workpiece.

To clean the bottom waste from the miter-cut piece, align your fence with the square offset line, hold the bottom edge flush with the workpiece then nibble away the waste. Work slowly from the point to the fence.

With the waste material removed from both workpieces, your joint will slip together with both shoulders tight. The increased glue surface adds strength to the joint and when viewed from the top, the joint appears to be mitered. This is a great technique for base frames, picture frames or anywhere else your woodworking calls for a mitered corner.

Make Accurate Half-lap Joints

by Bill Hylton

A half-lap joint is strong, versatile and easy to cut. You simply cut recesses in both mating pieces, then nest them together, forming an X, L or T.

Half-laps can be used for all sorts of flat frames. Doors, for example, but also face frames, web frames and picture frames. An intermediate rail half-lapped to the stiles "looks" right because it visually abuts the stile (the way a mortise-and-tenon joint would) rather than crossing it (the way a bridle joint would). On the other hand, a rectangle of end grain is exposed in assembled end laps and T-laps, which can be regarded as unsightly.

The half-lap can be used in post-and-rail constructions to join rails or aprons to legs. You usually see this joint in worktables rather than fine furniture. But even in the most traditional table construction, the half-lap is used where stretchers cross (a cross-lap).

From a practical perspective, the half-lap enjoys an advantage over the mortise-and-tenon joint in that one tool setup can suffice for both parts of the joint. (There's more than one way to cut the joint, of course, and some do require two setups, as we'll see.) You can join parts at angles quite easily. The joint accommodates curved parts, too. You can join curved pieces,

The half-lap is made by cutting dados of equal width and depth on two pieces of wood so that the face surfaces are flush when assembled. Each piece is trapped between the shoulders of the other, so it's a can't-fail joint. The wood will break first.

or you can shape the half-lapped frame after it's assembled.

Despite its simplicity, this joint is strong if properly made. The shoulder(s) resist twisting and there is plenty of gluing surface.

But be wary of using half-laps on wide boards. Wood movement can break the joint, so confine the joinery to members no more than 3" to 3½" wide.

You can cut half-laps using several

different power tools. Let the job suggest the tool to use and the way to use it, too.

On the Router Table

Everyone has favorite approaches, and mine involves the router. I cut end-laps on the router table using a lapping sled I originally made for tenoning. This shop-made device looks like a T-square on steroids (see the drawing on p. 65). The stout

Cutting a half-lap on the router table is fast and accurate using a lapping sled to guide the work and a large-diameter mortising bit to cut it. The guide references the edge of the tabletop and a stop sets the length of the cut.

Adjustable stop

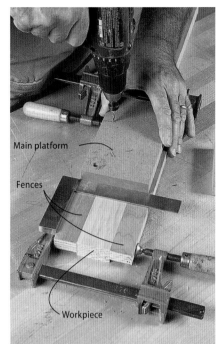

Main platform

Fences

Workpiece

To assemble a lapping platform, capture a workpiece between the fences and align the primary platform on them. The edge of the platform must be square to the work. You can build the simple version of this jig for cross-laps as shown in the photo or add a work stop as shown in the illustration to also cut end-laps.

fence is long enough to extend from the tabletop edge to well beyond the bit. The shoe rides along the edge of the tabletop. An adjustable stop clamps to the fence to control the length of the cut.

Construction is simple, but pay attention to the details. The fence must be square to the shoe. The edge of the fence must be perpendicular to the tabletop. The adjustable stop also needs to be square to the fence. If any of these is off, you won't get consistently sized, square-shouldered laps.

What bit to use? Well, a straight bit is the obvious choice, and it will work fine. I use what's variously called a planer, mortising or bottom-cleaning bit. The several bits I have range in diameter from ¾" to 1½", and the vertical-cutting edges range from ⁷⁄₁₆" to ⅞". The bit is designed to clear a wide, smooth recess. Perfect for laps!

The first time you use the lapping sled you'll cut into the fence. This cut is what you use to position the stop for the length of lap you want. Measure from the shoulder of the cut (include the cut itself in the measurement, of course). The stop prevents

you from making a cut that's too long.

Be mindful of the size of the cut and of the amount of material you will remove in a pass. You don't necessarily want to hog out a ⅜"-deep cut in a single pass, especially if you are using a 1¼"- to 1½"-diameter bit.

You probably know there are two ways to moderate the bite: Reduce the depth of the cut or the width of the cut. Here, the most expeditious approach is the latter. Form the full cut in small steps. The first pass should be about ⅛" wide, produced by holding the workpiece well clear of the stop, so only ⅛" of the workpiece extends over the bit. Make pass after pass, shifting the workpiece closer and closer to the stop. One last pass with the workpiece dead against the stop and your lap is complete.

This approach works well for end-laps, but not for laps midway between the ends of the workpiece. For a cross- or a T-lap, the router table accessory to use is the dadoing sled shown in our April 2003 issue (# 133). You need to use a stop with this sled to keep the work from moving as the bit cuts it, and that helps you place the cut as well. Set the stop

to position the final cut, and use a spacer between the stop and the work to position the first cut.

Personally, I think it's fussy to do Ts and crosses accurately on the router table. Given my druthers, I'd do them with a hand-held router and a job-specific (and thus disposable) jig, such as the lapping platform shown in the drawing at right.

Hand-held Router

When cutting this joint with a hand-held router, I prefer a fixed-base router, rather than a plunge. I use the same planer-mortising bit, but I mount a pilot bearing on the shank of the bit. The lapping platform I make from four scraps and a dozen drywall screws. I use the actual workpieces to scale it.

Begin by clamping the jig's two fences to the edges of a workpiece. These fences need to be a bit less than the thickness of the workpieces and their edges need to be straight and parallel for the jig to work well.

Next, set the main platform on the workpiece and the fences. I usually use some ¾" medium-density fiberboard for this, but plywood is OK for this application. Square it on the jig, then screw it to the fences.

Finally, lay your mating workpiece across the first, tight against the platform's guiding edge. Set the support platform in place and clamp it tight against the second workpiece. Screw it to the fences.

The gap between the platforms is the width of the lap. It is easy to position: You just set the platform edges directly on your layout lines. The bearing rides along the edges of the two platforms while the bit just below it excavates the lap. The bit is trapped, so you won't get a lap that's too wide. The fences tight against the workpiece edges prevent tear-out. The platforms support the router and keep it from tipping. Assuming the workpieces are equal in width, you can use one jig on both.

I'm touting this for T-laps and cross-laps, but you can use it as well for end-laps. For this use, add a fifth scrap as a work stop. Attach it to the underside of the support platform so the workpiece end can butt against it.

Sawing Half-laps

Not everyone is as enamored of router woodworking as I am, of course. Saws such as the band saw, the table saw, the radial arm saw, the sliding compound miter saw and, yes, even the carpenter's workhorse – the circular saw – all can be used.

Doing the job with a circular saw or miter saw is a "wasting" process. You adjust the saw's cut depth to half the stock thickness, carefully kerf the margin(s), then waste the material between the margins with lots and lots of kerfs. Typically, you get a ragged cheek. It has to be smoothed somehow to glue well. But if you're using a circular saw, you are probably doing something rough, where nails or screws work as well as glue.

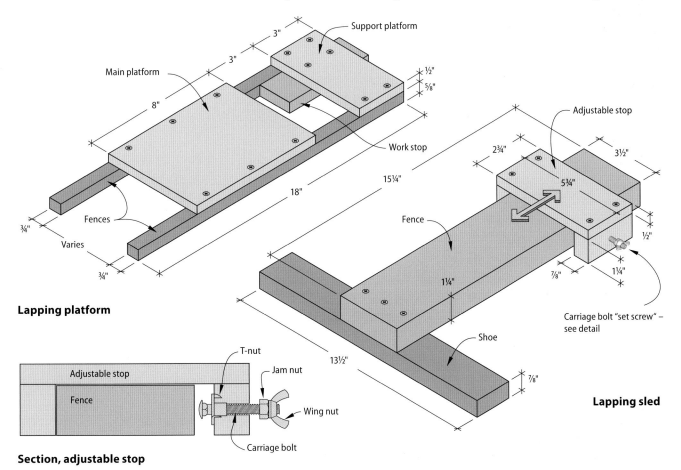

Lapping platform

Support platform · 3" · 3" · Main platform · 8" · ½" · ⅝" · Work stop · Fences · ¾" · Varies · ¾" · 18" · 15¼"

Lapping sled

Adjustable stop · 2¾" · 3½" · 5¾" · Fence · ½" · ⅞" · 1¼" · Carriage bolt "set screw" – see detail · Shoe · 1¼" · 13½" · ⅞"

Section, adjustable stop

Adjustable stop · Fence · T-nut · Jam nut · Wing nut · Carriage bolt

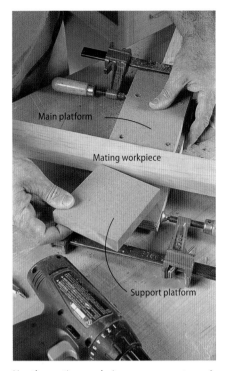

Main platform

Mating workpiece

Support platform

Use the mating workpiece as a spacer to position and align the support platform. Screw the support platform to the fences and you're ready to get to work.

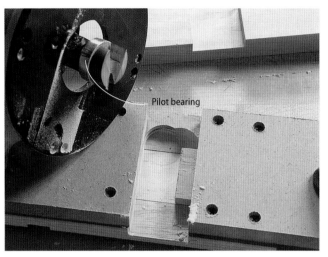

Pilot bearing

Make the cut with a mortising bit with a shank-mounted pilot bearing. Trapped between the platforms, the bit produces a smooth, square-shouldered cut that perfectly matches the width of the workpiece.

The band saw roughs out end-laps very quickly, but it leaves you with a rough surface that needs to be flattened and smoothed to glue well. Some woodworkers opt to rough out half-laps on the band saw, then finish them with a router. To me, that's extra setups and extra work. Besides, you'll be hard-pressed to effectively band saw a lap that isn't at the end of a workpiece.

The radial-arm saw can be an effective tool for half-laps. Set up with a dado head, a well-tuned radial-arm saw will cut end- and cross-laps quickly and cleanly. You

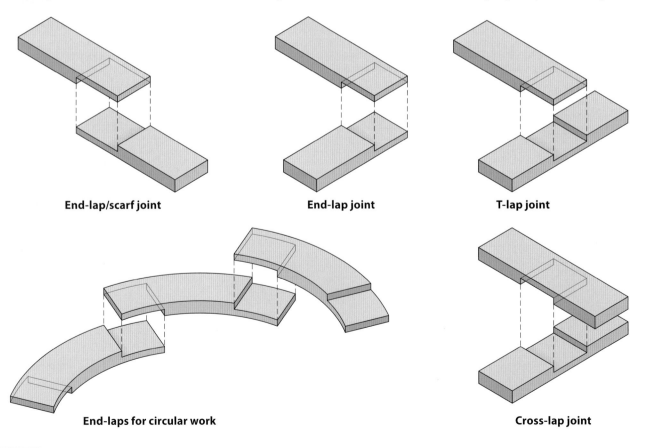

End-lap/scarf joint

End-lap joint

T-lap joint

End-laps for circular work

Cross-lap joint

can see your layout lines, so locating the cut precisely is easy. You can do angled laps easily; just swing the arm right or left for the cut. You can set stops to expedite production jobs.

The table saw gives you some options. You can use your everyday saw blade or a dado head. Guide the work with the miter gauge, a cutoff box or a tenoning jig.

I'm sure you can figure out how to use the dado head with either a miter gauge or the cutoff box. This is the fast, single-setup approach on the table saw.

But if you don't have a dado head or you don't want to switch from blade to dado set, you can use the blade with a tenoning jig to cut the laps. The routine is to saw the shoulders using the miter gauge, then saw the cheeks using the tenoning jig.

The cut depth on the shoulder cut is critical, of course. If you cut too deeply, you will have a kerf that shows on the edges of the assembled frame. If you cut too shallow, it isn't ideal but you can correct this with the following cheek cut.

Use whatever tenoning jig you have for the cheek cut. Delta's block-of-iron model is great, but I don't think it works any better than the shopmade fence-rider I use. Mount the jig on the saw and position it for the cut, adjust the blade height and saw those cheeks, one after the other.

Assembly

It's not difficult to assemble a frame joined with half-laps. You must apply clamps to the individual joints, however, in addition to using clamps that draw the assembly together. Use bar or pipe clamps to pull the joints tight at the shoulders. Then squeeze the cheeks of individual joints tight using C-clamps or spring clamps.

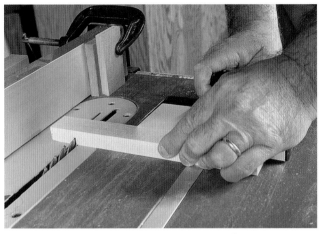

Set the height of the blade to half the stock thickness and cut the half-lap shoulders.

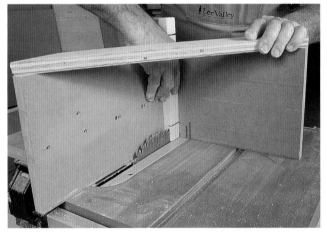

Cut the cheeks using a tenoning jig – this one is shopmade. For the cut, adjust the blade to match the width of the stock. Position the jig and the work so the waste falls to the outside of the blade.

Gluing up a half-lapped frame requires the usual complement of pipe or bar clamps to pull the shoulders of the joints tight. Each joint also requires a C-clamp or spring clamp to pinch its cheeks tight together.

Better Dados for Casework

Robert W. Lang

Dados are a "bread and butter" kind of joint. They're simple and strong, and a router with a straight bit and a way to guide it are all you need to make them quickly and accurately. Of course, dados can be made with the table saw and a dado set, but more often than not, this is an unwieldy operation if you are working with long pieces. Much of the time it's easier to move the tool across the wood, than to move the wood over the tool.

The "T-square" jig is an ideal way to guide the router for cutting dados. It can be put together quickly, and adapted to many different circumstances. In its simplest form, there are only two pieces: The guide that goes on top of the work and the bar that goes against the edge of the work, which provides a place to clamp and to accurately locate the cut. Additional pieces can be added to the jig to make clamping easier and more secure, to allow you to stop and start the cut, to make an odd width and to keep your router from "jumping" out of place when you switch it on.

I've made a lot of these jigs. While they are simple in form, making a good one requires attention to detail and a few tricks. Too often, these T-square jigs aren't quite at 90°. Or there is no easy way to clamp it to your workpiece. Both problems lead to sloppy work. Here's how to avoid those common pitfalls.

Select the materials for your jig with care. I like to use ⅜"- or ½"-thick Baltic birch plywood for the guide – it's a stable and strong material, and the multi-ply edges wear well. I'll make a couple of cuts on the table saw and check the edge against a reliable reference (such as a machinist's straightedge or my table saw's fence face) to ensure I have a straight edge to run the base of the router against. The other advantage of plywood is that it is thin enough to be out of the way of the handles of the router, and can be easily cut wide enough to provide plenty of surface

area for clamping.

I usually make the bar from solid wood that is about ⅛" thinner than the workpiece (i.e., I use a ⅝"-thick bar to cut dados in ¾"-thick wood). This ensures that the guide part of the jig lays flat on the surface to be dadoed, and that the jig and the workpiece can be firmly clamped to the bench. Before putting the jig together, I like to run the guide bar stock over the jointer to make sure it also is straight and true. With both parts straight, it's time to put this jig together.

Square the Square; Choose a Router

Of course, if the jig isn't square it won't be worth using, so here's how I make sure that it goes together precisely. With a bit of glue and one screw I fasten the guide and bar together, as shown below. Using only one screw at first lets me adjust the angle between the guide and the bar to a perfect 90°. Then I clamp a speed square across the two parts. Once the square is in place, I drive a second screw through the two pieces to make the attachment permanent, and then I wait for the glue to dry.

While the glue is drying, I set up a router with the appropriate bit. A router with a flat area on its base plate (as shown below) is the one to use, because a round-base router is likely to have the bit off center. If the bit isn't perfectly centered, and the exact same spot on the router base isn't run against the edge of the guide, the cut will be off the mark. If a round-base router is all that is available, I replace the factory base plate with a square or rectangular shop-made one. Even with a square-

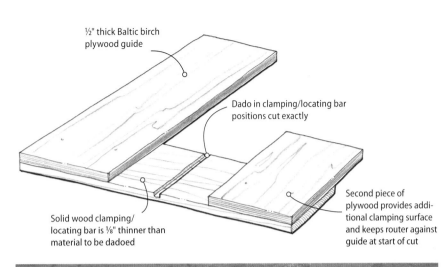

½" thick Baltic birch plywood guide

Dado in clamping/locating bar positions cut exactly

Solid wood clamping/locating bar is ⅛" thinner than material to be dadoed

Second piece of plywood provides additional clamping surface and keeps router against guide at start of cut

Make sure the jig is square – secure the parts with glue and one screw, clamp a square in place, then fasten with a second screw.

Flat edge of router base

Use a router with a straight, not round, base and run the same edge against the jig every time. Make a mark on the router with a permanent marker as a reminder.

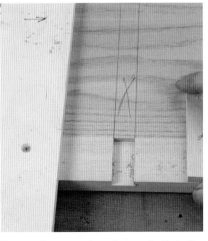

Use your layout marks to line up the jig in the exact location.

base router, it's prudent to always run the same edge of the router base against the guide, as there can be some variation in the distance from the bit to the edge. Some routers will have a different distance from the bit to the end of the base plate, and this may cause problems if you're making a stopped cut. Draw or mark on the router base plate, and on the jig, an indication of the proper orientation.

With the depth of the router set to the correct dimension, I make a test cut, letting the bit cut through the bar. This cut through the guide bar can now be used to locate the cut exactly on the work, as shown below

– no adding the distance from the base plate edge to the bit or any other fussiness. Lay out the location on the workpiece, locate the cut in the guide bar against the marks and clamp the jig in place.

Secure the Work and Fix the Location

Two clamps are needed to keep the jig from shifting. I place a clamp on the guide that clamps both the guide and the work down to my bench, as shown at right. A sliding bar clamp will securely hold the guide bar to the edge of the workpiece. Making the bar as long as possible provides

plenty of room for your clamps. An alternative location for the second clamp is to clamp down on an additional piece on the opposite side of the router from the guide.

When making a jig, keep in mind that it may need to be placed near the end of a board on either the right- or left-hand side, or in the middle of a board. Carefully plan your clamp locations before you put the jig together. It's no fun to spend an hour making a jig only to find that it isn't possible to securely clamp it down, or that the only locations available for clamping interfere with some part of the router.

If you want to locate the cut a specific distance from the end of a board, a block of wood can be added to the underside of the plywood guide, to butt against the end of the piece. Plus, if you're making a series of regularly spaced dados, you simply can adapt the jig by making a wider guide, and attaching a piece to the bottom of the guide that is the exact width of the dado. After you cut the first dado, place the piece on the bottom of the guide in it and then clamp the jig down. Then you can cut the next one.

Blocks can be added on top of the plywood guide to limit the travel of the router and make a stopped dado at one or both ends of the piece. These can be located by drawing the dado directly on the workpiece, setting the depth of cut of the router to zero, and locating the router in place. The blocks can then be placed to catch the ends of the router base plate at the beginning and end of the cut, as shown on the next page.

In use, the router needs to be

Make the jig big enough to give you room to clamp it down without the router interfering with the clamps. Clamp in two places to be certain that the jig doesn't slip.

You can also attach a stop on the bottom of the jig to locate dados at a consistent distance from the end of the board.

Stop

Stop dado cut here

With the depth of cut set at zero, you can use layout marks on the workpiece to accurately locate stops.

Attach a second guide on the other side of the router to make dados of any width wider than your bit. This also prevents router drift.

pushed firmly along the plywood guide. Often, especially when starting or stopping the cut, there is a tendency to let the router drift away from the guide. A second guide can be located on the opposite side of the router that will trap it in place (shown at right), preventing it from drifting away from its intended path.

The second guide bar can also be used to make dados of different widths. If you're routing a dado for a piece of plywood that is slightly less than its nominal dimension, you can use a smaller diameter cutter, set the second guide the right distance from the first, and make the cut in two passes. Again you can set the distance by clamping the guide to the work, setting the depth of the router bit so it just touches the surface, then locate the guides by positioning the router on your layout marks. This

second guide is also the easiest way I have found to place a second clamp.

You're not limited to square cuts, or to any profile of router bit for that matter. If you need to make an angled cut, simply fasten the guide to the bar at the angle you want. If you're using two guides, one on each side of the router, you can even make dados that taper in width. This is a good trick if making a relatively wide sliding dovetail joint. You can make one end slightly wider than the other so that the joint slides easily together, and then locks in place the last inch or two. This jig offers many possibilities.

Make Your Cut

Once you have the jig clamped in place, cutting the dado is simply a matter of turning the router on, and pushing it against the guide as you

move it across the board. You need to be careful as you start the router that it doesn't jump back towards you. When you hit the edge of the workpiece, you'll encounter some resistance, and you don't want the leading edge of your cut to be away from where it is supposed to be. A small block, can be placed on the opposite side of the guide to prevent the router from wandering at the start of the cut. You may also need to clamp a piece of scrap on the edge of the board where the cutter exits to prevent tear-out. The alternative is to back in to the far edge of the dado for the same reason.

A T-square jig is the key to perfectly precise dados for all your casework needs.

Mortises by Router 3 Ways

by Gary Rogowski

My old friend from college is a physicist who launches rockets into the sky for a living; let me just say that he is a very bright fellow. But he has also told me that the router is the quickest way for him to ruin a piece of wood. Well that can be true for anyone who doesn't pay attention to some simple facts about the tool. Proceed with accuracy and clarity, and the router makes flawless cuts every time.

Here are three methods for router-cut mortises that guarantee success.

Cutting Geometry

Routers pull themselves into a board and cut the softest wood available, tearing a path without regard for the beauty and simplicity of a straight line. You need to restrain them and show them the way to cut to get good results.

First, you must understand cutting geometry. When making a top-side cut the bit spins clockwise. If you are using a fence or bearing-guided bit, this direction of rotation pulls the bit in tight to the work as you move the router from left to right along the piece.

All this gets reversed when you move to the router table because there, your router is mounted upside down. As you look at the router table, the bit spins counterclockwise, so you then move your work from right to left into the rotation of the bit.

Now that you understand the cutting dynamics of the router, let's look at three ways to use it to make mortises.

Router Table Shim Method

I use the router table for one of my mortising methods. With this approach I prefer to take tiny nibbles – about ⅛" deep in a hardwood such as oak or maple. But the problem with making a series of cuts is that I would often get a step on one side of my cut due to slop between the motor and the base as I adjusted the depth of cut upward. If, like me, your router doesn't move precisely and without a hitch, there's a trick to get good mortises using a router table – shims.

To achieve the smoothest mortise cuts, choose a spiral flute bit. Set the bit to its final depth of cut. There can be a scary amount of bit showing, so clamp as many ⅛"-hardboard shims as you need around the bit until only ⅛" of it shows.

After each pass, simply remove one shim.

Work between stops on the router table fence and never move backward in the cut (left to right). The bit could grab your piece and pull it away from the fence – and even send it shooting across the shop.

To set the fence stops, use this simple trick: Unplug the router and hold a piece of scrap so it touches both the bit and the fence. Rotate the bit backward or clockwise, and it pushes the scrap piece away. When it stops moving, mark that position on the fence. That's the starting point of your cut.

Do the same thing on the other side of the bit to find the end point. These two marks are equal to the diameter of the bit. Mark the mortise on the top of your board to see where your cut starts and stops. Align those

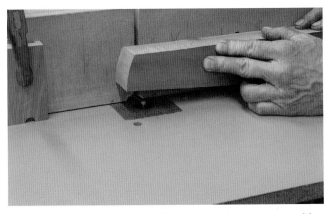

Cutting geometry. Move right to left when cutting at a router table.

Shims step your cuts. Set your bit for its final depth of cut and use shims to surround it. Remove a shim after each cut to make the next cut deeper.

Bit of rotation. As you rotate the bit by hand, it pushes your scrap piece away. When the scrap stops, you've found the starting point of your cut. Align your mortise layout on these marks.

Stop it. To set the length of your mortise, clamp stops to the fence. Start with the workpiece tight to the right stop and plunge down onto the bit. Once you are at depth, move across the bit to the left stop.

Rabbets join the jig. Cut a rabbet into the side walls of the universal jig for support. Clamp the joints together, but check to make sure your sides line up square to the base.

Three stops. A fixed stop attaches at one end with an adjustable stop at the other end. An adjustable stop on the inside of your jig registers your workpiece.

Line 'em up. After the end of the mortise layout is aligned with the bit, lock the workpiece in place using wedges.

marks to the marks on the fence to set your stops.

Universal Mortising Jig

The plunge router was designed to cut mortises. It pushes straight down into a cut. When routing with a fence attached, you can cut a decent mortise. For accuracy and repeatability, a plunge router works better with a mortising jig set up for a variety of cuts.

Make the jig from flat, ¾" Baltic birch plywood or MDF. Cut a rabbet into the bottom edge of the side walls to make gluing it to a base more accurate. My jig is approximately 6" tall x 18" long. At this height, I usually need shims to raise the workpiece closer to the top edge

of the sides. (You could make the sides shorter but you then limit the variety of stock thicknesses the jig accommodates.)

On the outside of your jig, glue a stop at one end then mount an adjustable stop at the other. On the inside of the jig, add a second adjustable stop to index the end of every cut.

Mark the mortise on your workpiece then set the part in the jig tight against one side wall. Attach a guide fence to your plunge router then place the unit on top of the jig with the guide fence riding against the jig's outside wall. Slide the router until its bit lines up with your mortise layout area. Lock the router fence in this position. Move the jig

fence into the fixed end stop; this is one end of the mortise.

Adjust the workpiece to align your mortise end with the bit, then clamp the part against the walls of the jig using wedges.

Move the router along the jig until the bit lines up with the other end of the mortise layout, slide the adjustable stop tight to the fence then lock the stop.

Making the cut is straightforward, but if your attention wanders or if you make too heavy a cut, you could push your router away from the jig. Make sure the fence stays tight to the jig throughout the cut. Also be sure the bit is fully retracted before lifting the router off a cut.

Mortise Templates

It may take a little extra time to make a dedicated mortise template, but once you're done you always have it ready to cut a particular sized mortise. Start by mounting a template guide in your plunge router's base and again, use a spiral flute bit. The template guide follows the template as you cut. Because there is an offset of the bit to the template guide edge, you need to know how much that offset is and make allowances for it in your template opening.

The template consists of a piece of ¼" MDF and a fence for use as a reference edge. The fence must have parallel sides and one square edge. Nail the MDF to the fence. It need not align perfectly. Just make sure it doesn't overhang the outside face of the fence.

To cut the mortise opening in the MDF, set up your router table with the outside face of your fence against the router table fence.

Mark out the slot on the underside of the MDF. If, for example, your mortise is centered on ¾" and is ½" wide x 1¼" long, and you are using a ½" bit and ¾" template guide,

there will be a total of ¼" offset. The slot is cut with a ¾" bit to match the diameter of the guide and is 1½" long to make a 1¼" mortise. Mark out the slot. (To more easily see the bit in the router table when starting the cut, drill an undersized hole at the start point.)

Set the router table fence at the proper distance. I always make a practice cut at the top of the template then measure to confirm I'm in the right spot. Start and stop the slot cut by eye.

Mark your workpieces for the mortises then add the offset mark for the longer template slot. In this example it would be ⅛" at each end. Align the template to your layout marks and clamp the template to

your wood. (You can make the cut with your router moving in either feed direction because the router is captured in the template slot.)

I use what I call a ramp cut. I slowly plunge the bit as I move back and forth in the template. I feel the plunge depth with my fingertips on the router base columns.

The only downside to the mortise template technique is that chips can clog the template slot. You need to clear the chips after a few passes so the guide bushing can fully engage both ends of the template slot.

Whatever router mortise method you decide to employ in your shop, you'll get repeatable accuracy and smooth mortise walls while knocking them out in no time at all.

Do the math. The difference in the diameters of your guide bushing and your router bit figures into your template opening size.

Draw it & drill it. Mark out the template slot on the inside of the template. Then drill a hole at the starting point of your mortise template.

Get the feel of it. Use your fingertips against the columns to feel how deep each new pass is as you ramp cut your mortise.

Compensation. Clamp the mortising template into place remembering that its slot is longer than your mortise.

Router-made Mortises & Tenons

by Bill Hylton

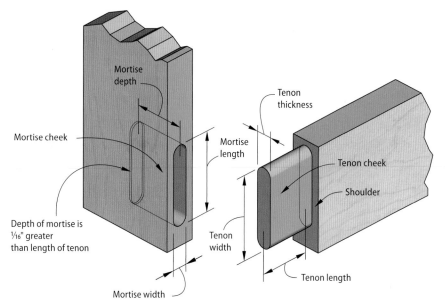

Anatomy of a mortise-and-tenon joint

Mortise
depth

Mortise cheek

Depth of mortise is
¹⁄₁₆" greater
than length of tenon

Mortise
length

Mortise width

Tenon
thickness

Tenon cheek

Shoulder

Tenon
width

Tenon length

The traditional way to make a mortise is to chop it out with a chisel and mallet; the matching tenon is cut with a backsaw. Fitting is done with a shoulder plane. Every joint has to be marked out. The work is slow and time-consuming, but quiet. Doing it well demands skill.

However, the router can do both jobs. It can do them faster, and it can do them better.

With the proper setups, you can minimize layout, which saves time. The cuts are accomplished faster (but with more noise). Machine setups produce uniform cuts, which minimizes the need for fitting individual joints. And the mortise cheeks will be smooth, which means the joints will glue well.

I always make the mortises first, then cut the tenons to fit those mortises. The reason is simple: It's easier to adjust the size of a tenon than that of a mortise. Before I show you how I cut this joint, study the illustration below to familiarize yourself with its parts.

Disposable Mortising Fixture

Successfully routing mortises requires a good plunge router and a good fixture to hold the workpiece. Over the years I've tried a variety of fixtures. In designing one, you have three challenges. You must:

• Provide adequate bearing surface for the router base to keep it from tipping.

• Position the router and control its movement so every mortise is identical.

• Minimize the workpiece handling.

The drawing and photos at right show that this fixture is simple to build and use with a plunge router and an edge guide. The more precise your edge guide, the more accurate your mortises will be, particularly in terms of placement on the edge. The width of the mortise is determined by the diameter of your bit. The router's plunge mechanism controls the mortise depth.

The basic fixture, made from scraps, has five parts: a base, two supports (or fences) and two stops. The supports are attached to a plywood base with drywall screws. The router stops are screwed (or clamped) to the top edge of the long support.

A setup line is squared across the edge and down the face of the long support, equidistant from the ends.

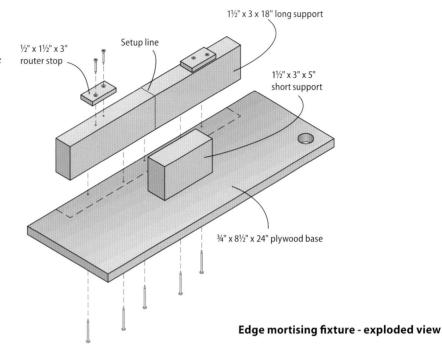

Edge mortising fixture - exploded view

Align the midline of the mortise – the only layout mark needed on all but one of the workpieces – with this line. Your router, edge guide and the stops will ensure that each mortise is uniform in placement, width, depth and length.

The upshot of this fixture is that it's easy to make and is disposable. Make one for a particular job, use it, then dismantle it and recycle the scraps for something else.

If you are so inclined – and I haven't been so far – you can make a spiffy model with sliding stops and a built-in work clamp.

Using the Fixture

Clamp the fixture to your bench and chuck the bit you want to use in your router's collet. Mount the edge guide on the router.

Lay out a sample mortise on a scrap, including the midline men-

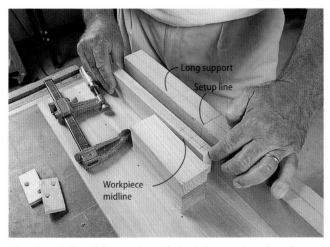

Align the midline of the mortise with the jig's setup line, then clamp the work to the jig's long support using an F-clamp.

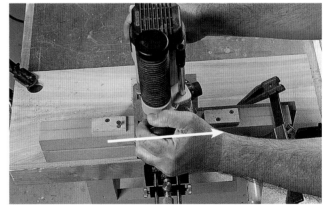

The jig provides support under each plunge post, which enables you to plunge your router smoothly. When cutting, move the router in the proper direction, so the bit's rotation pulls the edge guide against the support.

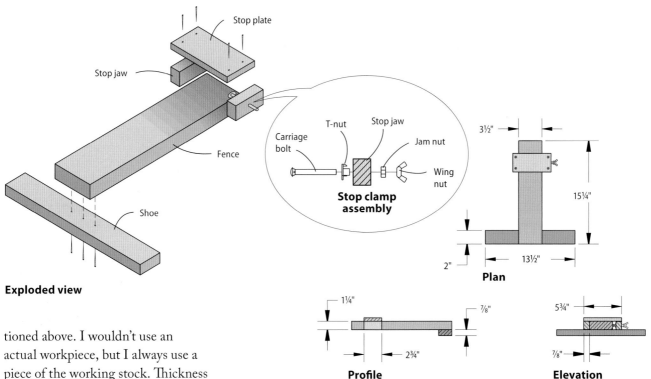

Exploded view

Stop plate

Stop jaw

Fence

Shoe

Carriage bolt

T-nut

Stop jaw

Jam nut

Wing nut

Stop clamp assembly

3½"

15¼"

2"

13½"

Plan

1¼"

⅞"

2¾"

Profile

5¾"

⅞"

Elevation

Router table tenoning sled

tioned above. I wouldn't use an actual workpiece, but I always use a piece of the working stock. Thickness is critical to the setup. The mortise layout must clearly define the mouth of your mortise.

Set the sample in the fixture, align it with the setup line and clamp it to the long support. Set the router on the fixture and plunge the bit down to the stock. Align the bit within the layout lines and set the edge guide, cinching down its screws.

With the bit still bottomed against the work, zero out the router's depth adjuster and reset it for the depth you want.

Finally, set the router stops, which control the mortise length. Move the bit so it aligns with one end of the mortise. Set a scrap on the long support against the router's base and attach it to the fixture. Move the router to the other end of the mortise, align the bit, then attach the second stop.

Move the router to the appropriate end of the mortise for bit rota-

tion, switch it on and plunge the bit about ⅛" into the work. Make a cut and retract the bit.

At this point, you can remove your sample from the fixture and measure the mortise shoulders. Assuming the mortise is to be centered, you want them equal. Adjust the edge guide as necessary to center the cut.

(If the mortise is intended to be centered on the work and your edge guide is less than precise, here's a trick. After routing the mortise to its full depth, unclamp the work and turn it around. Align the setup lines and reclamp the work. Re-rout the mortise. While it now will be wider than the bit, it will be centered. When you rout the matching tenons, simply cut them to fit the mortise.)

Now you can clamp a fresh sample in the fixture and make a full-depth mortise. Never remove more than about ⅛" of material in a single pass with your plunge router.

If the sample mortise is properly located and it's the correct length and depth, you should be ready to rout the good stuff.

Routing Tenons

A good tenon has straight, square shoulders and smooth cheeks (smooth surfaces glue best). Gaps and misalignments at the shoulder not only degrade the joint's appearance, they weaken it. You want a clean and square intersection of the shoulder and the cheek – no ridges of waste, which could prevent the joint from closing completely. The

Position the stop by measuring from the shoulder of the cut in the sled's fence. Use the same bit for tenoning so the shoulder cut remains accurate for setups and for backing up the tenon shoulders.

Cutting your tenon takes only one pass per cheek. Lay the work on the table, pull it against the sled's fence and stop and feed it across the bit. The bit cuts the cheek and shoulder simultaneously.

shoulders must be in the same plane all the way around the workpiece so they'll seat tight against the mortise's shoulders.

Router-cut tenons meet all these criteria and they're easy to make. While there are a variety of ways you can rout tenons, my favorite is with a router table and a simple jig. You can set this up in just a few minutes, you don't have any layout to do, and you can cut a typical tenon in four passes.

The key is the bit. Most manufacturers call it a mortising bit (intended for hinge mortising), but some call it a planer bit. The bit is designed to cut on the horizontal surface as well as the vertical. Thus it's perfect for tenoning, where you want shoulders square to cheeks and both surfaces smooth.

Mortising bits are available from many manufacturers with both ¼" and ½" shanks and in diameters up to 1½". With the biggest size, you can cut a typical tenon's cheek in a single pass. Even a bit that large can be run safely at the router's full speed.

I guide the work with an easy-to-make sled that's essentially a short, stocky T-square. The sled rides along the tabletop edge so you get a straight, consistently placed shoulder cut. The fence holds the workpiece and backs up the cut, so you don't get tear-out. A stop clamped to the fence sets the tenon length.

The sled is simple to make, but be careful about some details. Specifically, the shoe must be perpendicular to the jig fence, the edge of the fence must be perpendicular to the tabletop and the stop must be perpendicular to the edge of the fence and the tabletop. Misalignment of any of these reference surfaces can result in skewed tenons and shoulders.

Using the Sled

The first thing is to install the bit in the router and set its elevation. Use a rule to measure the exposure of the cutting edge above the table. I set the bit just under the width of the mortise's shoulder; that way, I can creep up on the right setting (determined by fitting a test tenon in a mortise) with test cuts.

Set up the sled next. Set the stop on the sled's fence to establish the tenon length. To do this, measure from the cut made into the fence by the bit. (You always want to use the same bit with the sled; otherwise you

will get tear-out.) If the tenon is to be 1⅛" long, as shown in the photo at right, align the 1⅛" mark on the rule at the edge of the cut. Slip the stop onto the fence and bring it against the end of the rule. Seat it firmly so it's square to the fence and the tabletop. Tighten its clamp.

Then cut a sample tenon to check the setup. Make one pass, cutting the first cheek and shoulder. Roll the workpiece over and cut the second cheek and shoulder.

Check the fit of this tenon in your mortise. You need a close fit for the joint to glue well. If you have to hammer the tenon to close the joint, the fit is too tight. Hand pressure should close it. But don't make it too loose, because the joint should stay closed until you separate the parts.

Obviously, "plain vanilla" tenons, which have the same width of shoulder all around, are the easiest to cut. An offset tenon or one with wider or narrower edge shoulders takes one or two more setups.

In any case, your square-cornered tenon doesn't match your routed mortise, with its rounded ends. You can resolve this problem in one of several ways. Some address it by squaring the ends of the mortise with a chisel. I've often rasped the tenon's corners to roughly match the mortise.

A third option is to scale the tenon width to fit the mortise. The primary glue surfaces are the broad cheeks, and you've got the shoulders working to resist twisting and racking. If the narrow edges of the tenon aren't in contract with the ends of the mortise, it doesn't significantly impact the strength of the joint.

Template Mortising

by Bill Hylton

Template mortising is an excellent technique for all sorts of special mortising challenges. It works for everyday mortising applications as well, but most of us already have an established setup for making door frames, leg-and-apron constructions, and the like. Where I use templates for mortising is any application that can't easily or accurately be done with a hollow-chisel mortiser or my setup that uses a plunge router, edge guide and mortising block combination (see the previous chapter). For example:

• Any mortise in the face of a panel.

• A difficult-to-position mortise, such as one in a round part, one cut into the arris of a leg, one cut into an already-shaped part, or one to be cut at an angle. In these situations, the use of a template allows you to make a cradle that immobilizes the workpiece and provides a flat, sound, bearing surface for the router.

• Multiple mortises, such as those needed for spindles in a chair backrest, twin mortises that join stocky rails to posts, double mortises that join a very wide rail to a leg. A template eliminates the little variations in mortise size or spacing that can make assembly of these constructions especially trying.

• A mortise in a part, such as a chair leg, that itself is shaped using a template. You can incorporate the slot for the mortise into the template for shaping the part.

Here's how a mortise template works: The template is a flat piece of plywood or Medium-density Fiberboard. It has a slot or a window that's actually larger than the mortise you want. To make the cut, you use a router (preferably a plunge router) fitted with a template guide. The guide's protruding collar is trapped in the template slot, limiting the router's movement. The only cut the router can make is exactly the cut you want.

Templates are an effective way to make multiple, identical mortises. With them, you control both size and location in one step.

This template slot is ¾" wide, and the mortise is ⁵⁄₁₆" wide. The big differential between bit size and guide bushing size, coupled with dust extraction on the router, helps clear the chips as you cut.

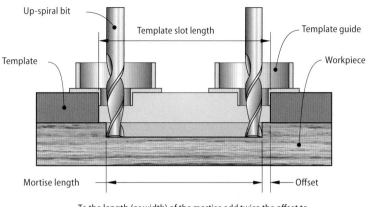

Up-spiral bit

Template slot length

Template guide

Template

Workpiece

Mortise length

Offset

To the length (or width) of the mortise add twice the offset to determine how long (or wide) the opening in the template must be.

Guide Bushings

The pivotal gadget in the operation is a template guide, sometimes called a guide bushing or guide collar. It looks a lot like a big washer with a short tube projecting from it. The "washer" fits into the bit opening in the router base and the bit extends through the tube, which usually is called the collar.

The collar rides along the edge of the template, just the way the pilot bearing on a bit does. But unlike a pilot bearing, this guide doesn't move when you change the extension of the bit. Consequently, you can contact the template edge with the

guide, then plunge the bit into the work and make a cut. Plunge deeper and deeper to excavate the mortise, and all the while, the guide is in contact with the template, controlling the router.

Obviously, the bit has to be smaller than the inside diameter of the collar.

A number of issues come into play in pairing a guide with a bit for template mortising. One is the flow of chips out of the cut. Unless there's a good reason for keeping the guide as small as possible, I like to provide good clearance between the bit and collar to allow the chips to clear the

cut – using a ⅝" or ¾" guide with a ⅜" bit, for example.

Guide bushings are manufactured with collars (those projecting tubes) ranging in length from ¼" to ⁹⁄₁₆" (the larger the diameter, the longer the collar). This is intended to help stabilize the router on edge cuts, when most of the router base is largely unsupported. That little extra length can be beneficial. The trade-off is that with the larger guides, you have to use templates at least ⅝" thick, and that extra thickness is subtracted from the depth-of-cut capacity of your plunge router.

If this becomes a problem, you

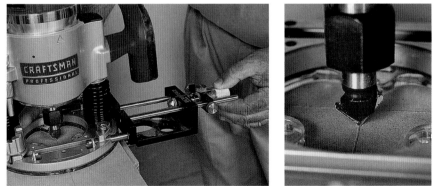

Success with template mortising begins with a precision template. Lay out the mortising slot on a line drawn parallel to an edge of the template blank. Before routing the template slot, use a V-groove bit in the router to align the tool on the line (inset) and set the edge guide (left). Then switch to a straight bit to rout the slot.

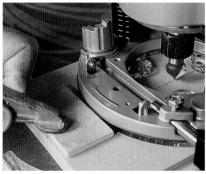

With the bit aligned for the end of the slot, set a scrap against the router base and clamp it. Note that the template blank is set on a sacrificial piece of plywood that protects the benchtop.

If you have a string of shallow mortises to cut in several parts, using a template to rout them can ensure the mortises are uniform across the run of parts. Invest the time to make a precision template. Typically, workpiece layout is eliminated, as are minor variations in mortise size and spacing.

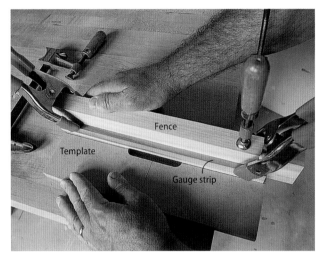

In most cases, you'll want a fence on the template so you can position the template quickly and accurately on a workpiece. Plane a gauge strip to half the working stock's thickness. Clamp it to your fence, then align it at the centerline laid out on the template. Clamp the fence to the template. Run two or three screws through the template into the fence.

can easily cut down a collar. Use a hacksaw or a bench grinder. I've trimmed most of my guides to just less than ¼", so I can use them with ¼"-thick templates. That adds ½" to the depth of a mortise I can rout with a template, and in a few instances, that's been a big help.

What bit should you use? If you are routing a commonplace mortise, say ⅜" wide by 2" long and 1" deep, you'd use a ⅜"-diameter bit. In this regard, template mortising is no different than other approaches.

For mortising, I do prefer up-spirals, but I'm not doctrinaire about it. I've often used regular straight bits in one- and two-flute configurations. But spirals cut cleanly, reduce the stress on the router, and help

pull chips out of the cut. (This can be especially helpful because the template-guide can block the escape of chips. They can only exit through the clearance gap between the collar and the bit.)

Making the Template

First calculate the size of the slot or window that's necessary to produce the desired mortise. If the mortise width matches the cutter diameter, the template slot should match the diameter of the guide being used.

To determine the slot length, you have to add twice the offset to the mortise length. Offset is the difference between the radius of the guide and the radius of the bit. If you're using a ⅜" bit in a ½" guide, the offset is 1/16". Thus, if the mortise is to be 2" long, the template slot must be 2⅛" long. If you opt for a larger-diameter guide, then the slot must be both wider and longer.

Making the template is as simple as routing a blind slot. Lay out the slot, then cut it with a plunge router and edge guide. Or cut it on the router table. In most instances, the mortise length isn't a critical dimen-

sion. By that I mean, the exact length – to the 32nd of an inch – is not as important as having all mortises be the same.

Some woodworkers are completely comfortable briskly laying out the slot, then cutting it by eye from mark to mark. I guess I'm just a little compulsive, so I use a V-groove bit in the router to set the edge guide and to set stops for the router to govern the slot length, as shown below. Hand-tighten the V-groover in the collet and plunge it to the template surface. Set the point right on your layout line and bring the edge guide against the edge of the stock. Slide the router along the stock to be sure the bit tracks on the layout line. Then position the V-groover on the end point. Set a stop block against the router base and clamp it to the stock, as shown below. Move the router and set the second stop block. (Bear in mind that the cut will be longer than this setup by the diameter of the bit. You have to account for the bit when you lay out your marks.) With the edge guide and stops set, swap bits to actually cut the slot.

If you have more than one slot

to make in the template (for doing twin mortises or double mortises, for example) you cut them similarly. Making a second slot in line with the first is a simple matter of moving your stops to new locations. Making a parallel slot can be easily accomplished by switching the reference edge or adjusting the edge guide.

Locating the Template

Your next hurdle is locating the template on the workpiece and securing it. You should know exactly what you're going to do, of course, because that was all part of your initial plan. Right?

How you do it depends, obviously, on the size and shape of the workpiece.

A template for a mortise in a panel may be positioned using the cross hairs of a center line and a midline, laid out to aid in routing the slot, as shown below. You might use carpet tape or hot-melt glue to attach the template for the cut. I've actually screwed the template to the part in a few cases.

For commonplace work such as stiles or legs, you can mount a fence to the template. Then you clamp the part to the fence. A stop attached to the fence can position the work so you don't have to lay out each piece. Or that midline can be your registration mark.

Use the laid-out centerline as a reference for mounting a fence and a gauge block to position the fence in relation to the line. Plane a piece of stock to the appropriate thickness. If the mortise is to be centered across the edge of the workpiece, that thickness would of course be half

that of the working stock. Align an edge with the layout line and clamp the block to the template, as shown above. Apply glue to the edge of the fence. As you press the glued edge to the template, slide the fence tight against the gauge, and clamp it to both the template and to the gauge. Then you can turn the assembly over and run a couple screws through the template into the fence. (Just don't glue the gauge to the assembly!)

Cutting the Mortise

Cutting the mortise is a job for a plunge router. Install the guide bushing and chuck the bit in the collet. Set the router on the template, guide collar captured in the slot. Bottom the bit against the workpiece, zero out the adjuster, then set the depth of cut.

The routine is to move the router back and forth, cutting progressively deeper. "Proper" feed direction becomes irrelevant. The template reins in the router, allowing it to move only on a defined line and distance. Release the plunge mechanism to raise the bit before lifting the router from the template.

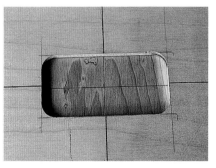

Where a mortise is located in the face of a panel, use cross hairs to position the template. Lay them out on the template blank to guide the cuts that create the "window." Lay them out on the panel, to delineate where the template must be placed.

What's going to happen is that chips will clog both the cut and the slot in the template. You need to interrupt the cutting periodically to vacuum out these chips. If you don't, and you focus doggedly on getting it routed, you'll get chips packed so tightly in the ends of the template slot that you'll need to dig them out with a narrow chisel or an awl.

Dust extraction as you rout is a major boon. I almost always use DeWalt's DW621 for mortising, primarily because of that router's dust extraction system. (This isn't a knock against built-in or add-on dust extraction available on other brands and models, few of which I have actually tried. The 621's system works for me and that's what I use.) In most instances, dust extraction reduces interruptions.

A plunge router with some form of dust extraction is best for template mortising. Without it, chips can foul the template slot. The template is a solid platform that supports the router under both plunge posts.

Half-Blind Dovetails by Jig

by Bill Hylton

Dovetails are prime joints. Long history, great appearance and cachet. Used in boxes, drawers and carcases. But for many woodworkers, cutting dovetails the traditional way – with saw and chisels – is an insurmountable challenge.

Dovetail jigs can produce excellent results in a short amount of time. The key is knowing how to adjust the jig to achieve a perfect fit.

If you aren't ready to tackle hand-cut dovetails, there are plenty of router accessories on the market to help. There are so many in fact, and they have so many variations in setup and operation, that I'm going to narrow my focus to the most common: the half-blind dovetail jig.

The typical half-blind dovetail jig consists of a metal base with two clamping bars to hold the workpieces. A comb-like template rests on the top to guide the router in cutting both pieces at once. The appropriate bit and bushing are packaged with the jig. Usually you use a ½", 14° dovetail bit and a 7⁄16" guide bushing to make the cuts.

Use any router, which is to say, the one you have. I typically use a 2-horsepower fixed-base model. The ability to plunge is irrelevant, and plunge routers generally are awkward for work on the edge owing to their high centers of gravity. Brute power doesn't contribute anything. When the urge to rout half-blind dovetails seizes you, get out your jig and clamp it at the edge of your workbench. Presumably, you'll have stored the instructions and the right bit and guide bushing with the jig.

Select your materials and make sure all like parts are jointed and planed uniformly. Not all the parts must be the same thickness. The fronts can be ¾" thick, and the sides and backs ½" thick, for example. Or ¾" and 5⁄8". Everything can be 11⁄16". Just be certain the fronts are consistently sized, the sides are consistently sized, and so too the backs.

Set Up the Router

Install the guide bushing. (If you have a centering mandrel, use it to center the bushing to the bit's axis.) Adjust the router so the collet is relatively close to the bushing. Carefully insert the dovetail bit through the bushing and into the collet. Tighten the collet nut.

Adjust the depth of cut next, as shown on the facing page. When you do this, turn the bit slowly by hand to absolutely ensure that the bit doesn't contact the bushing. The cutting end of the bit is too large to pass through the bushing. If you use

a steel bushing, it will damage the bit's carbide, so you want to avoid accidental contact.

Check your jig's instruction for the recommended depth-of-cut setting. It's often in the $^{21}\!/_{32}$" to $^{23}\!/_{32}$" range, depending upon the thickness of the template. A good generic starting point is $^{3}\!/_{8}$" plus the template thickness (to get an accurate measurement of the template, use dial calipers).

Clamp the Work in the Jig

The work has to be clamped in the jig in a particular way. When you cut following the template, tails are formed on the front board in the jig, and sockets into which the tails nest are cut simultaneously into the top board.

So the socket piece – and that's always the drawer front or back – is on top. The tail piece – the drawer side – is at the front. Alignment is critical: The tail board overlaps the end of the socket board, and its end must be flush with the upper face of the socket board. The boards must be

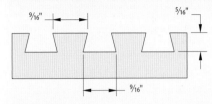

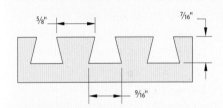

OPTIMUM:
Pin formed matches slot cut by dovetail bit.

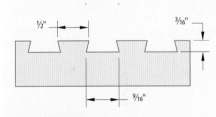

TOO DEEP:
Pin formed is wider than slot.

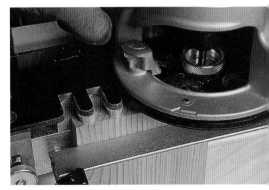

TOO SHALLOW:
Pin formed is narrower than slot.

In setting the depth of cut, you must account for the template thickness as well as the cut itself. Use a small machinist's square to set the bit extension from the baseplate.

Line up the workpieces carefully as you clamp them in the jig. Snug the end of the socket piece (it's on top) against the inner face of the tail piece (it's on the front). Make sure the pieces are flush against the guide pins or stops. (The pin on the jig is hidden by the socket board and clamping bar.)

Chipping along the shoulder of the tail piece is a problem. To eliminate this, make a shallow scoring cut across the tail piece first. A climb cut – where you feed the router from right to left – is most effective here. Just be sure the router doesn't get away from you.

Move the router along the template, feeding the router into each slot and keeping the guide tight against the template as you come out of one slot and round the finger into the next slot. Any little bump on either tail or socket will prevent assembly of the joint.

perpendicular to each other. In addition, the tail board is offset. Both boards are clamped in the jig with their "inside" faces out.

Here's an easy way to do it. Roughly position the tail piece in the jig, with its top end well above the jig. Slip the socket piece under the top clamping bar, and butt it tightly against the tail piece. Clamp it firmly. Now loosen the clamp holding the tail piece and lower it until its end is flush with the other workpiece. Clamp it firmly.

Both pieces need to be against the alignment pins or stops. These pins align the parts so they are offset exactly $\frac{7}{16}$", which is half the center-to-center spacing of standard router-cut half-blind dovetails ($\frac{7}{8}$").

Every jig has these pins on the right and on the left. Use those on the left for now.

The template must rest flat on the work. Its fore-and-aft alignment is critical to the fit of the joint, but don't worry about it for now. Use the out-of-the-box setting for your initial test cuts, and adjust as necessary.

Cut a Test Joint

Rest the router on the template with its bit clear of the work. Switch on the router, and make a quick, shallow scoring cut across the tail piece, feeding from right to left (yes, this is a climb cut).

The purpose of this cut is to prevent tear-out along what will be the inside shoulder. What often happens

is that the bit blows out splinters as it emerges from each slot of the jig's template. If there's no shoulder established first, these splinters can run down the face of the drawer side, defacing it.

Now rout the dovetails, slot by slot, beginning on the left and working to the right. Feed the router into each slot of the template, then back it out. Keep the router firmly against the template as you round the tip of each template finger; you want to completely form each tail – no little lumps.

I usually zip back through the slots after the first pass, just to be sure I didn't pull out of a slot too soon, leaving that socket only partially cut. Don't just lift the router from the template. The bit will ruin both the cut and the template. Instead, turn off the power and pull the router toward you, getting it well clear of the jig before lifting it.

Take a good look at the work and be sure you haven't missed a spot. If you have, re-rout it before moving anything clamped in the jig. Remove

Organizing the Parts. Keep the pieces organized by marking the parts of the drawers as shown in the drawing above. Mark your jig with the letter combinations that are shown on each side of the dovetail jig.

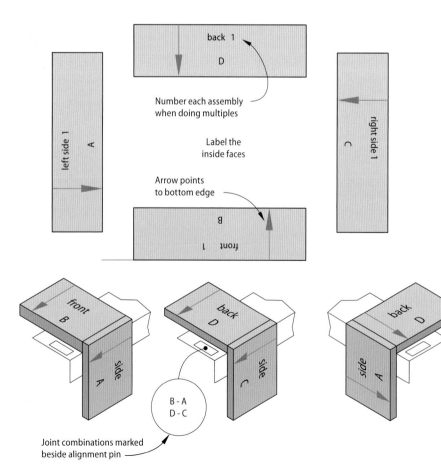

the template, unclamp the work, and test assemble the joint.

Fine-tune the Setup

Slip the test pieces together. Maybe something's not quite right. Perhaps the fit is too loose. Or too tight. Or the sockets aren't deep enough. Or the parts are a little offset. All of these ills are cured with some fine-tuning.

The bit's cut depth is the primary control of fit. The way it works is shown in the drawing, "Setting Depth of Cut," above. The cut – the socket – is always the size of the cutter. But when you alter the depth of the cut, the width of the material left between sockets changes. Because you are cutting both tails and sockets at the same time, the material between the sockets is in fact the tail.

In practice, this aspect of the setup is at the same time deceptive and frustrating. The transition from "no fit" to "perfect fit" is abrupt – just a ⅟₃₂" change can make all the difference. What often happens is that you lose confidence in the adjustment regimen after one or two incremental changes with no apparent effect. "Well, this isn't getting me anywhere!" you think, and start adjusting in the other direction. And you seesaw between increasing and decreasing the cut depth, never hit the right setting, get totally frustrated, and shelve the jig, never to use it again.

Take heart. Remember that woodworkers have been using these jigs for decades, and that routers have been pretty primitive tools for most of that time. You can do it. Be patient, methodical and persistent. Here's what you do:

• Reduce the cut depth to loosen the fit.

• Increase cut depth to tighten the fit.

Once the depth of cut is dead on, analyze a new test cut and determine if other adjustments are needed.

The relationship of the joint surfaces is controlled by the template's fore-and-aft position. Ideally, the surfaces are flush when the joint is seated tightly.

• If the side is recessed, the pin is short and the socket is long. Shift the template back.

• If the side is proud of the front's end, the pin is long and the socket is short. Shift the template forward.

Your jig's instruction sheet should explain exactly how to accomplish this. Generally, the template bracket sets against a nut on the mounting stud. Turn the nut and the template moves. These studs usually are ¼"-20 bolts, so a full turn of the nut will move the template in or out 50 thousandths of an inch.

Look at the edges next. When the joint is assembled, the adjoining edges should be flush. If they aren't, you may not have had the workpieces snug against the alignment pins. Or the pins may be slightly misadjusted.

Any other problems you have will have stemmed from misalignment of the workpieces in the jig. Make sure the top surface of the socket piece is flush with the top end of the tail piece, that they are at right angles to each other, that the template is square to the workpieces, and so forth.

When you've successfully fine-tuned the setup using the alignment

If your test joint doesn't fit exactly, the nature of the misfit cues you how to correct it on your next cut. If the tails are tight or loose in the sockets, adjust the cutting depth. If the tails fit, but aren't flush, adjust the position of the template.

pins on the left, cut a test joint at the other end of the jig. Do any additional tuning needed there.

Dovetailing the Good Wood

Before starting on the actual project parts, make sure you're organized. The parts are worked "inside out." If you are doing drawers, the sides always go on the front of the jig, and the fronts and backs always go on the top. Some joints are cut on the right side of the jig, others on the left. It's easy to get mixed up, whether you're dovetailing one drawer or 50.

A good way to avoid confusion is to label the parts on what will be their inside faces, as shown in the drawing "Organizing the Parts" at left. Where you put the labels is as important as what they are. The letters are always associated with a particular part. Put the letter at the bottom so you know which edge goes against the alignment pins. On the jig itself, mark the two-letter combinations beside each pair of alignment pins, as indicated in the drawing. As you clamp the parts into the jig, orient the letters toward the pins, and check the combination. If it isn't on your list of two, you are at the wrong end of the jig.

Sliding Dovetails

by Glen D. Huey

PHOTO BY AL PARRISH

One of the defining features of 17th- and 18th-century furniture is the dovetailed horizontal case divider. Case dividers are the rails that separate the drawers, or the door and drawer sections. Attaching these dividers to a case's sides using sliding dovetails is probably the strongest way possible to assemble a carcase.

However, reproducing this detail is daunting to many woodworkers. Not only is a sliding dovetail seen as complex joinery, but it can be made in different ways. The basic sliding dovetail, shouldered sliding dovetail and through sliding dovetail (shouldered or not) are just a few of the options.

Each type of sliding dovetail requires a different jig. I've used a variety of these jigs in my many years of building reproduction furniture. Some jigs capture the router base and are specific to a certain router bit. If you need to use more than one bit (to make a shouldered dovetail, for example) this can be a problem – unless you own two identical routers.

Other jigs are as large as the entire case side, making them hard to handle and store. But I've found a better way. Using a ¾" top-bearing flush-trimming bit (often used for pattern routing), a ¾" dovetail bit, a template guide with a ¾" outside diameter and a shop-made straight-edge, any of these joints can be made easily.

From Dado to Dovetail

To understand how this works, let's start with a simplified version of the joint: a dado. With a straightedge clamped across a cabinet side and a flush-trimming bit in your router,

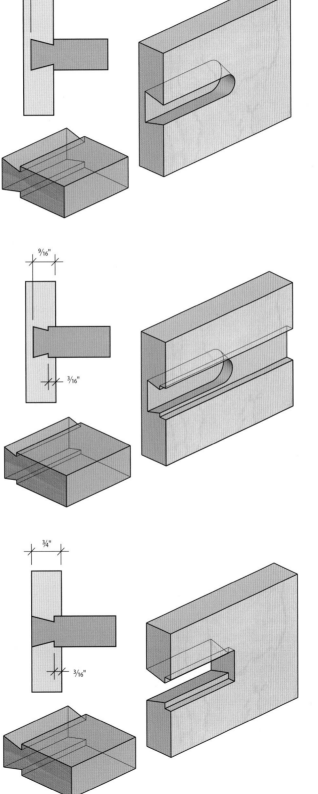

Basic sliding dovetail. The simplest option in sliding dovetails. The socket or trench requires only a single pass with the dovetail bit.

Shouldered sliding dovetail. This joint adds a shoulder to the dovetail and requires you to make a first pass with a pattern-making straight bit. Then the dovetail bit (set at the same depth as on the joint above) is used to cut the dovetail.

Through sliding dovetail. A more complicated joint, this is made in three steps. First the straight bit forms the shoulder, then the dovetail bit shapes the divider pin. The final dovetail socket is hand cut to avoid tear-out.

you can cut a dado for case dividers or web frames. Simply position the straightedge where you want your dado, set the depth of cut on your router and plow it out. The bearing on the bit follows your straightedge.

By using a dovetail bit with a template guide and this same setup, you can use the straightedge to make the basic sliding dovetail shown above left.

Use a template guide that has the same outside diameter as your dovetail bit to make measuring simple. Next, clamp your straightedge exactly where you want the sliding dovetail to go.

Set the proper depth for the bit, ($\frac{9}{16}$" in $\frac{3}{4}$" material, for example) then rout the dovetail trench or socket in a little further than the width of the divider. The trench doesn't need to extend all the way across the side. But because the dovetail trench will have a rounded end, the trench must extend a little further so the square-shouldered tail on the divider will fit.

Two-step Shouldered Joints

A shouldered dovetail is ideal for casework that uses web frames, which support drawers. The straight shoulder, which supports the web frame, is cut just as you would cut a basic dado.

First align your straightedge as you did with the basic sliding dovetail. With a $\frac{3}{4}$"-diameter flush-trimming bit in your router, plow out the dado to $\frac{3}{16}$" deep. Next, take your router with a template guide and dovetail bit, set it to $\frac{9}{16}$" deep (without moving the straightedge) and make the cut into the case side. The cut should be a bit longer than the width of your front divider.

Thanks to the template guide (and keeping the straightedge in one fixed location), the dovetail portion of this cut is centered in the dado automatically.

Through Sliding Dovetails

For an even fancier look, you can create through sliding dovetails. These joints allow the end of the case's divider to be seen on the outside of the case.

Start once again by plowing the dado as explained above. You could cut the socket portion of this joint with a router, but there's much less chance of tear-out if you cut the socket using a handsaw.

If you go with this hand-tool route, you should first cut the male portion of the joint (called the tail) on the end of your horizontal divider using the dovetail bit in your router table. The process is explained on the next page. Then use the tail to lay out the location of the socket on the case side.

Now you can saw out the socket.

THE STEPS TO A SHOULDERED SLIDING DOVETAIL

Making a shouldered sliding dovetail begins by cutting a dado in the case's side. This dado is easily made with a pattern-cutting bit and the right jig, which I call a straight-edge guide.

The bed of my jig, shown at right, is simply two pieces of plywood cut slightly longer than the width of the case side, then glued or screwed together face to face. (Depending on your router and bit, you might need only one thickness.) To complete the jig, screw a third block to the underside of the straightedge guide to hook it square against the front edge of the case side. The hook should be sized so you can clamp the jig in place without interfering with the base of the router. As you cut the dado, make sure you move the router in the correct direction (against the rotation of the bit) to keep it tight against the jig.

Next, install a template guide in your handheld router and the dovetail bit. I should mention one important detail: To use a template guide that is the same diameter as the pattern-cutting bit's bearing collar (in this case $\frac{3}{4}$"), it will be necessary to attach the guide first, then insert the bit afterward. Because of the identical diameters, the router base can't be slipped over the bit with the template guide in place. The guide is the same diameter as the collar to allow the dovetail to run exactly down the center of the dado cut.

With the template guide in place and the depth set on the dovetail bit, you're ready to cut the dovetail socket, as shown below.

With the socket created, it's time to make the mating tail on the end of the drawer divider. Mount the dovetail bit in a router table and run both sides of your divider on end between the fence and bit. You will need to make a few test passes to get the perfect fit. Note that I'm using a push block behind the divider for safety and to stabilize the piece during the cut.

Orient the saw to match the two tail sides, then cut in from the front edge the width of the divider. Finally, chisel out the waste between your saw cuts.

Don't Forget the Tails!

To make the mating joinery on the dividers (the tails), I use my router table. Use the same dovetail bit you used to cut the dovetail sockets to form the tails to ensure that the joint fits well. Set the fence to adjust the size of the tails, cutting on both sides of the divider. I like to sneak up on the final cut to ensure a snug fit.

Set the bit to cut at the appropriate height for each joint style. For the basic sliding dovetail, that height should be about two-thirds of the width of the case side. If you're making a shouldered dovetail, allow for the ³⁄₁₆" shoulder depth in your layout.

The through dovetail is cut with the height of the tail equal to the thickness of the case side (if you are adding a shoulder, remember to allow for the shoulder).

Your through dovetail doesn't need to expose the whole width of the divider. For example, you can show only ¾" on the sides if you like. After cutting the tails on both ends of the divider, use a saw to trim the end ¾" back from the front of the divider on both sides. Then cut from the back of the divider right at the point where the tail begins from the divider to remove the unneeded tail section. Repeat this cut on both ends.

With the back portion of the tail removed, slide the divider into the dado in the case and mark, then cut, the matching socket.

Whatever Size You Need

While these techniques work great with the standard ¾"-thick drawer dividers that are common today, they also work with other thicknesses of dividers by using different-sized template guides and bits. The guides are readily available in a wide variety of sizes, including ⁵¹⁄₆₄" and 1" if you need thicker drawer dividers.

You should consider using sliding dovetails for any number of woodworking tasks. The possibilities are endless.

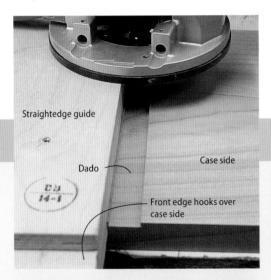

Straightedge guide

Dado

Case side

Front edge hooks over case side

The first step involves plowing out a simple dado with a pattern-cutting bit, shown above.

Use a dovetail bit, to make your shouldered dovetail socket.

You can easily rout the tail of the joint on your router table with the matching dovetail bit.

Cope & Stick Joinery

by Jim Stuard

Cope-and-stick joinery today is all about tungsten carbide. But the origins of this important door-joinery method are rooted in the world of moulding planes, chisels and backsaws. A little history is in order as to the origin of the terms "cope" and "stick." According to Graham Blackburn, a noted author on woodworking and its history, frame-and-panel construction came into its own back in the 14th and 15th centuries. Different methods evolved for joining a rail and a stile together and capturing a panel. The object is, of course, to circumvent wood movement and make stable panels and doors for furniture.

When the frame required a profile on the inside, it was made with moulding planes. This is referred to as a "stuck" moulding. As in, it's not an applied moulding, it's "stuck" on or made on the existing edge. Hence the term "stick." The rail and stile were joined using a mortise-and-tenon joint with a miter on the

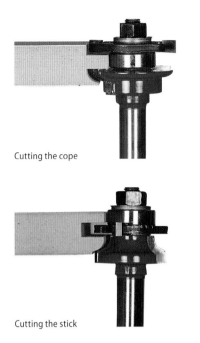

Cutting the cope

Cutting the stick

Set your fence. Setting up and using a cope-and-stick set of bits is relatively easy after the shimming is done. First, make sure the bearing on the bit is flush with the fence on the router table. Flushing the bearings makes sure that the profiles will match up. Use a straightedge that spans the two fences and tap the fence flush to the bearing. If possible, close the fence faces so there's about ⅛" clearance on both sides of the cutter.

moulded edge, where the rail and stile met. This is commonly referred to as a "mason's miter." "Coping" comes from its actual definition: "to deal with a problem." In the case of rail-and-stile joinery, the problem was dealing with the stuck edge. The solution was to make an opposite of the stuck profile that fit over the edge, filling the profile.

With the advent of mechanization in the 19th century, different, faster methods had to be devised to join those pesky rails and stiles. Enter high-speed cutting tools. They could be set up to make thousands of feet of stuck moulding and then the opposite of the cutter could be made to cut the cope on the rail ends.

Which Bit is Right for Me?

You can still make cope-and-stick doors using moulding planes, but most people use a router in a router table. Router bit catalogs are filled with cope-and-stick bits that are priced anywhere from about $50

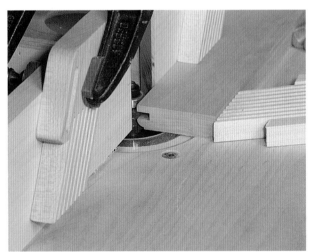

Cut the stick profile. Using fingerboards to keep your stock in place, press the stock into the fence and down onto the router table. Which profile you cut first isn't critical. Use test cuts to get your bits in the ballpark. I cut the stick first. For door construction, you can cut your stock to finish length, but I prefer to leave the stiles a little long for trimming later.

to $150. Essentially there are three types of bits to choose from. The least expensive is what is called a reversible cope-and-stick cutter. This single bit has two cutters, a bearing and shims to adjust it. You cut the stick part of the moulding, then you disassemble the bit and stack the pieces in a different order to cut the

cope. These are decent entry-level bits, but keep in mind that disassembling the bit can be a hassle, and you have to remember exactly how many shims go between each part or your joints won't fit. Also, wear on the cutter is doubled, necessitating re-sharpening more often.

The other "single-shank" solution

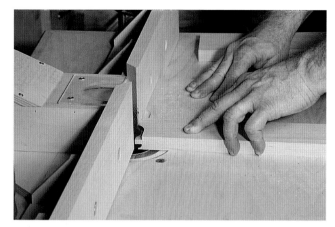

Cut the cope. Next, cut the cope profile on the ends of the rails. Make sure to use a backing piece (sometimes called a "cope block") of scrap. Because of the usual narrow width of a rail and the force of a router, the rail can easily be pulled into the bit. Hold the rail tightly to the cope block to avoid this. It's not necessary to push the entire setup through the cutter, just the rail ends. Once the front of the push block is touching the outfeed fence, gently pivot it away from the fence from the outfeed side.

Cut the panel. Once you've got rails and stiles that are sized properly, fit the parts using light clamp pressure and take the measurements for the panel. Leave a ⅛" gap all around to allow for seasonal expansion. Run the panel on the router by pressing it flat to the table. Cut the end grain sides first, then the long-grain sides. Make the cut in several passes, adjusting the height of the panel cutter after each pass. If you're using a big panel cutter such as the one shown here, you'll probably want to slow the bit's speed (if you have an adjustable-speed router).

is the non-adjustable combination bit. This one-piece bit is basically a chunk of metal on a ½" shank. It has a bearing on top and bottom. You cut the stick part of the moulding with the top section of the bit, then you raise the bit to cut the cope. The only drawback to these bits is they are a little long and will exaggerate any runout problems you might have with your router.

Last but not least expensive is the matched set. In a matched set, each bit has a fixed cutter close to the shank, a bearing and another matched cutter. These bit sets have advantages over the other sets. When they're sharpened, it's just a matter of proper shimming to get them back to an airtight fit. There's two separate sets of cutters, giving them longer life between sharpenings. They're relatively shorter than combination bits so they'll be more stable in a router. And once you get them set up, you won't have to take them apart until they're resharpened. The only real drawback is that they are

usually the most expensive solution.

Which bit is right for you? If you make an occasional door, use a single-shank solution. It's cheaper and you won't be sharpening the bit any time soon. If there are a lot of doors in your future or you just want a

setup that will last a long time, a real time-saver is having two bits in two tables and running all your stock at once. The price differences between one-bit and two-bit sets is around $20 to $50 dollars, depending on the manufacturer and quality.

CMT 891.521
$100.

Freud 99-260
$140

MLCS 8852
$40

The three types of cope-and-stick bits. On the left is a matched set of cutters. One bit for the stick; another for the cope. In the center is a non-adjustable combination bit. You change from cope to stick by changing the height of the router. On the right is a reversible bit. After cutting the stick profile, you disassemble the bit and rearrange the pieces to cut the cope.

THE EASIEST WAY TO SET UP A TWO-BIT SET

If you're one of those people who plunked down your hard-earned dollars on a two-piece bit set, you may test it out and find that the joint isn't tight or aligned. Some sets require some fine tuning upon arrival. Here's how it's done:

Get Familiar With the Parts

Many two-bit sets work great right out of the box; others make joints that are too loose or too tight. You can fix the problem, but you're going to have to disassemble the bits to adjust the cutters. Plan on this taking an hour or two of your time. It's a pain, but remember you won't have to do this again until you get your bits resharpened.

The easiest way to take these bits apart is to chuck them into a router. Use a wrench on top of the bit to loosen the cutters as you hold the bit in place with one of the router wrenches on the collet. Two-bit sets have a fixed bottom cutter, a bearing and a grooving cutter that are separated by thin shims. To get your two-bit set (or your reversible set) working you're going to have to figure out which shims go where for a perfect fit.

Step One: Align the Shoulders

Start by chucking the cope cutter in a router and making a test cut on a piece of scrap. I use MDF for setup because it is made up of small particles that have no grain direction. This gives accurate, highly visible test cuts. Cut the cope leaving about ¹⁄₁₆" on what will be the top shoulder of the cut. Next, chuck the stick cutter into the router and remove the grooving cutter, bearing and shims. Start the alignment process by placing the shoulder cut of the sample cope cut up against the fixed cutter in the stick bit and matching shoulder heights by raising or lowering the router (see the photo at left).

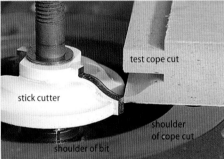

test cope cut

stick cutter

shoulder of cope cut

shoulder of bit

Step Two: Tighten the Top of the Tenon

The next step is to tighten up the joint between the tenon and the cope. Using your test cope piece as a guide, mount the grooving cutter and shim it as best as you can to match the tenon on the test cope piece.

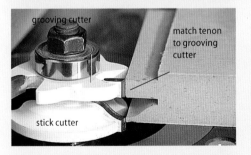

grooving cutter

match tenon to grooving cutter

stick cutter

Result: Top of Tenon is Perfect

After properly shimming the grooving cutter, you'll get a tight fit on the cope and the top of the tenon. Keep a test cut from the stick cutter. This is the finished, shimmed setup for the stick cutter.

Step Three: Shim the Cope Cutter

Remove the stick cutter from the router and chuck up the cope cutter. It also has a grooving cutter on top that needs to be shimmed to get the bottom of the tenon to fit snugly. Disassemble the bit and shim the grooving cutter so it is flush with the bottom of the tenon on the stick test piece. Now your joints should be tight.

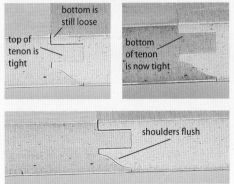

bottom is still loose

top of tenon is tight

bottom of tenon is now tight

shoulders flush

Result: Flush Shoulders

At this point the joint made by these cutters would be pretty sloppy, as shown in the photo at left. You can see, however, that the cut is flush on the shoulder (bottom) of the joint, which is the point of this important first step.

Lock Joint Holds Drawers Tight

by Bill Hylton

Two ways to cut a drawer-lock joint: The joint at top was made using a drawer-lock bit; the one at bottom was made using a miniature glue-joint bit. Both are strong and quick to make.

Two bits will cut a drawer-lock joint. The miniature glue-joint bit (left) is less flexible on stock thickness but produces a joint with more interlock. The drawer-lock bit (right) is more flexible in terms of the thickness of wood it works with. It cuts joints for both bottoms and corners.

A couple of hundred years ago, most drawers were assembled with hand-cut dovetail joints – half-blinds up front, through dovetails at the back.

But it's the 21st century now. Many of us don't have time to hand-cut dovetails. We want something that can be cut fast, assembles quickly and, of course, will stay strong.

The drawer-lock joint is just the ticket. It has an interlock that holds the front and back to the sides and it resists the main stresses administered to a drawer – tension, compression and racking. The finished drawer might not have the pizazz of one assembled with dovetails, but it goes together a whole lot faster.

The Best Bit to Use

While the routed drawer-lock joint can be produced with two kinds of bits, I am going to focus on the more familiar one, which I call the drawer-lock bit.

This bit is about 1¾" in diameter with a low body (about ½" high). Each cutting edge has a protruding tab to cut a single dado.

The other bit you can use is a miniature glue-joint bit. It's smaller in diameter (about 1") and the body is taller, about ¾". It's designed to

If you're using a miniature glue-joint bit, tweak the fit by adjusting the height of the bit. The point where the front meets the side must be tight.

Test cuts, made with the stock flat on your table-top, help you zero in on the correct height setting of the drawer-lock bit. If the samples won't mesh (top), the bit must be lowered. If they are gappy (bottom), the bit must be raised. When the setting is right (center), the joint closes tight.

produce a routed glue joint on thin stock. While the joint produced is stronger, thanks to the extra shoulder it produces, and it can also cut a glue joint on solid-wood stock, I prefer the drawer-lock bit. It's easier to set up and will cut all the joinery you need to make a drawer, including the groove you need to hold the bottom in place.

Neither bit has a pilot bearing, so you must do the work on a router table using a fence. Because the bits are small, you can use either in a low-powered router run at full speed.

Both bits work the same way. One height setting is used for all cuts. The fence is used in one position for the fronts and backs, and in a slightly different position for the sides.

Setting Up the Drawer-lock Bit

Start by setting the bit about ⅜" to ⁷⁄₁₆" above the tabletop. As you slide the fence into position, either adjust its facings for zero clearance or apply a strip of ⅛"-thick hardboard to it (put the hardboard in place with the bit running so it cuts through, creating your zero-clearance opening).

Adjust the fence so it's tangent to the bit's small cutting diameter – just the tab should protrude from the fence.

Make cuts in the edges of two pieces of your stock, turn one over and fit the two together. While the pieces won't be flush, the interlock should be nice and tight.

If the fit is too loose, raise the bit to tighten the joint. If the fit is too tight, lower the bit. After each adjustment, make additional test cuts to check the fit.

The only subsequent alteration you'll need during setup is to shift the fence back when you cut the fronts and backs to expose more of the bit. Use a piece of the side stock as a gauge. Hold it on end against the fence and move the fence until the protruding tab is flush with the exposed face of the stock.

It's easy to move back and forth between cutting sides and cutting fronts or backs. Check out the series of photos below to see how I make these cuts.

Cutting the Joinery

Before cutting the joinery for your drawer parts, mill your stock to the final thicknesses and lengths. To determine how long to cut the pieces, especially the sides, make sample cuts in scraps of the working stock.

The thickness of your stock will have an impact on this. If you're

using ½" stock, for example, the sides generally will be about ⅛" shorter than the desired drawer length (front to back). Figure out what it's going to be before crosscutting the parts and routing the joinery. A workable routine is this:

• Rout the sides. To cut a side, stand it on end with the inside face against the fence and slide it past the bit. Cut one end, then the other. I've never found a tall fence to be necessary, nor do I bother with featherboards. If you're more comfortable with these accessories, feel free to use them.

• Rout the fronts and backs. First, adjust the fence position. The workpiece will rest flat on the

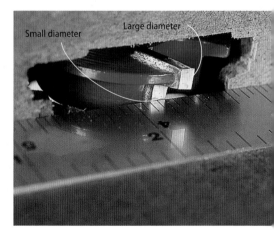

To rout the sides, set the fence tangent to the small diameter of the bit, leaving just the tab protruding. Check the setting with a rule.

Stand a side on end, braced against the fence, and feed it past the bit. The zero-clearance tabletop and fence surfaces minimize tear-out and prevent catches in the work's movement.

Lay a drawer front or back flat on the tabletop, its end butted against the fence, then feed it past the bit. A back-up block minimizes tear-out and helps keep the workpiece square to the fence.

tabletop with its end butted against the fence. A square scrap used as a back-up block helps keep the work moving squarely and smoothly along the fence.

Bear in mind here that the thickness of your stock doesn't impact the joints' fit. You can mix ¾"-thick fronts with ½"-thick backs, routing all with the same setup.

• Rip the parts to their final widths.

• Rout the groove for the bottom. Return the fence to the place used to cut the sides. Position the inside face of each part against the fence and

cut from end to end with the drawer-lock bit just as it is set. This groove won't be visible after assembly.

• Mill the bottom so it fits the groove. Keep the bit and fence setting as they are. The ¼" bottom should be face-down on the tabletop as you cut this rabbet.

Putting it All Together

Assembly is pretty straightforward. After doing a dry fit, apply glue to the joints and put the parts together. I glue a plywood bottom into place, regardless of the stock used for the sides, front and back.

In keeping with the "make 'em fast" mind-set, I've taken to shooting two or three brads into each joint. Glue holds the parts together, but the brads eliminate the need to clamp up each drawer, saving a lot of time.

To do this, first join a side to the

front. Then set the bottom into its grooves and add the back. Next, drop the second side into place. Check for square, shoot brads into the two remaining corners and your drawer is assembled and ready for fitting.

If you don't have a pneumatic brad nailer, you can use masking tape to "clamp" small drawers. But if you're making larger drawers, you ought to use parallel-jaw clamps or bar clamps. Just apply pressure from side to side; front-to-back clamping is unnecessary.

In the end, when the drawer is fitted to the case, shellacked and loaded up with whatever you've decided to store there, it'll perform as well as the ones you devoted hours crafting with dovetails. And the proof is in the performance, right?

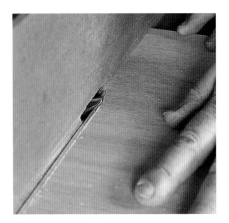

With the drawer bottom face-down on the tabletop, rout all four edges. The rabbet will fit the bottom to the grooves cut for it in the fronts, sides and backs using the same bit.

The drawer-lock joint works on inset drawers with integral fronts (shown here) as well as on drawers with lipped false fronts.

Complementary Curves

by Bill Hylton

If you rip a board in two, you can easily rejoin the pieces along the line of the cut. But you can't rejoin two pieces that have been cut along a curving line. Because of the material removed by the saw kerf, the contour of one piece will differ from that of the other.

You can visualize this more clearly if you think about routing a circle. The disk removed is smaller in diameter than the hole. The difference is twice the diameter of the bit you used. But suppose you did want to join two boards along a curved line. How would you go about it?

If the curve is a simple, fixed-radius one, all you need is a router and trammel. Cut the arc on one piece with the bit inside the radius, and on the other piece with it outside the radius. The two pieces should mate perfectly.

But that won't work for a sprung curve or an undulating curve. If the curve is very gentle, varying no more than about ¾" from a baseline, you can shape the mating edges by guiding a router along a fence with the contour of the joint you want. I described this process as an edge-jointing technique in issue #137 (November 2003). It produces positive and negative copies of the fence contour.

Just be forewarned: The more curve you use, the less perfect the fit. The contour of one curve is offset from the contour of the other by the bit's diameter. When the curve is gentle, the contours of the two pieces should be sufficiently close to fit together nicely, forming a clean joint. Using a small-diameter bit minimizes the mismatch between contours.

Lay out your curve on the fence and cut it. Trace the curve onto the two workpieces. Remember that the second piece must be the reverse of the first piece, not a duplicate. Trim the workpieces shy of the lines.

Clamp the fence atop the first workpiece. Guide the router along it,

Joining stock edge-to-edge along a wiggling, squirming line may be purposeful, but mostly it's for fun. Templates and a shop-assembled offset pattern bit are the secret.

A mildly curved joint line can be produced with a fence-guided cut. Saw the desired curve on the fence and the first workpiece. Guide a router along the fence, trimming about ⅛" from the sawed edge. The feed direction for this cut is toward the camera. (The work is blocked up on scraps so the bit doesn't cut into the benchtop.)

Without changing the setup, position the mating piece opposite the first. An approximation of the curve is sawed on its edge, and it's carpet-taped to scrap. The gap between the pieces is less than the bit's diameter. Make a pass in the opposite feed direction.

The seam is close to perfect – certainly close enough for a tight glue line.

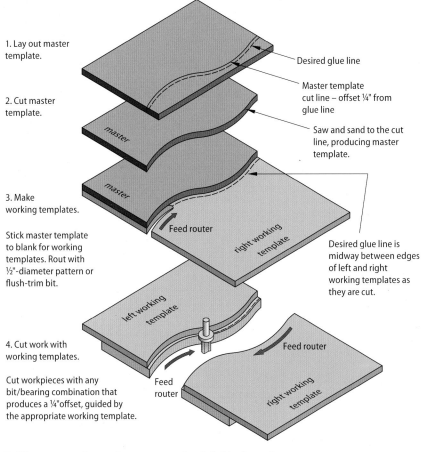

1. Lay out master template.

2. Cut master template.

master

master

3. Make working templates.

Stick master template to blank for working templates. Rout with ½"-diameter pattern or flush-trim bit.

4. Cut work with working templates.

Cut workpieces with any bit/bearing combination that produces a ¼"offset, guided by the appropriate working template.

Desired glue line

Master template cut line – offset ¼" from glue line

Saw and sand to the cut line, producing master template.

Feed router

right working template

Desired glue line is midway between edges of left and right working templates as they are cut.

left working template

Feed router

Feed router

right working template

Cutting a complementary curve-edge joint in four steps

trimming about 1⁄16" from the work. Then plant the second workpiece directly opposite the first, with a gap between them about 1⁄16" less than the bit diameter. Guide the router along the same fence – you haven't moved it – trimming the second workpiece and producing an edge on it that's a negative image of the edge milled on the first workpiece. The two boards should fit together perfectly.

As you set up, elevate both of the boards slightly so the router bit doesn't groove the support surface (most likely your workbench). Both should be in the same plane, so the router remains square to the workpiece edges throughout both cuts. You also have to work out a setup that enables you to secure both workpieces.

If the curve you want is more pronounced, more radical, then you should turn to templates to rout mating contours. It's all about taking out the kerf, and templates give you a means of doing that accurately.

The Template-based System

In this system, you contour the mating edges of the workpieces guided by a pair of "working" templates. The drawing shows the sequence of steps you follow to make and use them.

In a nutshell, you lay out your curvy joint line on a piece of template stock then cut it. Next, you stick that "master" template to another piece of template stock and rout. The resulting two curvy-edged pieces are your working templates.

Butt those working templates together and you'll see that they don't meet along the entire curved contour. Crest will touch hollow, but on the whole, it'll be a gappy fit. It's the kerf, of course. The larger the diameter of the bit you used to cut these two templates, the more prominent the gaps will be.

To get a perfect joint, you have to fill in that kerf, putting back the material that was wasted by the cutter. You do that as you use the templates to cut the mating workpieces. The trick is an offset pattern bit that you assemble using a standard straight bit, a bearing and a lock collar. The difference between the radius of the bit and the radius of the bearing is the offset. The offset you need in this instance must equal half the diameter of the bit used to make the working templates. By this means, you regain half the kerf from each mating workpiece. The resulting joint line fills in the center of the kerf.

Let's crack open this nut and pick out the contents. You make the master template first. This template

You have to assemble your own offset pattern bit. Use the correct bearing: Its diameter equals the cutter diameter plus twice the needed offset. Slide the bearing onto the shank and capture it against the shoulder with a collar.

If the final glue line must duplicate the drawn joint line, you have to offset the drawn line to delineate the guiding edge of the master template. Use a compass set to the "offset" dimension to do this. Then saw along the offset line to produce the "master" template.

Here's a good match of bit, bearing and template. The template's thickness provides a measure of vertical adjustment and the bit is just long enough to work the edge.

One pass along the "master" template creates the two "working" templates. Screw the blank to scraps so it's elevated above the benchtop. And clamp both sides so neither drops as the cut is completed! Screw the master to the blank. Use a straight pattern bit and make the cut in one continuous pass. The scrap under the router keeps it upright.

needs to be about 6" longer than the workpieces, and 6" to 8" wide. The extra length enables you to begin and end cuts with the bit clear of the work.

I recommend using ½" Medium-density Fiberboard (MDF) for all the templates. Yes, MDF yields talc-like sawdust when you saw or rout it. But it has desirable characteristics: It is flat and has crisp edges that are easy to work with files and sandpaper. You can power through it in one

pass with a router. It's cheap and it's widely available.

Near the right edge, carefully draw the joint line. It can be a sinuous curve, a series of straight lines and arcs, or whatever contour you desire. The only restriction is that none of the curves can have a radius smaller than that of the largest bearing or guide bushing you use. In this instance, that minimum is a ⅝" radius.

If the line you've laid out must be

Saw the rough contour on the work, so the template-guided router is only trimming. Lay the template on the work and trace the line using a washer measuring ¼" from rim to bore. Saw to the outside of the line.

in one pass. The resulting offset is manageable; the offset pattern bit you make up won't be wacky, with a huge bearing on a tiny bit. If you want to risk using a smaller bit for the initial cut, you'll have a smaller offset, which would be good. On the other hand, using a larger bit might be better for the initial cut, but it would mean having to deal with a larger offset. The ½" choice is a workable compromise.

You must choose the bit and figure the offset, but you don't have to offset the layout line. If the exact joint line isn't critical, just cut to your first-drawn contour. If you compare the master template to the completed joint, you'll find the joint is offset from the undulating edge of the template. But that hasn't been a concern in the work I've produced with this technique.

With the line drawn, cut on the band saw or with a jigsaw, then sand

the edge smooth. Clearly mark this as the "Master Template."

Make the Working Templates

You produce both working templates with a single cut. As the drawing implies, the blank for them ought to be at least twice the width of the master template. I'd make it wider than that; you can easily cut each one down, but you can't stretch them. The length should be about 3" longer than the workpieces, which makes it about 3" shorter than the master. The point here is to be able to start and end the cut with the bit clear, both when you make the templates and when you cut the workpieces.

Clamp, screw or stick the master template to the blank. Use a ½"-diameter pattern bit or flush-trim bit to cut along the contour of the master. The master goes on top if you use a pattern bit, and that makes it easier to follow the contour. You can

the exact line of the final joint, you have to draw a second line, offset to the left of the first. This second line marks the edge of the master template. To draw it, set a drawing compass to the offset distance and trace along the joint line with it. Pivot the compass around curves as necessary to maintain parallel.

The offset distance is half the diameter of the bit you intend to use with this template. The joint line is going to be the centerline of the kerf formed as you rout the working templates. And the offset distance is what you have to put back as you rout the workpieces with the working templates.

I use a ½" bit. It's a common size, and strong enough to make the cut

Directional arrows marked on work

Stick the template to the work with screws or carpet tape, block the sandwich up on scraps, and guide the router along the template edge, following the direction arrows. An offset baseplate on your router helps you balance the tool and pull the bearing tight to the template throughout the cut.

see where the router has to go. With a flush trimmer, the master must be beneath the blank.

As you rout, keep the pilot bearing tight to the master template. A sharp bit, especially one with a shear angle to the cutting edges, can plow through ½" MDF in a single pass.

Keeping the router steady through the cuts is essential. Use an offset baseplate and its outboard knob to pull the router firmly against the master. In addition, you can attach a support block under the outboard sector of the baseplate. That will keep the router upright.

A goof doesn't necessarily mean you've got to start over, since the mistake will impact both working templates simultaneously. A gouge in one template is complemented by a bump on the other.

When the working templates are done, mark them clearly "left" and "right." On each, note the bit and bearing or bushing that must be used with it.

Routing the Workpieces

This is standard template-guided work. Use the same bit and bearing for both workpieces. Any bit-bearing combination that produces the necessary offset will do. If you've followed my recommendations so far, try using a ¾" straight bit with a ½" shank and a 1¼" bearing. The bit is large enough to produce a good-quality cut finish without needing to use an excessively large bearing.

A word on making up this offset pattern bit. Most bit vendors sell bearings as well as bits. Look for the bearing with a 1¼" outside diameter and a ½" inside diameter. Buy a ½"

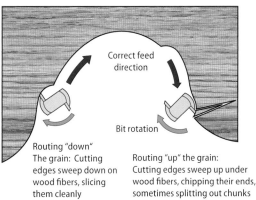

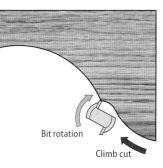

Routing "down" The grain: Cutting edges sweep down on wood fibers, slicing them cleanly

Routing "up" the grain: Cutting edges sweep up under wood fibers, chipping their ends, sometimes splitting out chunks

Climbing the uphill sections: Cutting edges sweep down and in on wood fibers

Avoiding tear-out

diameter lock collar, which should come with an Allen wrench for its set screw. Slide the bearing onto the shank, right up against the cutter. Add the lock collar. Install the bit in the router, and you are ready to rout.

Before attaching the templates to the respective workpieces, transfer the curve to the work. Add the offset, of course. Saw away the waste, cutting just to the outside of the line marked on your work.

Attach the template to the work with carpet tape, hot-melt glue or even screws. Clamp the assembly so it can't shift as you rout, elevating it as needed so the bit doesn't cut into your benchtop.

Be wary of the interplay of the joint contour with the grain of the workpiece. It is very easy to chunk the edge when routing across the grain. Perhaps you've already experienced that. As you feed the router along the template, the tool jerks and you hear a scary CRACK! You look at the cut, and there's a chunk missing from the edge. Perhaps the work has a piece split off.

When routing obliquely across the grain, you always want to be cutting "down" on it. It's like rubbing your hand across a rug. Move your hand one way and you raise the nap. Move

it the opposite way, and you lay it down. As you rout, you want to be laying down the nap, not raising it.

If you faithfully observe feed-direction rules, you're always feeding the router against the bit's rotation, thus moving your hand-held router roughly counterclockwise. Routing a curve that sweeps back and forth across the grain presents a dilemma, because on roughly half the curve you'll be routing against the direction of the grain.

You'll have to violate one rule or the other. I opt to violate the feed-direction rule. Before beginning the cut, I look at the contour and the wood grain, and I pencil some arrows on the template to remind me which sections to rout in the "correct" direction and which sections to climb-cut. Then I switch on the router and cut.

If you've never done cross-grain routing, it's best is to start with mild curves and get experience with the dynamics. As you progress to steeper slopes and tighter curves, you'll be better prepared to deal with the difficulties these contours present.

Routing the mating edges is most of the battle. What follows is a simple, standard edge glue up.

Quarter Columns

By Charles Bender

If you want to add a little punch to your next traditional furniture project, try adding quarter columns. They help narrow the look of any piece by drawing your eye inward. This usually gives the piece the appearance of being more compact and vertical, and gives it a more powerful stance.

So you'd like to give quarter columns a try but you only have a benchtop mini lathe? In 35 years of making furniture, I've only turned quarter columns once – and I'll never do it again. I make my quarter columns at the router table.

Why? Well, the time-honored method for making quarter columns on the lathe has many drawbacks: You need to mill and accurately glue pieces together with paper between so you can easily separate them once you've turned the columns. And if you don't get them precisely lined up in the gluing process, you need to start over or you won't end up with four equal columns.

Quarter columns the easy way. All you need to make quarter columns is a router in a router table, a roundover bit, a fluting cutter, some layout tools and wood. This method can turn circles around the traditional lathe method.

Once you get the columns turned, you need an indexing head for your lathe to make the flutes. And once you've got that handled, you need to either make a scratch stock with a guide box or a router jig in order to cut the flutes into the freshly turned column. All of this can take from several hours to a couple of days. The process is time-consuming, messy and prone to errors.

With just a few simple setups on the router table, you can make fluted quarter columns in no time – without all the fuss. The best part is, if you don't like the layout or you make a mistake, it's easy to start over and get exactly what you want with very little time invested.

Time to Buy Some Tools

To make quarter columns on the router table you'll need only a few tools, some of which you probably already own. You'll need a router and a router table, neither of which needs to be very big or expensive. A 1-horsepower (hp) router and a shop-made table should do the trick. I have only 1½-hp routers in my shop.

The next things you'll need are some flute-cutting router bits. I have sizes from ⅛" through about ⅜" in my collection. The bits can be with or without ball-bearing guides. Bits without ball-bearing guides give you a little more flexibility as to the depth of cut, but if you already own ones with bearings they'll work fine. If you're looking to buy only one bit, I'd go with a ¼" flute cutter.

You'll also need some roundover bits. I try to make my quarter columns ⅛" smaller than the opening in which they'll be placed. So, for

a 1"-square opening, you'll need a ⅞"-radius roundover bit for the column itself. I have sizes ranging from ¾" through 1½" in my collection, but the ⅞" and 1" roundover bits see the most use.

And that's about all the tooling you'll need to make quarter columns at your router table. Of course you'll also need some stock for the columns and a few pieces of scrap to help position the stock on the router table, as well as some basic layout tools, but not much more.

Materials Prep

Let's begin by making a 1" quarter column that fits into a 1⅛" opening. This means you need to mill a board to 1" thick. In order to get two quarter columns for a piece of furniture, mill the blank to approximately 3" wide. This allows for one quarter column along each long edge of the blank with some space between for a saw kerf to separate the columns from the blank. It also allows a little extra space in case the layout isn't perfect or you make a mistake in routing and need to trim back the edge and start over.

Install a 1"-radius roundover bit in the router table so it will round the edge of the blank without leaving a fillet behind on the edge or the face. You want a smooth curve from the corner of the blank to the theoretical corner of the column. It's good practice to lay out the 1" square of the quarter column on the blank to help set up the router table.

Now run the roundovers on the edges of the blank. I usually run the roundovers on opposite corners to give the blank more stability when

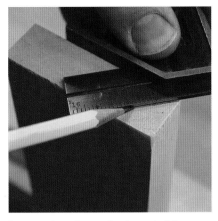
Lay out the column. On the end of the quarter-column stock, mark off a 45° angle to begin the layout process.

Find the extremity. At the point where the 45° line meets the face of the board, square a line across the thickness to define the largest point of the column.

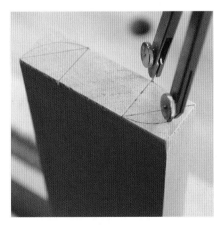
Draw the face. Using a compass, set the point at the extremity then carefully strike the arc of the column face.

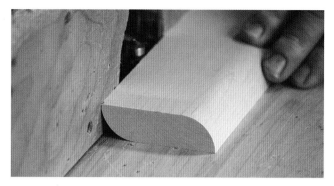

Play it safe. For added stability round over opposite corners of the quarter column blank.

running the flutes and when cutting off the columns on the table saw.

Layout & Setup

Now that the blanks are rounded over, it's time to decide how many flutes you want and the spacing between them. Using the layout line from the 1" square, begin by drawing a 45° angle from corner to corner of the column. Depending on how many flutes you want in the column, you'll need this line to help divide the rounded surface properly. (Adjustments can be made by eye if the mathematical results don't look quite right.)

For three flutes, the layout is simple. Begin by drawing a 45° angle from the corner of the quarter column through to the curved face of the column creating two quadrants. Then draw a 22½° angle from the corner of the column to divide

each of the two quadrants into two additional quadrants that are equally divided. At this point you should have three lines that intersect the curved face of the column approximating the centers of the flutes.

Take the fluting bit you'll be using and trace the flute's shape by holding the bit at a tangent to the arc of the column face. This is where you'll place the flutes when you set up the router table.

For four flutes, the division becomes a little trickier. Because you're creating four flutes, there will be five spaces created (two along the outside edge of the column and three between the flutes). Divide 90° by five, and each flute is 18° apart. Set a bevel gauge at 18° and mark the two outermost flutes on the columns, then reset to 36° and mark the two innermost flutes.

If you are having trouble set-

ting bevels to those degree marks, divide the curved face into five equal segments with dividers. You've just divided the column for four flutes. Trace the flute shape from the bit as before.

Five flutes function the same way as four, except the degree multiple is 15. So, each flute is 15° apart – one flute at 15°, one at 30°, one at 45°, one at 60° and one at 75°. You can divide the column using the alternative method above but you'll need to divide the curved face into six equal segments (two spaces along the edge of the column and four divisions between the flutes).

The degree angles are important to know because you'll need to make angled wedges on the table saw in order to flute the column blank. This means for three flutes you'll need a pair of 22½° wedges and one 45° wedge. For four flutes you'll need a pair of 18° and a pair of 36° wedges, and for five flutes you'll need a pair of 15° and 30° wedges and a single 45° wedge.

Time to Rout

With the end of the column blank marked out and the wedges made,

Center flute. Once the flute face is divided in half, use the fluting cutter to mark the center flute location.

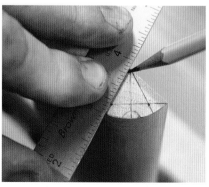

Divide again. Once you have the rounded shape of the center flute drawn in, lay out the remaining flutes.

Outer flutes. Using the fluting cutter again as a template, draw in the outer flutes, adjusting as necessary to keep the fillets between even.

Stick 'em down. With the layout complete, use double-sided tape to attach the wedges to the router table and fence.

Two flutes, one setup. Run the first pass with the blank vertical against the wedge then run the second pass with the column blank horizontal to rout the other outermost flute.

Choose your wedges. On three- and five-flute columns, use the 45°-angle wedge and set up to rout the centermost flute first. On four-flute columns, use the 18° wedges and run the outermost flutes first.

Fine-tuning. You may need to juggle the placement of the wedges, the height of the cutter and the fence placement, but you should end up with equal-sized flutes and fillets.

it's time to set up for and run the flutes. The first thing to do is grab some double-sided tape and the appropriate wedges. Tape one wedge to the router table fence making sure to leave enough space for the router bit. Put the fluting bit into the router and, with the column blank held against the wedge and down to the table, adjust the bit to the proper flute. On a column where you'll be using a 45° wedge (for a flute in the middle of the column – that is, for a three-flute or five-flute column) line up the bit so it is centered on the column. On a four-flute column you'll line the bit up with the top-most outside flute. For the four- flute column, you'll then tape down the second wedge to the table. This way,

you will run the two outside flutes first – one with the board raised along its long edge against the fence and the second pass with the board lying down flat on top of the wedge on the table.

Once you have the first round of flutes cut, remove the wedges from the table and the fence, then set the next set of wedges in place with the tape as you did with the first set. Adjust your router bit height and run one pass with the board on edge then another with the board laying flat.

It's always easiest to run the center flute on an oddly numbered column followed by the outermost flutes, then divide up the flutes in between evenly. On evenly divided columns, run the outside flutes first then the

inner flutes. This way, if you have any variation of the spaces between the flats of the inner and outer flutes, it won't be as noticeable.

Most quarter columns in period furniture are separate from the capitals at the top and bottom of the column. You'll still have to glue up and turn the capitals, but running the fluted quarter columns on the router table is one way to speed up the process and achieve accuracy while keeping the process safe and simple. If you've ever tried to rig up a scratch box or router jig on the lathe, try this method. I'm sure you, like me, will never again go back to the "traditional" method of creating quarter columns.

Dirt-simple Router Jigs

by Glen D. Huey

I'm a power-tool woodworker. Sure I use hand tools for some parts of furniture building, specifically when cutting dovetails. But I doubt you'll ever catch me with a Bridge City Tool Works VP-60, Veritas router plane or a Lie-Nielsen shoulder plane if I'm trying to complete a project quickly. It's just not my thing. The jobs completed with those tools, I accomplish with my router and a router jig.

The next time you venture into your shop to work on a project, take a survey of what's stacked around your shop. I'll bet you have the material to create a boatload of simple, useful jigs that, when combined with your router, will increase your woodworking abilities. The routing techniques shown in this article are a combination of the correct router bits along with dirt-simple jigs made from leftover pieces from other projects,

such as scraps and plywood.

A Square-platform Jig

We all know you can guide your router by placing the router's base against an edge to make a straight cut, but who wants to calculate the offset of the base each time you go to use it or struggle with clamping requirements? If you use my favorite router jig along with a pattern bit, you have a setup that is a multi-

Tricky joint; simple jig. Three pieces of plywood are all you need to cut a housed sliding dovetail socket.

tasker and is as easy as can be to position for accuracy.

That jig I call a square-platform jig. To make the jig, start with two pieces of plywood cut to the same size. Attach the two with glue and a few brads (keep the brads away from the edges), then add a third piece to the front edge to act as a lip – similar to a bench hook – and the jig is ready for work. The key is to keep the edges of the jig straight and square with that third piece, which I call a catch rail.

This jig is best when used for cutting dados for shelves or for creating a dovetailed socket for drawer dividers. Due to its usefulness, I have more than a few of these jigs in my shop made in different sizes and thicknesses for different techniques and for use with different router bits, but my favorite setup is a 1"-thick jig (two pieces of ½" plywood). This thickness is perfect for working with a ¾"-diameter, top-mount bearing router bit with a 1" cutting length.

The greatest thing about this jig is the ease of clamping. No longer is it necessary to use more than a single clamp. One clamp holds the jig to the workpiece and does not allow any movement of the jig. When a clamp is positioned at the lower left-hand corner of the jig as shown in the photo below, the jig cannot move away from the workpiece due to the clamp. And the jig cannot slip to the left because the front piece acts as a catch. As long as the clamp is secure, no amount of force will allow a shift in the jig. This makes it easy to clamp and quick to adjust from one work area to the next.

To use this jig, do any layout

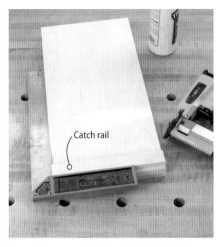

Keep it square. The key to this jig is to keep the edges perfectly square with the catch rail that is attached to the bottom face of the jig. Glue and brads are the joining force.

Quick and secure. The design of the platform jig allows a single clamp to hold the jig in place. This allows the jig to move to the next layout line quickly. Once the clamp is tight, it's all but impossible to slide the jig in either direction.

work, then slide the jig into position, always aligning the jig to the left of the work area because the normal operation of a router pushes the tool to the left (if the jig were set to the right of the work area, it would be a struggle to hold the router firmly against the jig in use). Next, add a clamp keeping a clear path for your router base and allow the pattern-bit bearing to ride along the edge of the jig. With this setup, wherever the jig is, the router bit follows.

Use the Same Jig for Dados

I began using this jig due to the ghastly dado bottoms produced by my older dado stack. My stack had exterior blades that were slightly higher than the chippers and this caused an unwelcome profile at the bottom of the dado. When bookcase shelves were routed through, that shape showed – and it wasn't pretty.

Because most bookcase units I built were 12" or less in depth, I made my first platform jig 16" long. At that length, the jig stretched

across the entire width of the sides and created a dado in a single pass.

To make the cut, allow the router base to sit on top of the jig while the bearing rolls against the jig's edge. Use a pattern-routing bit that is ¾" in diameter and the resulting cut is exactly ¾" wide with a bottom that's flat. There is no ghastly profile to try and hide. Cut one dado or 100 dados and the results are the same – predictable and accurate.

Perfect Sliding Dovetails

Having so much success creating dados with this jig, I wondered what other operations I could make easier by using this setup. One area that came to mind was drawer dividers. Most chests I build use sliding dovetails for joining dividers to the case sides. How could I adapt this jig?

What I discovered was that I had to change the router setup, not the jig. I typically use a ¾" dovetail bit when cutting the socket for my dividers, but I didn't have a bearing to ride against the jig. I had tried bearings on dovetail bits, but I wasn't satisfied with the results. So I turned to a ¾" outside-diameter bushing. You might think it's impossible to use a ¾"-diameter dovetail router bit with a ¾" outside-diameter bushing, but if the bit extends below the bushing (aim for at least a ½"-deep socket into the case sides), everything works perfectly.

Again, simply align the jig with your layout marks, add a clamp, then cut the dovetail socket into your workpiece. Cut into the case side to the width of your divider and you're golden. This creates a perfect sliding-dovetail socket, and it's a simple move from a completed socket to the next socket area. Additionally, remember to use the same router bit to create the male part of the joint. The second half of this operation is completed at a router table.

If you're wondering about hogging out the waste with a straight bit prior to cutting with a dovetail bit, I seldom, if ever, take the time to work this way. My router bits are sharp and able to make this cut without

Designed to fit. The equal width of the bushing and the widest portion of the dovetail bit is what makes this setup work. The dovetail bit cuts exactly to the outside edge of the bushing. As the bushing travels the edge of the jig, the dovetail slot is perfectly aligned.

difficulty. If this extra step is important to you, I would mount a ¾" bearing on a ½" straight bit so I was always registering off the jig.

How about housed dovetail sockets? The beauty of this jig is that you simply make a first pass with the ¾" pattern bit to make the shallow dado. Then follow up with the dovetail bit in a second router, as shown in the opening photo of this article. The entire operation is completed with one clamping setup.

Also, here's a tip: Create the dovetail slots while your case sides

are wider than the final dimension by ⅛". Once the joinery is complete, trim the extra material from the edges to leave a clean front edge.

Are you wondering why I suggested you keep the brads located away from the edges of the jig? When you nick the jig's edge – and you will ding it with your router bit spinning – you can simply take a pass at the jointer to straighten the jig's edge.

A Simple Jig for Smaller Router Bits

Another jig I use, which is not far from the design of the platform jig, is based off of a circular saw guide's jig. When using those saw guides, the base of the saw rides on top of the guide while the blade cuts at the edge. This setup is great for aligning the guide to the cut line. I adapted this idea to use with my small router bits in lieu of guide bushings or bearings. It works great for plowing small grooves or dados such as when routing out cubbyhole dividers in desk interiors.

Constructing jigs such as these is simple. Here, too, I have a few scattered about the shop that work with specific router bits. I even take the time to label each jig so I know with which bits it works. Begin with a piece of ⅛" tempered hardboard or ¼" plywood that's about 5" wide and 10" or so long. Next, add a piece of ¾" material along one edge of the plywood to act as a fence. Add a front piece to this setup just as in the platform jigs – it's important to keep the relationship of the front piece at an accurate 90° to the fence piece.

To complete the building of the jig, install a router bit into the router, set the depth of cut to a bit stronger

One-pass dado. The correct router bit along with this jig provides a simple and quick method for cutting dados that are through, or simply stop before reaching the end of the workpiece to create a stopped dado.

No bearing is no problem. Design this simple jig to have the base plate rub the fence as the cut is made. Make one for each router bit.

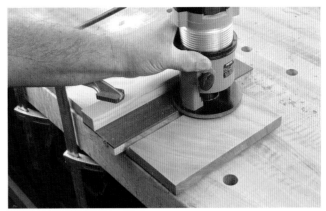

No guesswork needed. Once built, the jig is a snap to align with layout lines; hit the mark every time.

than the hardboard or plywood, then with the router base running against the fence, make a cut. The newly created edge is the exact cutline of the router bit and aligning this jig is as easy as clamping to your layout lines.

A Simple Straightedge Jig

Not all the best shop-made jigs are pieces of plywood arranged in some design. One of the most useful jigs is simply a straight piece of stock or two pieces stacked together, what I call a straightedge jig. There are a couple operations where these shine. One use is for simple straight cuts on pieces too large or too awkward to hoist onto the table saw. A second use is to create a tenon for installing breadboard ends on a tabletop. Or, you can use this to create everyday, run-of-the-mill tenons.

Each of these operations works with a pattern bit; the depth of cut determines the layers of plywood needed for the jig. If I plan to create a smooth cut across an edge, a single thickness of plywood is best. This style of jig allows the standard pattern bit with a 1" cutting length to extend completely through a ¾"-thick workpiece while the bearing rubs the jig.

For example, if I were trying to cut the angled slope on a case side of a slant-lid desk, it would be nearly impossible to hoist the panels up to a band saw, or to control a panel at a table saw. But trim close to the line with a jigsaw, clamp a plywood straightedge at the layout line, then make a pass using your router while the pattern bit rides smoothly along the guide. The completed cut is square and needs little sanding or

smoothing before finish – it's that smooth.

The same operation is perfect for squaring large panels, too. You know how hard it can be to trim a large top with a panel-cutting sled. Once you achieve parallel sides at a table saw, use a square to lay out one end cut, position a plywood straightedge at the layout line, clamp the jig in place and trim the end square. Repeat the same steps at the opposite end of the

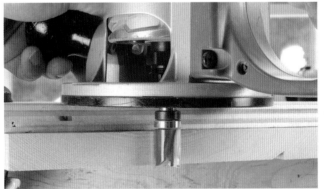

Ideal edge treatment. A pattern bit matched with a single layer of plywood is a perfect way to trim ends of wide panels or large tops. With the bearing running along the guide, a clean, straight cut is achieved.

Two layers for tenons. A second layer of plywood builds the jig to make it possible to rabbet the end. This is a great setup for the first step for breadboard ends.

Possibilities abound. Teaming plywood patterns with a pattern-routing bit opens the door to design and detail – and it makes repeatability achievable.

Fundamental pattern routing. A bottom-mount bearing follows the pattern as a smooth and accurate cut is made on the workpiece below.

top.

I don't like to perform this operation with a circular saw – as you may have seen done a number of times – due to the sometimes-wonky finish of the cut. It's easier to sand a routed cut than that of a circular saw – but I will trim the end close with a jigsaw prior to routing.

Change the Thickness, Change the Cut

If you require a cut that's not a through cut such as making a tenon, you will need to stick two pieces of plywood together because of the cutting length of the router bit. A single thickness of plywood is sometimes not thick enough to allow the bearing to ride against the guide without cutting into the workpiece too deeply. A second thickness of plywood remedies that problem. Now it's possible for the bearing to ride the jig and set the depth of cut where needed.

I use this two-piece setup to create tenons on large panels or table-tops. I cut a 1¼" -long tenon to create

a breadboard end (the ¼"-thick tenon slides into a matching slot formed in the breadboard end). To do this, just set the two-thickness guide on your layout lines, adjust the depth of cut on the router, then waste away the excess from each face, leaving a tenon intact and centered. By using a pattern bit and plywood jig or guide, you clamp directly on your layout lines and go for it. That's much easier than determining the offset for the router base.

More Work for a Pattern Bit

As you can tell, I use a pattern bit with plywood jigs for many operations. And bit diameter is not important. I use a ¾"-diameter bit as well as a ½"-diameter router bit. Additionally, I use bits with either a top- or bottom-mount bearing.

Until now we've primarily discussed work accomplished with straight jigs. However, plywood is also where I turn for intricate work with patterns. I've built quite a few tea tables over the years and the most fancy was a Massachusetts design

with extremely scalloped aprons at both ends and sides.

Instead of transferring the design onto each apron separately, I drew the design one time onto plywood – use a piece that's ½" thick at minimum – and used that to repeat the layout on each piece. But the plywood pattern did double duty. Not only could I use the piece to trace the pattern onto the aprons, I used the plywood and a pattern bit to cut the intricate design at a router table.

If you attach the plywood pattern on top of the workpiece, you'll need a bottom-mount bearing, but a top-mount bearing is used if the pattern is positioned below the workpiece. As you make the jigs for this type of work, make sure to extend the ends of the pattern an extra inch or more to allow contact between the bit and pattern prior to cutting the work.

There are a number of techniques where this setup works great other than table aprons. Before I added a spindle sander to my shop, I would create a pattern for bracket-style feet and cut the design using my router.

It's more efficient to create the feet other ways, but this works if needed. Furthermore, I use this technique for high chest aprons and sculpted drawer dividers such as those on block-front or serpentine chests.

Running in Circles

Step into most woodworking stores and you'll find many commercially made jigs for cutting circles of all sizes. In fact, these jigs are so involved that you have to read the instructions before beginning work (something we all hate to do). For the most part we use a few sizes of circles specific to our work. We don't need all those settings. I looked for something different.

My first circle-cutting jig was an elongated base added to my plunge router. I used the existing bolts to affix the base to the router, then cut a circle. Seemed easy enough. But I ran into an issue. With the router bolted to the jig, there's a point as you rotate and make a cut that you have to let go of the handles in order to complete the circle because the router doesn't turn as you spin the jig. Your hands should always be in control as you use a router.

To eliminate the handle problem, I turned to a guide bushing. Again using plywood, I fashioned a jig for circle cutting. This time, instead of affixing the jig to the router base, I positioned a ¾"-diameter hole where the router bit would be located. The hole, which could be sized to match any size guide bushing, allows the bushing that's installed in the router to spin freely as a circle is cut. The ability to spin during use means my hands stay in contact with the router

throughout the cut.

Using the jig is a walk in the park. Select a guide bushing that matches the hole in the jig, then install the desired router bit and the bushing to the tool. Measure accurately for your needed diameter and pin the jig to the workpiece with a dowel. All that's left is to cut a circle. Use a plunge router for this technique and step through the cutting process; don't try to complete the cut in a single pass.

You don't need scads of money. You don't need complicated commercial jigs. You don't even need to keep the jig once it serves its purpose. All you need is a few pieces of plywood used in conjunction with certain router bits and you can increase productivity in your shop. It's as simple as plugging in a router.

Another simple setup. One hole in the middle of the circle-cutting jig, plus a guide bushing, equals a great method for creating circles.

Safe and secure. The guide bushing turns in the hole as the circle is cut. At no time is it necessary to remove your hands from the router. Elevate the workpiece or the bench is will also get a groove.

The Magic Trammel Jig

by Nick Engler

The trick to learning to cut precise, professional-looking circular and oval shapes is to achieve a "fair curve." This is a curve with no bumps, divots or abrupt changes in direction – the curve must appear to be a single, flowing line.

While you can achieve a fair curve with a band saw and a belt sander, the best tool in your shop for making a fair curve is your router. With the aid of a trammel jig, you can rout circles and ovals more precisely than you can by laying them out and cutting them with any other tool in your shop.

Making the Trammel Jig

The trammel jig consists of three parts:

• A single fixed pivot for routing circles;

• A plywood plate with two movable pivots for routing ovals;

• A long beam with a mounting plate on one end to hold the router and swing it around the two pivots.

As shown, the beam is 32" long with pivot holes spaced every ½". This lets you rout circles up to 60" in diameter and ovals up to 48" long. For larger workpieces, all you have to do is make a longer beam.

At one end of the beam, attach a router mounting plate and drill holes to mount your router. Remember, the holes must be counterbored or countersunk so the head of the mounting screws do not protrude.

The circle pivot block is a square block with a pilot hole in the center of one face. The oval pivot block has two dovetail slots that cross at right angles in the middle of the block. To cut these slots accurately, first rout ordinary grooves with a straight bit to remove most of the stock. Then use a dovetail bit to create the angled shape. Cut the sliding pivot blocks to fit the dovetail slots, making them small enough to slide easily.

Depending on the size of the ovals you want to rout, you may have to adjust the size of the oval pivot block. I made mine 8" in diameter – this works well for a variety of small- and medium-sized ovals. To determine if this will work for you, subtract the minor axis of the oval (its width) from the major axis (its

Routing an oval with a double trammel setup. The resulting curve is perfectly fair.

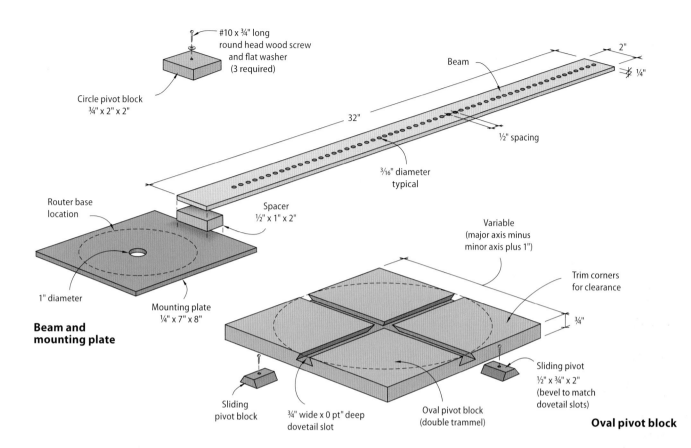

#10 x ¾" long
round head wood screw
and flat washer
(3 required)

Circle pivot block
¾" x 2" x 2"

Beam

2"

32"

¼"

½" spacing

³⁄₁₆" diameter
typical

Router base
location

Spacer
½" x 1" x 2"

Variable
(major axis minus
minor axis plus 1")

Trim corners
for clearance

1" diameter

Mounting plate
¼" x 7" x 8"

¾"

**Beam and
mounting plate**

Sliding pivot
½" x ¾" x 2"
(bevel to match
dovetail slots)

Sliding
pivot block

¾" wide x 0 pt" deep
dovetail slot

Oval pivot block
(double trammel)

Oval pivot block

---

length). Add 1" to prevent the sliding pivots from slipping out of the slots, and that's the minimum diameter of the pivot.

Cutting a Circle

To rout a circle, position the circle pivot block in the center of your workpiece (shown at right) and attach it with double-faced carpet tape (so you won't have to drive a screw or a nail into your work and mar the surface).

Mount a straight bit in your router and attach the router to the beam. Drive a roundhead screw through the beam and into the center of the pivot block.

The distance from the screw to the edge of the bit should be equal to the radius of the circle you want to cut. You can adjust this radius either

by varying the diameter of the bit or drilling new holes in the beam.

Swing the router and the beam around the pivot clockwise, cutting your circle. Make the circle using several passes, routing no deeper than ⅛" with each pass until you have cut through the wood.

Cutting an Oval

To rout an oval, you must swing the router around two movable pivots in an arrangement called a "double trammel." The pivots slide back and forth in their dovetail slots; one controls the length of the oval while the other controls the width.

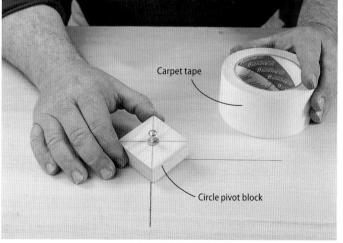

Carpet tape

Circle pivot block

When you mark the center of the circle on your work, draw a large crosshair. Fasten the circle pivot block to the work with carpet tape, aligning the corners with the arms of the crosshairs. This will center the block precisely. Attach the beam to the block and rout your circle.

Start by marking the center of the oval on your workpiece. Draw two lines at right angles that intersect at this point, then mark the length of the oval along one line and its width along the other.

Attach the oval pivot block to the workpiece with carpet tape, centering the slots over the lines you have drawn. Attach the router to the beam and align the beam with the major axis (length) of the oval.

Center the minor pivot (which is the pivot that moves along the minor axis, or width) and fasten the beam to it with a roundhead wood screw.

Next, swing the beam 90°, aligning it with the minor axis. Position the router so the bit is even with the mark for the minor axis, center the major pivot and attach the beam with a screw. The beam should not be fastened too tightly to either

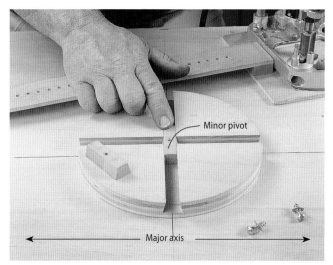

To rout an oval, position the minor pivot over the center of the oval where the two slots cross.

pivot.

To check your setup, swing the router once around the pivot block with the power off. The bit should pass over the end of the major and minor axes.

Once this is done, turn on your router, adjust the depth of cut for a

shallow bite and swing the router around the pivots. As you rout, pull gently outward. The slight tension will take any play out of the mechanical system, helping to create a smooth, precise oval. Rout in multiple passes, cutting just a little deeper with each pass.

Position the router so the inside cutting edge of the bit (the edge nearest the center) is even with one end of the major axis, then attach the beam to the pivot by driving a roundhead screw through one of the predrilled holes. If none of the holes are aligned over the pivot, you must use a different diameter router bit or drill a new hole.

Repeat, centering the major pivot and aligning the inside cutting edge of the router bit with the mark for the minor axis. Note that the minor pivot has slid to the opposite side of the pivot block from the router.

A Jig for Precision Trimming

by Nick Engler

Once upon a time I had the brilliant idea to use a strip of hardwood to trim out the edge of a laminate countertop. And not just any laminate, either. This stuff was so expensive that if you asked how much it cost, the salesperson presumed you could not afford it. So scratching it during installation was not an option.

The challenge, I realized the moment the glue set upon the wood trim, was that I had to plane the top surface of the trim flush with the laminate without touching the laminate itself. If the blade touched the laminate, I would remove the thin layer that held the color, revealing the dull substrate (which the manufacturer thoughtfully made a flat white to provide maximum contrast and advertise my slip-up to the world).

I searched the 40 billion tool catalogs I receive each month (give or take), looking for something that would shave the wood without touching the laminate. I found nothing that would do the trick.

Now, we all know what happens when you have a perfectly good excuse to buy an expensive new tool and you can't find anything suitable – you buy something that's unsuitable and make it work. As a result, I

bought a small laminate trimmer and built the jig shown here to turn it into a tool that I hoped would not mar the laminate.

Making a Router Cut Like a Hand Plane

What I made is sometimes called a "router plane," although it does something quite different from the hand tool of the same name.

An old-time router plane rides on the surface and reaches down into

a recess to trim the bottom. This jig lets you adjust the depth of the router bit to cut adjacent surfaces flush to or higher than the surface on which the router is riding.

In my case, I wanted the tool to ride on the laminate and shave the top surface of the wood trim ever-so-slightly higher than the laminate it was attached to.

The first thing to do is to make a mounting plate from clear acrylic. (This lets you see what you are plan-

Bottom view

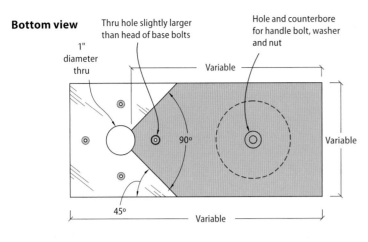

Thru hole slightly larger than head of base bolts

1" diameter thru

Variable

90°

45°

Variable

Hole and counterbore for handle bolt, washer and nut

Variable

Exploded view

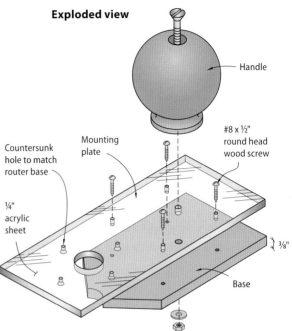

Handle

#8 x ½" round head wood screw

Mounting plate

Countersunk hole to match router base

¼" acrylic sheet

Base

⅜"

ing.) The plate should be rectangular and about twice as long as the laminate trimmer's base is wide.

Mount the router at one end of this plate, centered over a 1"-diameter opening for a bit. On the end of the plate, mount a ⅜"-thick wooden base and a handle, as shown in the drawing at right. The base rests on one surface and lets you cantilever the router over another surface that you want to shave parallel to the first.

The handle not only helps you control the router, it lets you counterbalance the router's weight and keep the base flat on the reference surface as you work.

The fasteners you use to assemble the plate, base and handle must not protrude below the bottom surface of the base – after all, you don't want metal hardware dragging over the surface you're trying not to cut.

Using the Jig

Mount a straight bit in the router. I commonly use a ¾"-diameter bit, but any bit smaller than the plate opening will do.

Adjust the depth of cut to the level you want to rout. If you want to trim one surface flush to another, raise or lower the bit until the tip barely touches the surface on which the base rests. If you want to cut slightly above a surface, as I did, simply raise the bit to the proper height.

I used a piece of paper as a feeler gauge to position the tip of the bit about .003" above the surface – close enough to look flush, but far enough away to make sure it wouldn't cut the laminate on which the jig rested. Then make a test cut to check your setup.

As you cut, pay close attention to the direction of rotation and the direction you move the trimmer. I cut with the router so the bit rotation pulled the router through the wood trim and away from the laminate surface I was trying to protect.

If you have to "back-feed" (where you move the router so the bit pulls in a direction you don't want to go), move the router very slowly and keep the base pressed firmly against the guiding surface. For delicate work, cut the wood in several passes, lowering the router a tiny fraction of an inch between each pass.

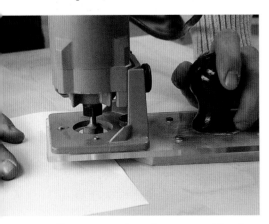

You can use a piece of paper to position the bit about .003" above the surface. This will look flush but still ensure you don't hurt the surrounding laminate.

This jig also will trim wooden plugs flush with the surrounding surface without cutting or marring that surface.

ILLUSTRATIONS BY MARY JANE FAVORITE

Super-Simple Dado and Rabbet Jig

by Nick Engler

When building a bookcase, you often must make a series of repetitive dadoes in the long uprights to support the shelves. You could do this on a table saw with a dado blade, but you'll find it's difficult to control the long stock as you feed it over the blade. If you have a router, you could clamp a straightedge to the stock and use it to guide the router, but it's time-consuming to measure and set up for each individual cut.

The dado-and-rabbet jig simplifies both the set-up and the operation. Lock the board between the base and clamping bar, then guide the router along the bar. The stock doesn't move, so you don't have to worry about controlling a large piece of wood. The straightedge is also the clamp, so the set-up is very simple.

And that's not all it does. The jig helps create any long dado, rabbet or slot. You can make repetitive cuts in multiple parts. And you can use it to guide other hand-held tools to make straight cuts, such as a sabre saw or a circular saw.

Making the Dado-and-Rabbet Jig

The jig is just two pieces of wood (a base and a clamping bar). The sizes of both parts is determined by your own needs. My jig is about as long as my workbench is wide. This allows

me to clamp the ends of the base to the bench. Not only does this keep the jig from moving around while I'm using it, it also keeps the base flat when I tighten the clamping bar against the stock to be routed.

Make the base from ¾" plywood and the clamping bar from a hard,

dense wood such as oak or maple. The bar should be fairly thick from top to bottom so it doesn't bow when tightened down. If it bows, the clamping pressure won't be even all across the stock. In fact, the bar will only press against the stock at the edges and the stock will be more

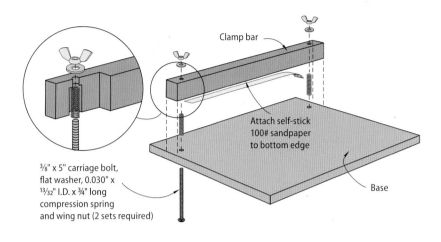

Clamp bar

Attach self-stick 100# sandpaper to bottom edge

Base

3⁄8" x 5" carriage bolt, flat washer, 0.030" x 13⁄32" I.D. x 3⁄4" long compression spring and wing nut (2 sets required)

in the base recess the heads of the bolts so the base will rest flat on the workbench. The counterbores in the clamping bar provide recesses for the compressed spring, allowing you to clamp thin stock.

The purpose of these springs, of course, is to automatically raise the bar every time you need to move or remove the stock. What do you do if you're routing thick stock and the springs don't reach far enough into the counterbores to raise the clamping bar? Simply turn the bar over so the springs are no longer recessed in the counterbores. (This, by the way, is why I crowned both the top and bottom of the bar.)

Making Dadoes and Rabbets

To use the jig, first you must position the stock on the base under the clamping bar. To do this quickly and accurately, it helps to make a

likely to slip. This becomes more and more of a problem the longer you make the clamping bar. To solve it, I crowned the top and bottom surfaces of the clamping bar, making it 1⁄32" to 1⁄16" thicker in the center than at the ends. Even though the bar flexes, the clamping pressure remains even. However, remember that the sides of the clamping bar (the surfaces that will guide your router) must be perfectly straight.

Tip: To keep the stock from shifting in the jig, apply self-adhesive sandpaper to the underside of the clamping bar. In some cases, you may also want to apply a strip of sandpaper to the base, directly under the bar.

Drill counterbored holes for the carriage bolts in both the base and the clamping bar. The counterbores

To make a positioning gauge, clamp a scrap under the clamping bar so you won't cut into the base. Rest a scrap of 1⁄4" plywood or hardboard against the bar and secure it to the scrap with a separate clamp. Then rout through the material, saving the strip between the router bit and the clamping bar.

Use the positioning gauge to align the stock underneath the clamping bar. The edge of the gauge indicates the inside edge of the cut.

ILLUSTRATION BY MARY JANE FAVORITE

You can rout multiple parts by stacking them edge to edge or face to face. However, you must be very careful that all the parts are secure under the clamping bar. If there is a slight discrepancy in the thickness of the pieces, one or more parts may shift during the cut. To prevent this, you may have to use additional clamps to secure individual pieces to the base.

To make multiple identical cuts, such as cutting the cheeks and shoulder of tenons in several rails, clamp a short fence to the base to automatically position the parts. Always check with the positioning gauge, however, before you make each cut.

positioning gauge from a scrap of thin plywood or hardboard. Lock the bar down on the base and place the scrap so one straight edge rests against the side of the bar. (The scrap mustn't be under the clamping bar.) Mount the bit you will use to make the cuts in your router, then rout all the way through the scrap, creating a strip about as long as the bar. This width of this strip is precisely the distance from the edge of the router to the cutting edge of the bit, and it becomes the positioning gauge for that specific router and that bit.

Lay out the cut you want to make, slide the stock beneath the bar, and turn the wing nuts so the bar is snug against the stock, but not tight. Place the positioning gauge against the clamping bar and line up your layout marks with the edge of the gauge. Then tighten the bar down and remove the gauge.

Rout the dado or the rabbet, keeping the router against the side

of the clamping bar. This is like any other router operation (feed the router left to right as you face the bar so the rotation of the bit helps hold the router against the guiding edge). Make deep cuts in several passes, routing about ⅛" deeper with each pass.

If your router has a flat side to its base, keep that pressed against the fence. If the base is round, you may want to mount the router to a square sole for this operation. Router bits aren't always perfectly concentric to the sole, and the bit may move in and out slightly from the clamping bar if the router turns as you make the cut. This will make the cut curved or wavy.

The jig is not only useful for cutting dadoes and rabbets in wide stock, it's a timesaver for making identical cuts in multiple parts. You can line up the parts under that clamping bar and cut several at once. For example, you can makes tenons

in the ends of multiple door rails by cutting four identical rabbets in the end of each piece. To do this, first position two parts under the clamping bar, one near each end. Then clamp a short fence, no taller than the stock is thick, against the ends of the parts. This will automatically position the rails for each cut you make.

Line up several rails edge to edge with the ends against the fence and lock the bar down on top of them. Check to see that each part is secure. If it shifts, you may have to add another clamp behind the clamping bar. Rout the faces of the rails, then turn them over and repeat. After routing the faces, make identical cuts in the edges. If the router seems unstable when routing the edges, either wait until you have enough parts to stack face to face to make a larger platform for the router or put spacers between the parts to spread them out.

Taming the Top-heavy Router

by Robert W. Lang

The router can be a great friend in the woodshop, but it's one of those friends with character traits that aren't welcome in all situations. Like the fraternity brother you want at your bachelor party but not necessarily at your wedding ceremony, the router is noisy, spews trash everywhere and is decidedly off balance. Lose control of it for a brief moment, and all kinds of damage can be done.

The problem. Most routers are top heavy and likely to tip (right). The standard baseplate doesn't leave much room to hold on with two hands.

Quick fix. A custom-made baseplate (below) provides a solid base for routing edges.

But the good things a router can do (that other tools can't) make it worthwhile to put up with some things you can't change, and look for ways to improve the situation. Put in your earplugs and put on your safety glasses because the noise and chips won't go away. But you can improve the stability of the beast. A router table is one way to do that, as is the addition of a custom base.

Adapt to the Situation

Custom router bases can be made in a short time out of simple and readily available material. Swapping the stock base for a custom one doesn't take long either, so there's no reason not to have a few dedicated to difficult tasks. If you struggle with holding your router steady and maintaining control, a larger base will overcome those issues.

The base shown here increases the surface area, and it provides a place for your off hand to hold the router down to the work. Commercial versions of this old standby are often in a teardrop shape, but we couldn't think of any good reason to do that, other than to make it look cooler. Keeping the shape a rectangle will speed fabrication, and leave you with useful reference edges for joinery.

We used a piece of ¼"-thick Plexiglas we had in our shop. You can find this material at the home-improvement store, or if you're in a larger town you can get offcuts from a plastics fabricator. The clear plastic is nice, but the only advantage it has compared to other materials is that you can see through it. Any material

Almost like wood. Plexiglas can be cut to size with standard carbide-tipped saw blades, and drilled with twist drill bits. Go slow and back up the work with a piece of scrap wood.

Big bit, same story. The larger bit clearance hole can be cut with a spade bit or a Forstner bit. A drill press is nice, but not necessary.

On the level. Countersink the holes so the screws are below the plate surface. You may need to make a trip to the hardware store for longer screws.

that is thin and stiff, such as plywood or hardboard, will work as well.

Use the same tools you use to work with wood to cut the plastic to size and to drill the required holes. Carbide-tipped saw blades are preferred, but don't spend $150 on a triple-chip-grind, 80-tooth blade until you go into the plastics fabricating business. What you have will work fine for the few cuts you need to make. Wear a dust mask and safety glasses as you work with it.

Good old twist drill bits will handle the holes; just use a slow drill speed to keep the plastic from melting. If the plastic you have comes with a paper covering, leave it on while you work on it. Our Plexiglas lost its cover years ago, so I put some painter's tape down the center to make marking possible.

Front & Center

Before removing the existing baseplate from your router, take note of how the switch and handle are oriented in relation to it. You want your custom configuration to be suited to your task and easy to use. After the screws are out, tape the existing plate down to your plastic to use as a pattern.

The solution. The extended base provides better control, eliminating the tendency of the router to tilt.

Find a drill bit that matches the diameter of the holes for the mounting screws, and drill a hole at each location. If you have a drill press you should use it, but if you don't, drill through with a hand-held drill into a scrap of wood beneath the plastic. When all the holes are in, remove the stock baseplate and carefully countersink the screw heads below the surface.

Now drill the center hole for the router bit clearance. I had a Forstner bit that was close in size to the original center hole, so that's what I used, but a cheap spade bit works as well if not better. Use your drill press if you have one, or clamp the plastic down on top of a scrap of wood and guide the drill by hand.

Any rough edges from cutting or drilling can be removed with a

few strokes of a file. The knob is a leftover cabinet knob, screwed to the plastic on the centerline. You can turn or whittle something fancier or more comfortable, or just attach a chunk of scrap wood.

Variations of the basic plate can be used for a variety of purposes. Increase the length and add a hole for a pivot pin to rout perfect circles or arcs. Attach a fence to the bottom to locate grooves or rabbets a set distance from an edge. Use a straight side of the baseplate against a straightedge to precisely guide the router to make dados.

Knowing how to use your tools includes knowing their limitations and discovering ways to overcome them. Most often the solution is simple, and waiting for you to uncover it and give it a try.

The Joint Maker

by Nick Engler

This horizontal routing jig, which I call "Joint Maker," holds the router to one side of the work. This setup offers several advantages over a standard router table for certain operations:

• You have more control when making mortises – you can rest the part on its face and feed the edge into the bit.

• When making tenons, the rotation of the bit doesn't pull the work sideways as it does on an ordinary router table. Instead, you cut directly against the rotation.

• And if you use vertical panel-raising bits, you'll find that with the panel resting flat on the worktable, gravity works for you.

I've built several Joint Makers throughout the years and I've noticed that the most serious limitation encountered is in routing small, narrow parts – your hands come too close to the bit for safe, accurate control. So I added a carriage on this one – essentially it's a sliding table. It works wonderfully. Just clamp the workpiece to the carriage and use it to feed the work into the router bit. Four stops on the carriage help position the work and control the cut. A unique cross slide keeps the work perfectly aligned with the bit, yet allows you to feed it front-to-back and side-to-side.

How Do I Build It?

In essence, the Joint Maker is just a Baltic birch plywood box with two flat work surfaces – one vertical, one horizontal – mounted to it. The vertical surface (or router mount) is attached to the back of the box and holds the router. The horizontal surface (or carriage) slides over the top of the box and holds the work.

Cut the parts to the sizes given in the cutting list. Rout ¾"-wide x ¼"-deep grooves in the top surface of the top and the bottom surface of the carriage, as shown in the illustrations on page 128. Note that the grooves in the top run front-to-back, while those in the carriage run side-to-side. The grooves fit around the cross slides.

Cut the shape of the top and cross-slide mount. The top has a "fixed stop" on one side and a cutout in the other.

Then cut a 2¼"-diameter dust-collection hole in one of the end pieces. Next, you should drill a 5⁄16"-diameter pivot hole for the router mount in the back side.

Assemble the bottom, sides, ends and baffle (which is a dust-collector diverter) with glue and screws. Insert the carriage bolt that serves as the pivot for the router mount through the pivot hole in the back side, then screw the top in place. But don't glue the top to the assembly – I found that out the hard way. If the pivot bolt happens to fall out, you can lose your religion trying to get it back in. (Of course, had I been smart, I would have epoxied the bolt in place.)

Mounting the Router

Attach the router to a clear plastic plate before putting it in the router mount. Because this router mounting plate is thinner than the board it attaches to, this arrangement gives you a fraction of an inch more depth of cut. More importantly, it lets you see what the router is doing as you cut.

To attach the plastic plate to the router mount, make a cutout and rabbet the edge to accept the mounting plate. Attach the router mounting plate to the router mount with #10 flathead sheet-metal screws. When installed, the router mount-

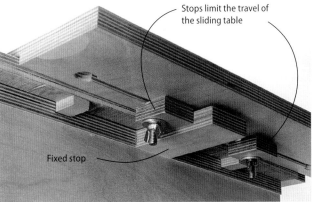

Stops limit the travel of the sliding table

Fixed stop

The sliding carriage has several straight slots with a ¾"-diameter hole at one end for you to mount the stops without having to remove the hardware. Just insert the head of the mounting bolt in the hole and slide the stop in.

ing plate must be flush with the work surface of the router mount. The heads of the screws must be countersunk in the mounting plate so they rest slightly below the surface.

Cutting the Slots

There are two types of slots in this fixture. The carriage has several keyhole slots – straight slots with a ¾"-diameter hole at one end. The holes let you mount the stops and clamps instantly, without having to remove the hardware. Just insert the heads of the mounting bolts in the holes and slide the stop sideways in the slot.

The slots let you position the stops and clamps wherever you need them when making cuts. Note that these slots are counterbored, which helps hold the heads of the bolts so they don't rub on the top of the fixture.

To make the keyhole slots, drill the ¾"-diameter holes first. Then rout ¾"-wide x ⅜"-deep counterbore grooves using a straightedge as a guide. Without changing the position on the router guide, change bits and rout a ⁵⁄₁₆"-wide slot through the middle of each groove.

The other slot used in this Joint Maker is the curved slot in the router mount. To rout this slot, attach the

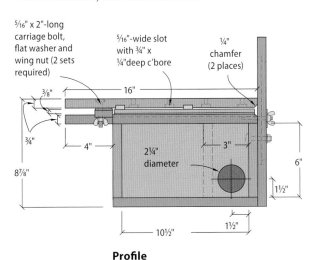

⁵⁄₁₆" x 2"-long carriage bolt, flat washer and wing nut (2 sets required)

⁵⁄₁₆"-wide slot with ¾" x ¼"deep c'bore

¼" chamfer (2 places)

16"

⅜"

¾"

8⅞"

4"

2¼" diameter

3"

6"

1½"

10½"

1½"

Profile

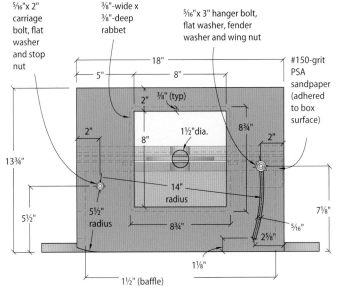

⁵⁄₁₆"x 2" carriage bolt, flat washer and stop nut

⅜"-wide x ⅜"-deep rabbet

⁵⁄₁₆"x 3" hanger bolt, flat washer, fender washer and wing nut

#150-grit PSA sandpaper (adhered to box surface)

18"

5"

8"

2"

⅜" (typ)

1½"dia.

8¾"

2"

13¾"

2"

8"

14" radius

5½"

5½" radius

8¾"

7⅛"

⁵⁄₁₆"

2⅝"

1⅛"

1½" (baffle)

Back view

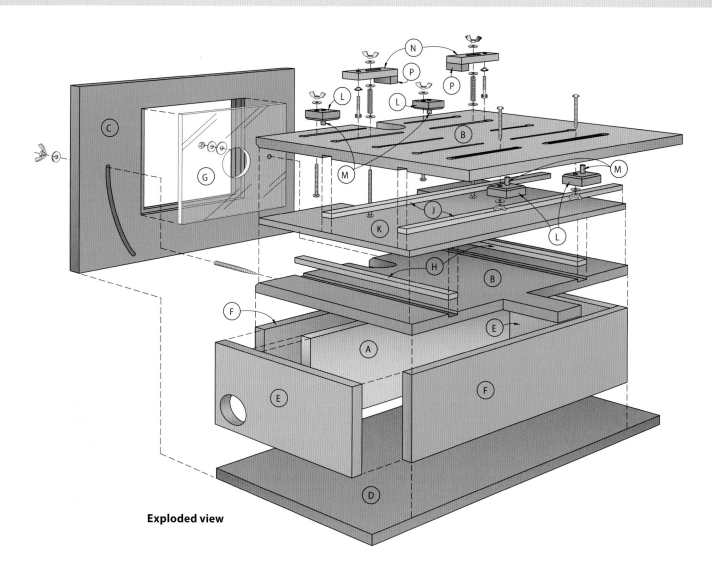

Exploded view

router to a router compass jig. Insert a pivot bolt through the compass and the mount, then swing the router in an arc as you cut.

Make the Cross-slide Mount

The cross-slide mount is a simple assembly, but you have to get all four of the slides positioned correctly for it to work well. The best way I found to do this was to use the tool itself as a glue-up jig.

Place a single layer of thin plastic in the grooves in both the top and the carriage (a plastic grocery bag works well). Then press the slides into their grooves on top of the plastic. Apply a thin bead of glue to

The Joint Maker

No.	Let.	Item	Dimensions (in inches)			Comments
			T	W	L	
1	A	Baffle	¾	6	16½	Baltic birch plywood
2	B	Top/carriage	¾	16	18	Baltic birch plywood
1	C	Router mount	¾	13¾	18	Baltic birch plywood
1	D	Bottom	¾	12	24	Baltic birch plywood
2	E	Ends	¾	6	10½	Baltic birch plywood
2	F	Sides	¾	6	18	Baltic birch plywood
1	G	Router mounting plate	⅜	8¾	8¾	Acrylic plastic
2	H	Front-to-back slides	¼	⅜	11¾	Baltic birch plywood
2	J	Side-to-side slides	¼	⅜	18	Baltic birch plywood
1	K	Cross-slide mount	¼	11¾	18	Baltic birch plywood
4	L	Stops	¾	1½	1½	Hardwood
4	M	Stop pins			1	⁵⁄₁₆" diameter
3	N	Clamps	¾	2	5¾	Baltic birch plywood
3	P	Clamp jaws	¾	¾	2	Baltic birch plywood

You can make a counterbored slot in two steps. First rout the wide "counterbore groove" that forms the step inside the slots .

Then rout a slot down the middle of the groove, cutting completely through the stock in four ⅛"-deep passes.

the exposed surface of each slide. Place the cross-slide mount on top of the slides in the top, then place the carriage (with the slides in place) on top of it. Don't worry if there's glue squeeze-out; the plastic will prevent it from accidentally bonding surfaces that shouldn't.

Make sure everything lines up properly and the back edge of the carriage is flush with the back of the Joint Maker. Then clamp the parts together and let the glue dry. After it sets, take the carriage, cross slide and Joint Maker apart, and trash the plastic.

Make the Stops and Clamps

The stops and clamps are all attached to the carriage by carriage bolts. The stops are just blocks of wood with dowels protruding from the underside to keep them from rotating while in use. Chamfers around the bottom edges prevent sawdust from interfering with the accuracy of your setup.

I found that as sawdust builds up around the stops, it prevents the parts from making full contact. This, in turn, keeps you from positioning the parts correctly. The chamfers give the sawdust somewhere to go. You will still have to brush the dust

away from time to time, but you don't have to get every little particle.

On the clamps, a compression spring around the mounting bolt automatically raises the clamp when you loosen the knob. A hex bolt threaded into a T-nut at the back of the clamp prevents the assembly from tipping when you apply pressure.

Make as many clamps and stops as you think you'll need. I made just

Router compass jig

To rout the curved slot in the router mount, first make a router compass jig to guide your router in an arc. Drill the ⁵⁄₁₆"-diameter mounting hole in the router mount and mark the ends of the curved slot. Use the mounting hole as the pivot and swing the router in an arc to cut the slot.

three clamps and four stops, which I've found to be adequate for the work I do. But if you think you'll need more, now is the time to make them.

As another option (if you've got a few extra dollars) there are a couple of hold-down clamps available from catalogs that will also work very well when attached to the Joint Maker (see "Some Store-bought Options to Improve the Joint Maker" on page 129 for more information).

Final Assembly, Finishing

Give all the wooden surfaces a light sanding, then apply a durable finish to all parts of the Joint Maker: the router mount, carriage, cross slide, clamps and stops.

Apply a thin coat to all exposed surfaces, then rub down those surfaces that will slide together (such as the back and the router mount, or the top and the cross slide) with steel wool or fine abrasive pads. Then apply a coat of paste furniture wax to the sliding surfaces of the top, cross slide and carriage, and buff it out. The thin layer of wax lubricates the surfaces and helps the parts slide much more easily.

Attach the router mount to the

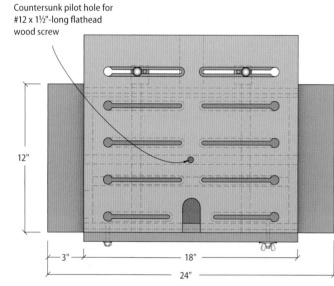

Countersunk pilot hole for #12 x 1½"-long flathead wood screw

Carriage layout - plan

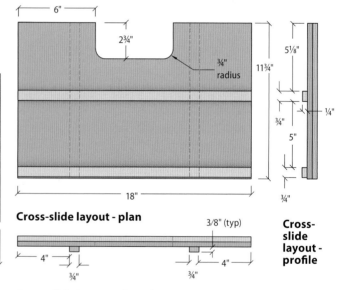

Cross-slide layout - plan

Cross-slide layout - profile

Cross-slide layout - elevation

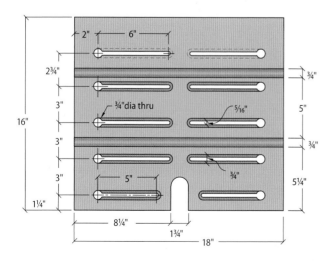

Carriage layout - bottom view

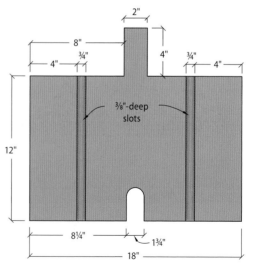

Top layout - plan

Joint Maker with a pivot bolt, washer and a stop nut. Using the curved slot as a guide, drill a ¼"-diameter pilot hole for the hanger bolt in the edge of the top. Install the hanger bolt, fender washer, flat washer and wing nut, as shown in the illustrations.

Also install the hardware in the stops and clamps. The carriage and cross slide are not attached; they simply rest atop and slide on the Joint Maker.

Once you've done that, you're ready to test it out on all your joint-making operations.

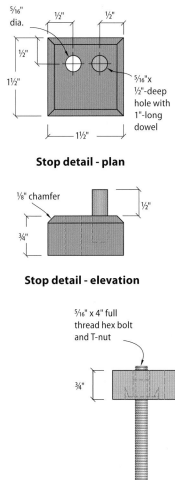

Stop detail - plan

⅛" chamfer
½"
¾"

Stop detail - elevation

SOME STORE-BOUGHT OPTIONS TO IMPROVE THE JOINT MAKER

When we had a chance to work with the Joint Maker in the Popular Woodworking shop, we were definitely impressed with the cleverness of the design. Our minds were spinning with the amazing number of operations that could be performed easily with this homemade jig.

We also let our minds wander a little further about some of the features of the jig. After adjusting the numerous wing nuts (especially when applying hold-down torque to such a small surface area), we decided that some very affordable handles would make the jig more user-friendly. T-handle, star and three-wing knobs are available for 50 cents to $2 each, and make gripping and tightening the adjusters a whole heck of a lot easier.

Another addition we felt would be useful were some optional manufactured hold-downs. While Nick's hold-downs function well, there are a number of other hold-downs available for less than $5 that offer slightly better performance. The store-bought hold-downs shown at right will work with the slots as shown in the plans, and by purchasing them you'll reduce the time necessary to build the jig and get you using it more quickly.

Both the knobs and hold downs shown here are available from Hartville Tool (800-345-2396 or hartvilletool.com). The knobs (right) are made from recycled plastic and available as two-prong (item #60946), three-prong (item #60866) or four-prong (item #60796). Each costs 99 cents. The hold-down unit below left (item #60736) costs $5.49 and includes a solid aluminum hold-down, a bolt and a ¼"-20 knob.

While the four-prong "star" knobs are easiest to grab, the two-prong "T" knobs require less clearance. The hold-down at left also works in the Joint Maker's slots.

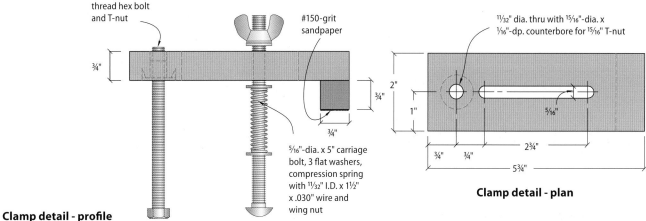

Clamp detail - profile

Clamp detail - plan

USING THE JOINT MAKER TO CREATE A HAUNCHED MORTISE-AND-TENON JOINT

1 You can cut grooves on the inside of edges of rails and stiles with a straight bit. Lock the carriage to the base with a wood screw and feed the parts past the bit, guiding them along the mount.

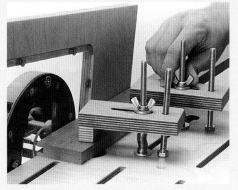

2 To cut the mortise, clamp a stile to the carriage so the inside edge faces the router. Adjust the hex bolts so the clamp jaws sit squarely on the work while you tighten the knobs.

3 Secure a stop against the end of the stile to quickly align the other stiles. This makes it a lot easier to make the same cut in multiple pieces without having to set it up each time.

4 Advance the router bit to cut the full depth of the mortise. Holding the carriage, feed the stock into the bit no more than ⅛" deep at a time, moving it side to side.

5 For the tenon, mount a rail on the carriage so the edge is perpendicular to the mounting plate. Secure stops against the rail to help you position the others for duplicate cuts.

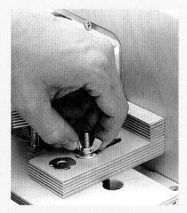

6 You can use the wooden clamp as a stop to prevent the bit from cutting into the carriage as you work.

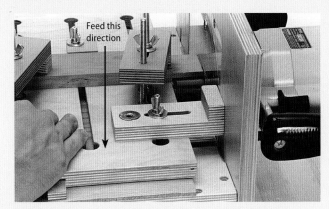

Feed this direction

7 Once you set up the stops and clamps to cut the tenons just as you want them, feed the rail across the bit, cutting the underside of the stock. With the cutter below the work, you need to pull the work toward you to cut against the rotation of the bit.

8 To cut the tenon's shoulders, turn the rail so the outside edge rests on the carriage and clamp it in place. Readjust the router bit and cut the haunch in the tenon, using the carriage to feed the work and control the cut.

Router Table-Mate

by Steve Shanesy

Commercially made router tables are everywhere these days. Some of them come with more gizmos and gadgets than a '59 Edsel. By the time you tally up all the add-ons, the price approaches a medium-duty shaper. Here's my short list of "must-have" features for a good router table:

• A table the size of a carrier deck.

• Compact design so it can store easily.

• A stout fence that's long and easy to adjust.

• Easy bit-height adjustment with no stooping.

• Great dust collection.

• A $60 price tag.

With all these features in mind, I hit on the idea of using my folded-up Workmate stored under the stairs. Can't I just make a top for it? Then I remembered the great idea from Contributing Editor Nick Engler in our January 2000 issue. Nick made the top of his router table tilt up for easy adjustments. Bingo. Now my Workmate/router table goes right back under the stairs and takes up only another 1½" of space, the thickness of the router tabletop. You can also use this router table without a

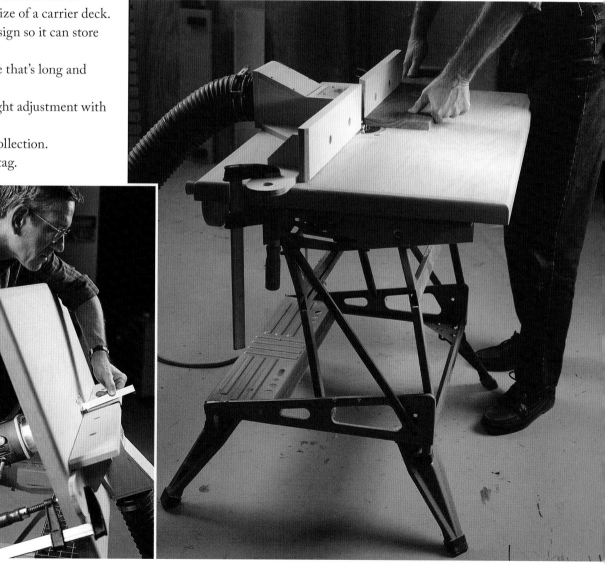

Workmate. A simple pair of saw-horses will suffice.

Customizing Your Table

While the fence is generic to any router table setup, the table needs to be customized for your needs. You may have a different brand router than mine, so you will have to relieve the underside of the table to accommodate the shape of your tool. You'll have to locate the mounting holes for the base to suit your router. You may prefer a different table height. If you are below average height, you'll want the make the angle at which the table props up less steeply.

The top is made from two pieces of ¾" birch plywood that are glued together and banded with ¾"-thick solid birch. Before gluing anything

together, it's best to work on the top plywood piece. Since you must rout out the underside of this top piece where the router base will be mounted, do it before gluing the two sheets together. The hole in the bottom sheet can be simply cut with a jigsaw.

First, lay out where you want your router base to be mounted and find the exact center of the base. I put the centerpoint on my table 8" in from the back edge and centered right to left. So once the point is established, drill a ⅟₁₆" hole straight through to the other side. You'll need this location for work later on.

Now set up a router with a circle-cutting jig and a ½" straight bit. Set the bit so it will cut to a depth that will leave a ⅜" thickness in the

plywood top. Cut a circle (assuming your router has a round base) on the underside of the top that is approximately ¼" larger in diameter than the router base. Place the circle jig's indexing pin in the center hole you just drilled. Rout the circle and the remaining waste inside the circle.

Next, turn the plywood piece over. Use your center hole and circle jig to cut a ⅛"-deep circular rabbet or ledge for your plastic inserts to fit into. The insert diameter is 4¾". But before you use this insert size, check the size of your router's base. You may need to make a smaller-diameter insert based on the size of your router base. The router I mounted in the table is a massive Porter-Cable 7518. I made the insert hole size large enough to accommodate the

A larger base for the router was the ticket for bridging the open areas left by routing out the plywood for the router's base. It was later used as a small circle cutting jig for the tabletop and plastic inserts. Use the same cutter and it's easy to keep track of dimensions for cutting inside or outside circles.

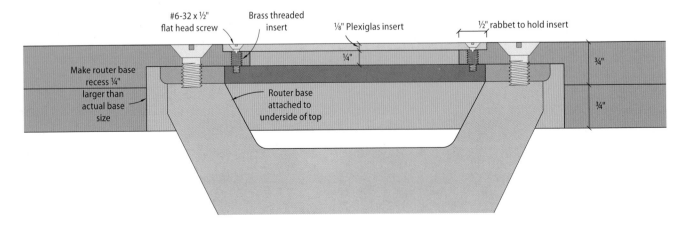

#6-32 x ½" flat head screw   Brass threaded insert   ⅛" Plexiglas insert   ½" rabbet to hold insert

¼"

¾"

Make router base recess ¼" larger than actual base size

Router base attached to underside of top

¾"

largest diameter router bits.

Now make the hole the router bits pass through. Leave a ledge about ½" wide all around for the removable inserts to rest on.

Now take the second sheet of plywood and jigsaw the cut to accommodate the router base. Also, make any cuts necessary to allow for your router base's handles. When done, glue the two sheets together. Keep the edges flush.

When the glue is dry, trim the top to finished size on the table saw. Now prepare some stock for the solid-edge banding. Miter the corners and glue it on. Make sure it is flush to the top. When dry, sand everything flush, then rout a roundover profile on the top edge.

Router Table and Fence

No.	Ltr.	Item	Dimensions (in inches)			Material
			T	W	L	
2	A	Table top	¾	23	35	birch ply
1	B	Top edge banding	¾	1½	11'	solid birch
1	C	Workmate board	¾	4	27⅜	any hardwood
1	D	Prop stick	¾	18¾		dowel stock
1	E	Prop bracket	½	11/2	4	Baltic birch
1	F	Fence bottom	½	8	41	Baltic birch
2	G	Fence sub fronts	½	3	2½	Baltic birch
2	H	Dust chute sides	½	4⅛	8	Baltic birch
1	I	Dust chute top	½	4	5	Baltic birch
1	J	Chute angled top	½	5	4¾	Baltic birch
1	K	Chute back	½	5	5	Baltic birch
2	L	End ribs	½	2⅝	3	Baltic birch
2	M	Mid ribs	½	2⅝	2⅝	Baltic birch
2	N	Fence adjust. front	¾	4	16	any hardwood

Hardware: 3, 6-32 threaded inserts and ½" 6-32 screws; 4 each ⅜" x 1½" round head machine screws, star washers, flat washers and wing nuts, 1 pr. medium-duty loose-pin hinges. Acrylic ⅛" sheet 12" square, 1 switched plug strip.

Tabletop Inserts

Make the round tabletop inserts from ⅛" acrylic. I made three inserts to cover most of the router bit sizes I'd encounter. First set the circle jig to cut a circle that is the same size as the insert hole. Set your router to make an outside cut instead of an inside cut. To rout the acrylic, just drill a hole to accommodate the circle-cutting jig's pin or nail.

The three hole sizes I made in the inserts were 1", 1¾" and 2¾". The smaller holes were drilled using hole saws but the larger size required the circle-cutting jig.

Complete the Top

To fasten the inserts to the table, install three threaded inserts in the rabbet. I used inserts for a 6-32 flush machine screw. Once installed, transfer their locations to the acrylic inserts, then drill and countersink the plastic.

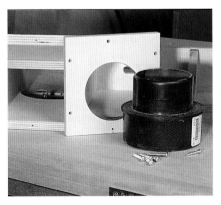

Inside view of the dust chute from the rear including the plastic 4" to 3" dust collection hose adapter. Rout the 3" hole for the adapter with the circle-cutting jig or use a "fly cutter" in your drill press.

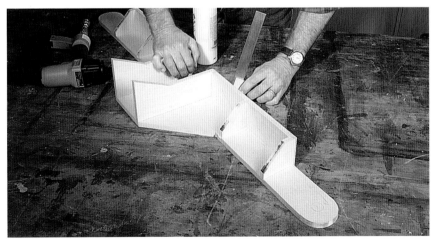

As you assemble the fence, make sure it is square along its length. Be sure and check it again after it is clamped up.

Next make a new piece to replace the rear board on the Workmate's table. The homemade board is narrower and allows the router to swing up unencumbered. Cut the board to the dimensions given in the materials list and locate holes that match those in your existing Workmate. The new board is slightly shorter than the original. Install the Workmate connecting hardware and place the board in the furthermost connecting hole of the Workmate.

On the underside of the router tabletop you'll need to install a piece of ½" material where the stick that supports the top in the open position locks in place. I used a ¾" dowel for a prop stick and drilled an oversized hole on a 25° angle in the block to nest it.

Once the tabletop is hinged to the Workmate's front board, it's easy to locate the positions for the prop stick and stick bracket. Note the shop-made replacement board for the Workmate top.

As mentioned earlier, the length of the prop stick will depend on how tall you are. On the end of the stick opposite the 25° angle, drill two holes that intersect each other to allow the stick to pivot in two directions, side to side so that it can be lowered when not in use and angled to allow you to tip it forward when propping the tabletop. Use a stout wood screw, a #10 or #12, to connect the prop stick to the edge of the new shop-made top board.

Next use a pair of hinges to connect the top to the Workmate's front board. Locate them about 4" in from each end.

Now Make the Fence

Keep in mind the most important factor in making the fence is that it is straight and square to the table. It could be shimmed later, but you'll be fussing with it forever.

Start by laying out the full size shape of the bottom piece on the material you will actually use. Be sure you have a true, straight edge for what will be the front.

Go ahead and lay out where the dadoes will be cut, including where the half-round throat opening for the router will be. It's best to do the layout by first establishing the center of the length of the fence and working out from there. When done, cut the back shape. It need not be pretty.

Next cut out the two subfronts for the fence. Install your dado blade on the table saw to cut the thickness of the Baltic birch.

Now set the dado blades to make a ⅛"-deep cut. While holding the front edge of the fence bottom against the slot miter gauge, cut the

six dadoes, following the layout lines already marked. When done, cut the center dado on the subfronts making sure it locates precisely where the dado in the bottom falls. Next raise the dado set to cut ⅜" deep and run the rabbets on the ends and bottom of the fence subfronts.

Remove the dado and cut the fence ribs and pieces that make up the dust collection chute. Use the diagram for the shape. Before assembling the fence, cut the half circle in the fence bottom for the throat opening, then use a rasp to slope the back edge for more efficient dust evacuation.

Assemble the Fence

Be careful when you assemble the fence to make sure it goes together square. First dry-fit all the parts to be sure you have a good fit. Then glue the ribs and dust chute sides to the bottom, making sure all the edges are flush to the front edge. If you have a brad nailer, set these in place with a couple short brads. Glue the fence subfronts to the bottom and ribs. Clamp front to back until the glue dries.

Now cut the three remaining dust chute parts: the top, angled top and back. Cut a half circle in the top similar to the one in the fence bottom.

After the glue in the fence assembly has dried, glue the dust chute top in place. Afterwards, install the angled top and the back piece. The angled top requires a steep angle cut on the lower edge to seat down to the flat top. I cut this angle on my band saw. The back of the chute requires a hole for dust collection. The chute

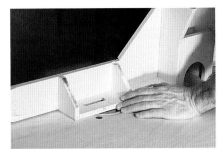

Break in your router table by milling the slots in the fence subfront that will allow the fence faces to adjust into or away from the router bit. Lay out the stop/start lines and plunge cut the slots.

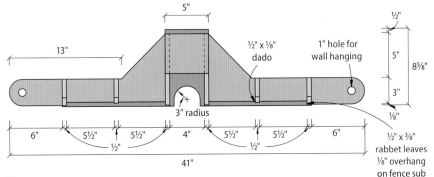

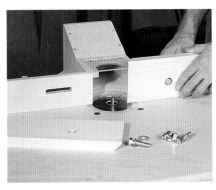

Attach the fence faces using ⅜" roundhead machine screws, a star washer, flat washer and wing nut. I tried using hex-head bolts but switched to screws because a screwdriver can be used and makes a more secure attachment with less trouble.

is set up to take a 3" hose or a fitting that reduces a 4" hose to a 3" hose. I used a "fly cutter" in my drill press to make the 3" hole. To complete the assembly of the dust chute, screw the angled top, then the back in place.

Use Your New Router Table

Now use your router table to mill the slots in the fence's subfronts that allow the fence fronts to slide left to right.

Set your router in the table with a ⅜" straight bit. Make a temporary fence from a straight piece of scrap

and clamp it to the tabletop. Use the fence diagram for setting the distance. Cut the 2"-long slots in the center of the openings between the ribs.

Make the adjustable fronts from a tight-grained hardwood such as maple. Be sure the material is flat and straight. Cut the two pieces to the lengths given. Make bevel cuts on the ends as shown in the diagram. Carefully locate the hole locations where the ⅜" machine screws attach the fronts through the slots in the subfronts. Drill and countersink the holes. For attachment, I used the screws along with star washers, flat washers and wing nuts.

The last detail is to cut a small piece of acrylic as a "window" on the top of the dust chute into the router opening area below.

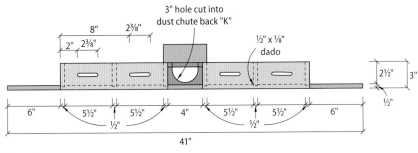

Plan

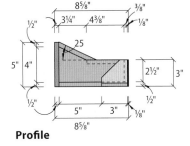

Elevation

Profile

Benchtop Router Table Stand

by Troy Sexton

At first it might seem a bit odd to build a cabinet base that will convert a benchtop router table into a floor model. But it really makes great sense for a couple of reasons.

This setup takes up less space than a commercial floor-model router table, yet it has just as much storage for accessories than the big boys; in fact, it probably has more. On the whole, this setup costs less than buying a floor-model router table, and it lets you easily remove the benchtop unit if you need to take it with you on a job or to the garage.

As you'll see, I've come up with an ingenious way to slip the router table into place without clamping. I also added an inexpensive power strip to the side to make turning on the router (and a shop vacuum) a convenient, single-switch operation.

How it's Built

While this stand is built using solid poplar, you easily could build this project from ¾" plywood.

The joinery is pretty simple, but I got a little fancy on the drawers. The case is held together with rabbets and dados. The bottom is held in place between the sides in ¼" x ¾" through dados. At the back edge of each side is a ¼" x ¼" rabbet to hold the back.

For the drawers, I took advantage of a joint-cutting router bit I've been wanting to try for a while: the drawer-lock bit. This bit cuts an interlocking rabbet that adds extra strength against racking and separation to a drawer joint. Because there were going to be a lot of heavy router bits in the drawers, I figured the extra strength was a good idea.

Case Joinery

I used solid poplar for my stand, which means I started by jointing and planing the wood into straight and true ¾"-thick boards. Then I edge-glued some together to make up the panels for the sides, bottom and top. If you've opted for plywood, you've saved yourself a couple of steps, but you're still going to have to cut all the pieces to size according to the cutting list.

With everything cut to size, it's time to make some rabbets and dados. I prefer making these cuts on my table saw, but you can certainly opt for a router.

First, you should cut the through dado that holds the bottom in place between the side pieces. After

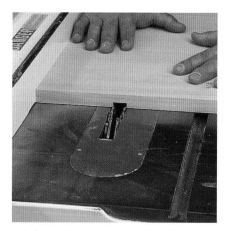

A dado stack in my table saw makes quick work of the dado for the bottom in each side. The cut is made 4¼" up from the bottom edge.

After resetting the dado height and adding a sacrificial fence to my rip fence, I was able to cut the rabbets for the back on each side.

installing a dado stack in my saw (and shimming it to a perfect ¾" thickness) I set the height of the dado to ¼" and set my rip fence to 4¼" up from the bottom edge of the side. Mark the bottom and inside surface of each cabinet side so you don't get confused, then cut each dado with the side's bottom edge against the fence and the inside surface of the side down on the saw table.

With that joint complete, it's time to cut the rabbets on the sides that will hold the back. Increase the height of the dado blades to ½" and add a sacrificial fence to your table saw's rip fence to allow only ¼" of the stack to be exposed by the fence. Then cut the two inside back edges of each side to form the rabbets.

Glue and Nails

Except for the drawers, you've completed all the necessary carcase joinery. Sand the inside of the case and decide how you want to assemble it. I chose glue and a pneumatic nailer, but you could use screws, or hammer

and nails.

Put one of the sides on your bench and glue the bottom piece into the dado. Add glue in the dado of the second side and then use one of the brace pieces between the two sides to temporarily prop the side piece up. Flush up all your joints and then nail the bottom in place.

Flip the assembled side and bottom over, and repeat the process for the second side. Then slide the brace to the upper back corner of the case, and glue and nail it in place (vertically) between the sides. Keep this brace flush with the rabbets in the sides.

The next step is to shape and attach the two lower braces. One brace goes in the front and the other one goes in the back.

By notching the lower braces and both sides of the stand, I formed sturdy "legs" for my cabinet. This makes it more likely that your stand will sit flat on an uneven floor. Mark the cutouts using the illustrations at right, then use a jigsaw to cut away the waste. Nail the braces in place.

Benchtop Router Table Stand

No.	Item	T	W	L	Material	Comments
		Dimensions (inches)				
1	Top	¾	18½	24	Poplar	
2	Sides	¾	17½	25¼	Poplar	¼" x ¼" rabbet at back
1	Bottom	¾	17¼	21	Poplar	
3	Braces	¾	4¼	20½	Poplar	
1	Back	¼	21½	25¼	Plywood	
4	Drawer fronts	¾	5	20½	Poplar	Drawer-lock joints
4	Drawer backs	½	4½	20½	Poplar	Drawer-lock joints
8	Drawer sides	½	5	15¾	Poplar	Drawer-lock joints
4	Drawer bottoms	¼	19	15½	Plywood	
2	Fixed mounting strips	¾	2¾	17	Poplar	
2	Short mounting strips	¾	2¾	4	Poplar	
2	Removable router table mounting strips	¾	2¾	13	Poplar	

Topping it Off

The next part of the cabinet is the top. Evenly space the top's overhang on the cabinet and start nailing it in place at the back of the cabinet.

Before nailing the top at the front, be sure to measure the drawer opening at the front of the cabinet to make sure it's the same at the top and at the bottom. Otherwise your drawers will be difficult to install because the case will not be square.

The last part to make is the back. Cut your back to fit in the rabbets, but don't nail it in place yet. It's a lot easier to put the drawer slides in with the back off.

A Bit of a Cavern

This cabinet has a remarkable amount of storage space; in fact, it gave me some room to grow my already extensive collection of router bits and accessories.

For shop furniture, I prefer drawers to shelves and doors because it's easier to organize small things in a drawer.

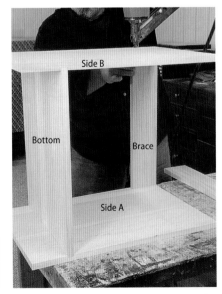

To assemble the bottom and sides, use one side to hold the bottom upright in the dado, put glue in the other side and install it. One of the braces makes a temporary support for the side piece as I nail it to the bottom.

After flipping the assembly and attaching the other side the same way, I take the brace I've been using as a support and shoot it in place at the upper back corner of the cabinet using my nailer.

Nail the other two braces in place below the bottom. The braces help square up the cabinet as you attach them – assuming they're cut square.

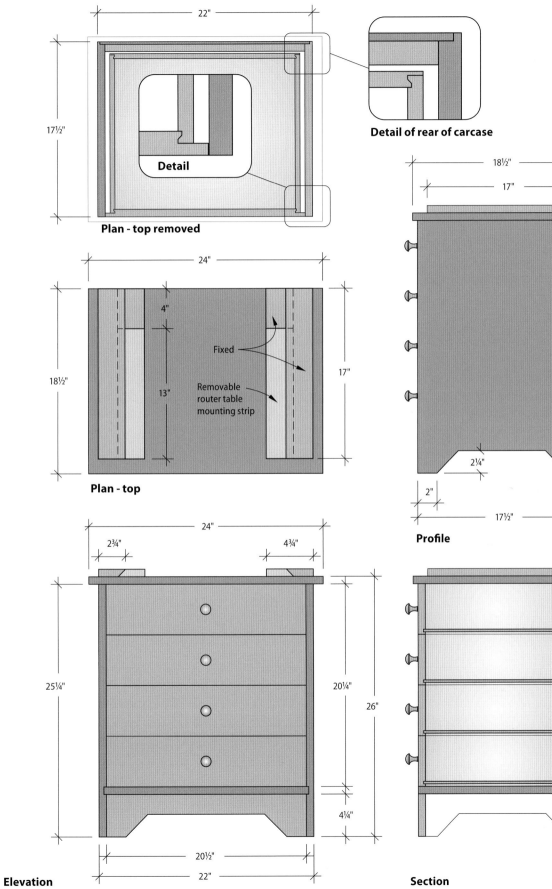

Detail of rear of carcase

Plan - top removed

22"

17½"

Detail

Plan - top

24"

18½"

4"

13"

17"

Fixed

Removable
router table
mounting strip

Profile

18½"

17"

25¼"

2¼"

2"

17½"

Elevation

24"

2¾"

4¾"

25¼"

20¼"

26"

4¼"

20½"

22"

Section

4¼"

4¼"

The carcase is essentially complete. All that's missing is the back, which I leave off until after I paint it and install the drawers.

Making the drawers for this piece is pretty simple: I used a drawer-lock bit in my router table. To keep my setups to a minimum, I ran both the front and back at the same setting, then trimmed the back to length before assembling the drawer. For the drawer fronts and backs, I needed to inset the joinery ½" on each end to accommodate the mechanical drawer slides I was using. This meant taking off a pretty serious amount of wood on each end, so I quickly notched each end on the table saw first (the dado stack was still set up).

Then, by working with the inside surface of the drawer backs and fronts down against the router table, I was able to make the compatible joinery parts on different thicknesses of wood.

With the front and backs of the drawers complete, I ran the drawer sides vertically to form the mating pieces.

Drawer Assembly

The last step before assembling the drawers was to cut a ¼" x ¼" groove along the inside face of the front and side pieces to capture the plywood bottom piece. I did this with a ¼"-diameter straight bit in my router table, but a couple of passes with a standard blade on the table saw also would work, if you prefer. I started the grooves ¼" up from the bottom edge of each piece.

The drawer backs are narrower than the other drawer pieces, allowing the bottom to slide into the groove after assembly.

Dry-fit the drawers to make sure everything fits tight. While the drawers are together, mark the extra length on the drawer backs with a pencil. Then take the drawer apart and cut the backs to finished length.

The drawers now are ready to assemble. Add some glue to the corner joints. One of the other nice advantages of the drawer-lock joint is that the drawers can be clamped together with only a couple of clamps across the drawer width. The joint itself will hold everything tightly in place.

After assembly, slide the bottom in place to square up the drawer before nailing the bottom in place to the back.

Not Just Paint

While poplar is a good, sturdy and inexpensive wood for building this type of shop cabinet, it's not exactly attractive. I build a lot of Shaker-style furniture, so I've become fond of milk-paint finishes. They brush on easily and look like a finish on the piece, rather than a coat of paint. My sister painted the outside surfaces (including the still-unattached back) and the drawer fronts.

I installed the drawer hardware by following the instructions supplied with the full-extension, 100-pound-capacity drawer slides I bought. When installing, the drawer fronts are held flush to the front edges of the cabinet.

Mounting a Table

Except for adding the Shaker knobs on the drawers, the cabinet essentially

Large rabbet cut before drawer-lock joint

With the bottom grooves cut and the back trimmed for length, shoot the drawers together. The drawer-lock joint (inset) pulls the parts tighter, so there's less need to clamp during assembly.

is complete. But to make it a router table stand, I still needed to add cleats to the top to secure the router table.

The cleats are a variation on a couple of very good ideas: the sliding dovetail and a French cleat. By mounting two strips of poplar cut lengthwise at a 45° bevel opposite one another on the top, you create the female part of a sliding dovetail. The mating strips then are mounted to the bottom of whatever portable router table already is in your shop.

To make a stop to keep the table from sliding front-to-back, I cut the second set of strips 4" shorter, then attached the 4" blocks to the rear of the cabinet, tight against the bevel of the longer, attached strips. Now the router table slides into place and stops where I want it.

OK, I have a confession to make. While I like the usefulness of being able to make my portable router table stationary and vice versa, it wasn't my only reason for making this stand. I'm guilty of owning more than one router table and leaving a set of routers ready-to-use for some joinery at all times. My router table stand allows me to switch out tables effortlessly. I know it's extravagant, but I like routers!

Supplies

Woodworker's Supply
800-645-9292 or woodworker.com
4 pair 16" drawer slides,
#860-835, $14.59/pair
4 Walnut Shaker knobs,
#938-503, $3.29
1 qt. Federal Blue milk paint,
#895-130, $22.99
Prices as of publication deadline.

Once the cabinet is assembled, use the dimensions provided in the illustrations to mark and cut the "feet" on the front and back braces, and on the sides. A jigsaw makes quick work of these cuts.

If everything worked out right, you'll have ½" clearance on either side of the drawer for the drawer slides. With the back off, it's a lot easier to attach the slides to the cabinet sides. Then it's some final fitting, paint and adding a back.

THE DRAWER-LOCK BIT

If you're shopping for a clever router bit for making drawers, add the drawer-lock bit to your list.

I used it to make the drawers for the router table stand, and I'm going to be using it a lot more. The cut created by the bit is a variation on a tongue-and-dado joint that is used a lot in commercial drawer-making. But the bit is quicker and looks nicer, too.

The photo below left shows the router table setup with the bit ready to cut. You should note that the drawer front I'm about to cut has a notch cut in it already. Because I'm using drawer slides, I needed to allow ½" clearance on either side of the drawer. This means the drawer front extends beyond the drawer to hide the slide hardware. So the drawer-lock cut is deeper on the front than it would be on a drawer without slides. Rather than try to hog off all that wood with the drawer lock bit in one pass (which would not be good for the router), I notched the drawer fronts and backs on my table saw first.

The photo below right shows the cut being made in the front. I run all the drawer fronts and backs with this setup. (Though the backs are thinner, I don't have to reset the bit height.) You also should note that I've added a build-up to the router table fence. This helps protect my hands during the cut, and it's also the setup needed for the next cuts on the drawer sides. By simply running the sides vertically against the fence, the mating half to the drawer lock joint is complete! It's a pretty slick system.

Pre-cut notch

Build-up on fence

No-nonsense Router Table

by Robert W. Lang

The original version of this router table was born out of necessity. I needed a router table at a job site, and I didn't have the space or the desire to carry my large one. I cobbled it together quickly, screwed the router's baseplate to the bottom of the tabletop, and made a simple fence. A dozen years later, it still serves me well.

It's easy to get carried away when making a router table, building something the size of a 5-horsepower shaper, full of drawers for storing every router bit in the catalog and accessories for every imaginable circumstance. If you'd rather keep things simple, or need a second table in your shop, this will do everything you need without taking much time or space. And if you want to jazz it up, this is a good starting point.

The top measures 16" x 24" – large enough to handle all but extremely large panels and small enough to store below a bench or on a shelf. The small size also helps to keep the top from sagging, a common issue with super-sized router tables.

The height of the table will be a compromise between a comfortable working height, and ease of getting the router in and out to change bits. I chose a router that clamps in a fixed base and can be quickly removed for changing bits. I left plenty of room

Not fancy, but functional. A good router table features a flat, solid top and a straight fence. With those in place, there isn't a need for much more.

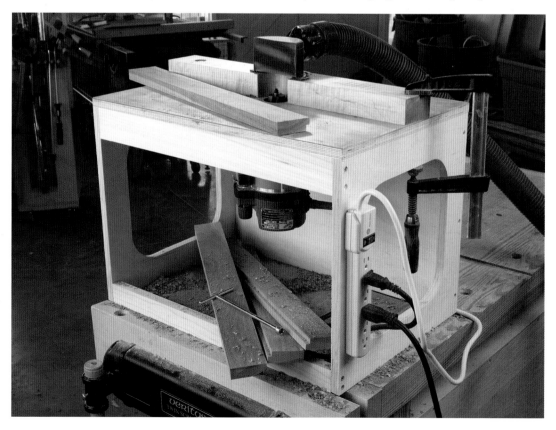

for this operation, which leaves the top a bit high when placed on my workbench, but just right when set on sawhorses.

Begin construction by cutting the top, sides and back from ¾"-thick plywood, particleboard or MDF. The two rails across the front are ¾" x 2½" hardwood.

On each of the two side pieces, mark a line 2½" in from each edge. Use a compass to draw a 2½" radius in each corner, and cut inside the lines with a jigsaw. The curves in the corners add strength, and these cutouts in the sides make the structure lighter. More important, they provide room for F-style clamps. Clamps are used at the top to hold the fence, and they can also be used at the bottom to secure the table to a bench or sawhorses.

The back goes in between the sides, secured with glue and #8 x 1¾" screws. To keep everything lined up, assemble the parts on the flattest surface available. The top of the table saw is a good choice for this. After the first three parts are assembled, cut the rails to length, and glue and screw them between the sides. The edge of the top rail is flush with the top of the sides.

I placed the lower rail so ¾" is below the bottom edge of the sides. This allows me to clamp it in my bench vise, quickly securing the router table. If you don't plan on using the router table in conjunction with a vise, place the bottom edge of the lower rail even with the bottom of the sides. Always secure the router table before using it; you don't want it sliding around in the middle of a cut.

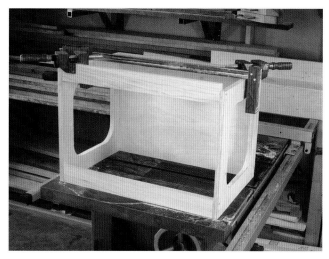

Start flat to end flat. Assembling the frame on a flat surface makes it easier to align parts, and ensures a flat surface for mounting the top.

Front and Center

Before attaching the top to the frame, decide where and how to attach the router base to the table. If you have a drill press, it will be easier to align the mounting and center holes, but these can be carefully positioned using a handheld drill. I centered the router front to back and side to side. This provides adequate area in front of the bit, and makes access to the router easier. Moving the router back a few inches will provide more table area in front of the bit, but be sure there will be room inside for the router.

Draw a center mark on the table-top, and position the baseplate of the router over it. Mark the locations for the mounting screws and with a Forstner bit, make a counterbore deep enough for the screw heads at each screw location. Different routers will use different size screws, and you'll likely need to make a trip to the hardware store to get some screws ¾" longer than the stock mounting screws. Drill the holes with a bit that is larger in diameter than the screws. The oversized holes and counterbores will allow you to move the router base around to help

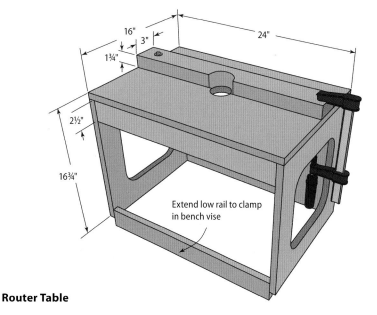

Router Table

16"
3"
1¾"
24"
2½"
16¾"

Extend low rail to clamp in bench vise

Insert? Don't need it. Foregoing a thin insert for mounting the router will yield a stronger top and save construction time.

Nice and flat. The weight of the router helps during final assembly, it keeps the top flat as the cleats are screwed in.

line up the holes.

The center hole should be about ¼" larger in diameter than your largest bit. Make the hole with a Forstner bit at the drill press, or with a hole saw and a handheld drill. If you need to enlarge the hole at a later time, cut around the perimeter with a rabbeting bit, then switch to a straight bit with a bearing mounted above the cutter. This will preserve the round shape of the hole, and if you want to use smaller inserts, they can be placed in a rabbet.

Mounting the router directly to the top involves a trade-off. It is quick and easy compared to making a large cutout for an insert plate, and keeping the top at full thickness means a stronger top that is less likely to sag over time. The disadvantage is that you lose some depth of cut.

How much depends on your particular router, the bit you use and the cut you want to make. For most cuts this won't be an issue, but if it becomes one, you can always add an insert plate later.

When the holes have been placed, go ahead and attach the baseplate to the bottom side of the top. The top can be held to the frame with screws from above, but a stronger and neater attachment will be to place ¾" cleats on the top inside edges of the frame, and attach the top from below with #8 x 1¼" screws.

Again, working on a flat surface is a must, so put the top face down on your table saw, then run a bead of yellow glue around the perimeter. Put the assembled frame on the top, screw the cleats down and leave it alone while the glue dries.

The fence is also simple, a 1¾"-thick x 3"-wide piece of hardwood, carefully jointed with flat faces and straight edges. One end is held to the table with a 5⁄16"-18 machine screw and nut. The fence swings on this screw to adjust the distance between the fence and the bit, and the opposite end of the fence is held down with a clamp.

I made the cutout in the fence by cutting a 2½"-diameter semi-circle at the band saw, smoothing the recess

with a spindle sander. If I want a continuous fence, I can flip this over, or if I want to close down the opening, I can screw a couple pieces of scrap on each side of the opening.

There isn't any need for the fence to be parallel to the edge of the table, nor is there a need for a miter slot. Operations that move the wood on end across the bit may be performed by using a block of scrap wood held against the fence as a guide.

Other than knocking off the sharp edges, the only sanding I did was to go over the top with #150-grit paper in a random-orbit sander. I ragged on a couple coats of shellac, and when that was dry I scuffed the top with a nylon abrasive pad and applied a coat of paste wax to reduce friction.

I added a fitting to the top of the fence for dust collection, and a power strip to turn on the router and the shop vacuum simultaneously. It isn't fancy, but it functions well, and it didn't take a lot of time or money to build.

One-weekend Router Table

by David Thiel

I think it might have been seeing a $1,000 router table setup at a recent woodworking show (it's very cool, but $1,000?). Or maybe it was realizing that our shop's router table's cabinet mostly takes up space and fills with dust. Either of these observations was enough to get us rethinking our router table needs.

Essentially you need a stable, flat working surface that can support most work. You need a fence that guides, supports and moves easily for adjustments (both the fence location on the table and the faces themselves toward the bit). You also need easy access to the router for bit changing and height adjustment. Other than that, it just needs to be up off the floor, hence the cabinet.

So we decided that a lightweight, easily stored router tabletop that would still offer all these benefits would be preferable. Oh, and we wanted to be able to make it in a weekend for a reasonable price. No problem! The hardware came to $110 and change, and you can purchase the plywood locally.

An Ingenious Design

For a stable, lightweight top the solution that made sense was a torsion box made of high-density plywood. The size that seemed most functional

was a 20"-deep x 24"-wide platform that only needed to be about 4" tall. The box itself has an open center section on the bottom to accommodate the router body. There are two lengths of T-track installed front to back on the tabletop to easily reposition the fence.

The fence itself is a variation of one we've built half-a-dozen times. The fence base is almost a torsion box – more of a torsion corner – that provides stable support for the laterally adjustable fence faces and allows for dust hook-up.

For the router itself, we went shopping. After looking at a number of router lifts and router table plates we chose the Milwaukee 5625-29, a 3½ horsepower router that offers through-the-base height adjustment.

Allowing the proper clearance for your router is critical. You can see that I've removed the handles from the tool to allow as much space as possible. Mark out the space and then assemble the frame to fit.

You don't have to use this router, but in our opinion it has the horsepower you want to swing large panel-raising bits on your router table, and the through-the-base adjustment means you don't need to buy a router lift. The variable speed is also a big plus.

We chose a circular router plate from Veritas because it replaces the sole plate on your router and allows you to still use the router freehand or in the table without changing the base. The base also fits into the table without the use of any tools, and slips in and out from above in seconds.

Now the fun part: To bring the router table up to height, but still make it compact, we designed a brace that is mounted to the table and then the entire thing is simply clamped in your bench vise. Instant router table!

Torsion Top Construction

The top itself is very simple to make. A frame made of ¾" x 3" plywood pieces is sandwiched between two pieces of ¾" plywood. The bottom piece is notched to accommodate your router (you'll need to test fit your router to locate the center frame pieces and the notch). The top piece extends 1½" beyond the frame on all sides to allow for clamping featherboards or other guides to the top surface.

Start by cutting out the top, bottom and seven frame pieces. If you opt to use the Veritas plate, the instructions are very clear on how to cut the hole in the tabletop to fit the plate. Otherwise, follow the instructions for your individual router plate.

One-weekend Router Table

No.	Let.	Item	Dimensions (inches)			Material
			T	W	L	
1	T1	Top	¾	20	24	Plywood
1	B1	Bottom	¾	17	21	Plywood
2	B2	Frame F&B	¾	3	21	Plywood
4	B3	Frame dividers	¾	3	15½	Plywood
1	B4	Frame divider	¾	3	10½	Plywood
2	B5	Support stems	¾	3	7	Plywood
2	B6	Support braces	¾	3	21	Plywood
2	F1	Fence faces	¾	4	14	Plywood
1	F2	Fence sub-face	½	3½	28	Plywood
1	F3	Fence base	½	3	28	Plywood
4	F4	Fence braces	¾	3	3	Plywood
1	F5	Hood top	½	5	3½	Plywood
2	F6	Hood sides	½	2½	3	Plywood
1	F7	Hood back	½	5	3	Plywood
2	H1	Fence T-tracks	⅜	¾	14	Aluminum
4	H2	Hex-head bolts	¼"-20	1½"		
4	H3	Star knobs				
2	H4	Cam clamps				
2	H5	Table T-tracks	⅜	¾	20	Aluminum

We chose to locate the router plate closer to the front of the table rather than in the center of the table. Most router table work happens within 6" of the fence and this location keeps you from having to lean across the table for operations. If you have a larger piece to run, the fence can be reversed on the table to give you a larger support surface.

With the router plate located in the top, suspend the router from the top and locate the two center frame members the necessary distance to clear the router. Make a note of that dimension, then lay out your frame accordingly.

I used glue and an 18-gauge brad nailer to assemble all the pieces for this project. While perhaps not the height of joinery, it's fast and reliable.

With the frame assembled, place the frame on the bottom, and mark and notch the center section to allow clearance space for the router body. You could leave the center section open, but the extra strength along the back of the tabletop is worth the effort.

Attach the bottom the same way you assembled the frame.

Before fastening the top to the table, you need to install the aluminum T-track inserts for fence adjustment. I used a dado set on my table saw to run the grooves before attaching the top.

Next, attach the top, centering it on the frame assembly. Pay extra attention when attaching the top to keep the fasteners below the surface of the tabletop. This will keep you from scratching your work, or worse, allowing your wood to hang up on a brad head during an operation.

Down and Dirty Fence

The fence is also absurdly simple to make. Accuracy is important to make sure it sits square to the table-top, but other than that, it's brads and glue.

Start construction on the fence by cutting out the base, sub-face, faces and braces. All but the braces are very straightforward. The braces are actually triangles. The best method is to rip a piece of plywood to 3" wide,

More marking: With the frame assembled and resting on the bottom piece, mark out the notch that will allow the router to extend through the top.

With the bottom notched, simply glue and nail it in place on the frame.

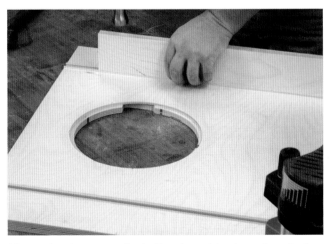

After cutting the grooves for the T-track, tap it in place using a backing block. If you have to tap too hard with the hammer, your groove is too small. Attach the track with ½" x #4 flathead screws. Pre-drill and countersink each hole.

Supplies

Lee Valley Tools

800-871-8158 or leevalley.com

4 Four-arm knobs, #00M55.30, $3.20 each

1 Veritas Router Base Plate, #05J25.01, $46.50

2 2' T-slot extrusions, #12K79.42, $9.90 each

1 3' T-slot extrusion, #12K79.44, $13.80 each

2 Cam clamp mechanisms, #05J51.01, $5.50 each

Available from any hardware store:

4 1½" ¼"-20 hex-head bolts

2 1¼" ¼"-20 hex-head bolts

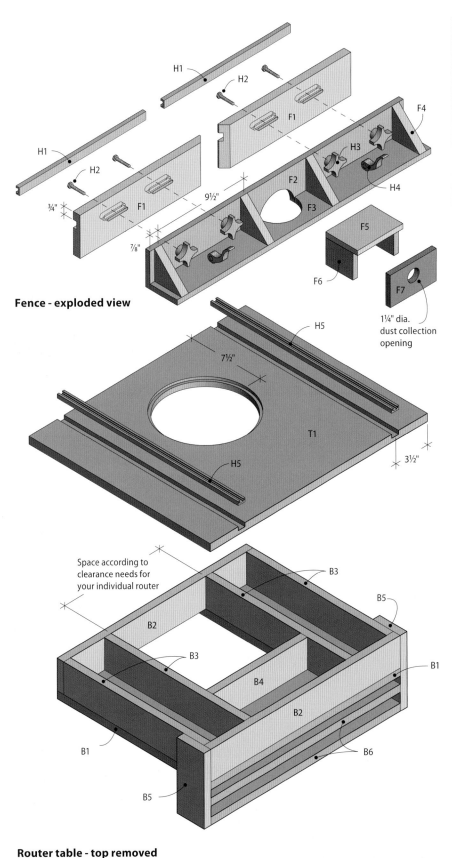

Fence - exploded view

H1

H2

F1

9½"

H1

H2

¾"

F1

7⁄8"

F2

F3

H3

H4

F4

F5

F6

F7

1¼" dia.
dust collection
opening

H5

7½"

T1

H5

3½"

Space according to
clearance needs for
your individual router

B3

B5

B2

B3

B4

B1

B2

B6

B1

B5

Router table - top removed

Cutting out the bit clearance hole on the band saw is made simple by first cutting "spokes" toward your line. These relief cuts allow the pieces to fall out in small chunks, rather than fighting with one bigger piece.

then head to the miter saw. First miter both ends of the strip at a 45° angle, then reset the miter saw for a 90° cut and cut the 3" triangles from the strip. Repeat this process and you've got four braces.

The sub-face and base need to have a 3"-wide half-circle cut at the center of each piece along one edge as shown above. This space will be the opening for the router bits.

The sub-face is then glued and nailed to the base. Then glue the braces into the corner formed by the sub-face and base. Make sure to locate the braces as shown to avoid interference with any of the fence handles. I again used brad nails to hold the braces in place.

For the router table to be as useful as possible it needs dust collection. This is achieved by building a simple hood to surround the bit opening in the fence. Drill a hole in the hood back piece. Adjust the hole size to fit your dust collection hose, usually 1¼" in diameter.

Then attach the hood sides to the

hood back, holding the sides flush to the top edge of the back. Then add the top to the box.

The next step is to locate and drill the holes for the cam clamps that hold the fence to the table and for the knobs that hold the faces. Place the fence assembly over the table and orient the cam clamp holes so they fall in the center of the T-tracks in the top. There can be a little bit of play, but not too much.

Secure the fence to the table with the cam clamps so it seats tightly. Use an engineer's square to check the fence against the top. If it's not square you need to adjust the base slightly, either by shimming or

removing material from the underside of the fence base to make it square.

Next, drill the holes for the fence knobs, again avoiding the braces so the knobs can be easily turned. The holes should be 2" up from the tabletop.

The fence faces are next. To allow the best fence clearance near the bit, I beveled the inside lip of each of the faces at 45°. Next you need to rout two, 2½"-wide stepped slots in the front of each fence face. These will allow the faces to be moved left-to-right to accommodate different bit sizes.

The easiest way to do this is on

a router table, but if you're building your first, you can use a drill press with two different bits. Use a ½"-diameter Forstner bit to first cut a ¼"-deep slot. Then change to a 5/16"-diameter bit to drill through to the back of the fence face. This will create a slot that will let a ½"-hex-head bolt drop into the slot, recessing the head, but capturing the sides of the bolt head to keep it from spinning.

I also added a T-slot fixture to the front of each face. This allows you to attach featherboards, a guard to protect your fingers and other guides. Again, you can use a router or your dado set in the table saw to make the slot (about 1" down from the top of the fence).

Attach the fence faces using the bolts, washers and knobs.

The Mounting Support

With the sub-face and base assembled, add the four triangular braces with glue and brads. Space them adequately to support the fence, but make sure you leave room for the knobs.

The dust collection hood completes the router table fence. It should seal tightly around the fence to provide the best dust collection, so don't skimp on the glue here.

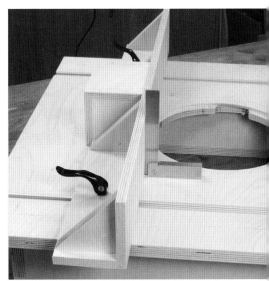

After installing the cam clamps, lock the fence in place on the top and check for square. If adjustment is necessary, you can do it by sanding the base or adding thin shims. You don't want to add shims behind the fence faces because they're moving parts. Adjust the base.

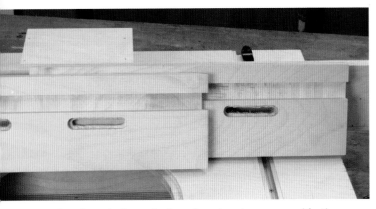

Seen from the front, the fence faces have been grooved for the T-tracks, and the clearance holes to attach and adjust the faces are drilled. Note that the face slot shows the rough edges from the overlapping holes made on the drill press. A few minutes with a file and some sandpaper will clean up the slots so the bolt will move smoothly.

After drilling clearance holes, you can locate the holes in the fence faces and add the knobs.

Here you can see the fences in place and the fence attached and ready to run. The T-tracks in the fence faces can be used for featherboards and you can use them to attach a simple guard to keep your hands a safe distance from the bit.

The support brace (customized for my bench vise) holds the router top firmly in place with plenty of clearance (and no wasted space).

To make the whole thing work, you need to be able to secure the table in your bench vise, but still have access to the router motor. We used a U-shaped support screwed to the sides of the table. The actual size of the support will depend on your bench vise, but you want the tabletop to rest on the vise as much as possible. In fact, if you can also get the top to rest on the vise at the rear of the table, that's even better support. Our larger router forced us to move the support all the way to the rear of the table. This is something else that can be individualized on your table.

You'll see in the photo that we used two support braces to catch the vise at both the top and bottom of the jaws for more support. Your vise may require a different arrangement, so give it a test run to make sure it's held tight.

Finishing Touches

With the support mounted you can put your table to work. But you may want to add a step – finishing. While a bare plywood surface will perform reasonably well, a slicker surface will make things move easier. You can add a topcoat of spray-on lacquer (as

we did), or simply add a coat of oil or shellac.

Some other simple additions for your table can include some shop-made featherboards (that will fit nicely in the T-tracks on the fence face) and if you're really industrious, you could actually add a couple of storage drawers to either side of the opening in the top. Customize the project to meet your needs.

The Incredible Tilting Router Stand

by Nick Engler

During the past 25 years, I've designed more than a dozen whiz-bang router tables for various books and articles, each one supposedly packing a bigger bang than the last. But what finally dawned on me a few router tables ago is what makes this fixture truly useful has less to do with the tabletop than the stand it rests on.

Whether you build or buy a router table, you're faced with the same dilemma. The router is designed to be a portable power tool. All the controls and adjustments are easily accessible when the router is resting upright on a workbench. Bolt it to the underside of a table to convert

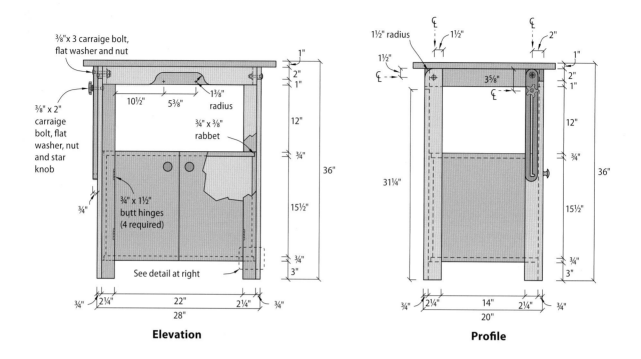

Elevation

Profile

it to a stationary tool and suddenly your router is a good deal less cooperative. Many of us spend a lot of time on our knees in front of our router table, fumbling underneath to change bits and adjust the depth of cut. A woodworker I know calls this "praying to the router god."

Some woodworkers solve this problem by mounting the router to a plate that rests in a rabbet, then removing the plate when they need to get at the router. Unfortunately, the sides of the rabbet wear as you pop the plate in and out. As the plate becomes loose in its rabbet, new problems arise with safety and accuracy.

A tilting router stand makes the router easily accessible and lets you secure the router to the table. The table swings up like the lid of a chest, exposing the router and bringing it up to a comfortable working height. You can change bits and make adjustments standing upright, just like the Deity intended.

Of course to get this amazing convenience, you have to build a complex mechanism and a special table, right? Nope. Most parts are rectangular boards, butted together and secured with screws or bolts. The design is easily adaptable to support whatever table top you're using right now; just change the width and depth of the stand to fit.

Begin with the frame under the table. It should be about 6" smaller side-to-side and 4" smaller front-to-back than your router table. If the table has slots to mount the fence, make sure that the frame members won't cover these or interfere with the fence movement. Also give some thought to how you will attach the table to the frame. I used two long cleats, one on each side. Brackets, table clips and pockets screws work equally well.

The legs should hold the table at countertop level – roughly 36". My router table is part of a "work

island" – the table saw, workbench and router table are all at the same level. So I cut the legs on my table a fraction of an inch longer than what the drawings show.

A plywood box is screwed to the legs below the table to brace the legs and provide storage for router accessories. There must be adequate room between the top of the box and the bottom of the router table to fit the router when the collet is fully retracted into the router base.

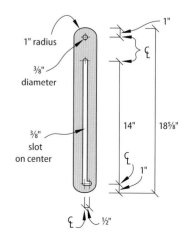

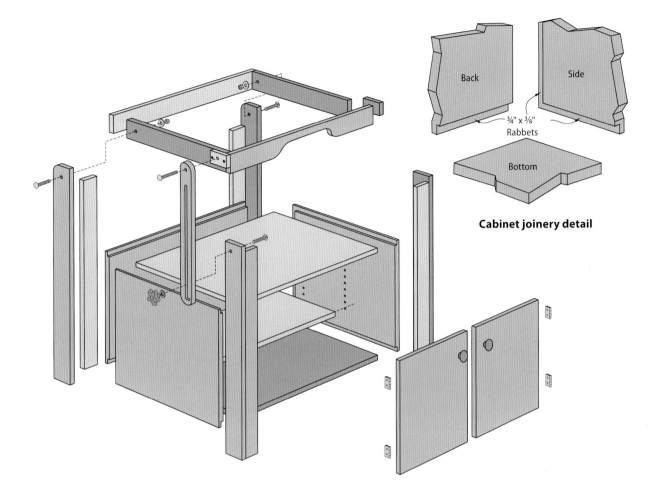

Back

Side

¾" x ⅜"
Rabbets

Bottom

Cabinet joinery detail

The sliding shelves shown in the photo are removable so you can take your bits where they are needed.

I mounted simple plywood doors on the front legs to enclose the box and keep some of the sawdust out.

The most complex part in the table is the support arm. It has a L-slot – a long slot with a little hiccup at one end. I made the "hiccup" first, drilling a few overlapping holes to create a short slot. I routed a long slot perpendicular to the short one, then cleaned up the edges of the short slot with a file. When mounting the support arm to the stand, the short portion of the slot faces front.

To help organize all my router bits and collars, I mounted two sliding shelves to the fixed shelf inside the storage box. You needn't purchase expensive hardware to get the sliding action. Make narrow hardwood rails to guide the shelves, then cut match-

ROUTER CRANK

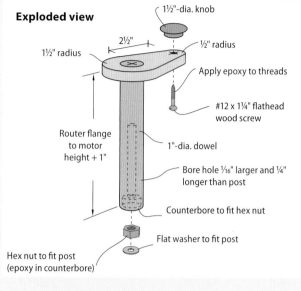

Exploded view

1½"-dia. knob

2½"

1½" radius — ½" radius

Apply epoxy to threads

#12 x 1¼" flathead wood screw

Router flange to motor height + 1"

1"-dia. dowel

Bore hole ¹⁄₁₆" larger and ¼" longer than post

Counterbore to fit hex nut

Flat washer to fit post

Hex nut to fit post (epoxy in counterbore)

If you use a plunge router with your router table, this little gizmo takes all the frustration out of setting the depth of cut. Just thread it onto the post, then crank the router up and down as needed.

There's an accessory on the market very much like this,

I know. But it has a simple knob at the top and takes a lot of wrist action to raise or lower the router. You'll find the crank action much faster and more comfortable. When used with the tilting router stand, the two fixtures create a truly user-friendly stationary routing system.

ing grooves in the sliding shelves and fixed rails. Glue splines in the grooves in the rails, then glue the rails to a fixed shelf. Fit the sliding shelves to the splined guides, enlarging the grooves in the edges and sanding a little stock from the bottom faces so the shelves slide easily. Wax

the grooves in the shelves to help them move smoothly. I drilled holes and mounted dowels in the sliding trays to help organize the bits and accessories and keep them in place. The shelves slide all the way out of the storage box so you can use them as a caddy or tray to carry the bits.

To raise the top of the router table, lift it all the way up and push down near the bottom of the support arm to slip the locking bolt into the short portion of the L-slot. Tighten the knob to make sure the top doesn't slam down unexpectedly.

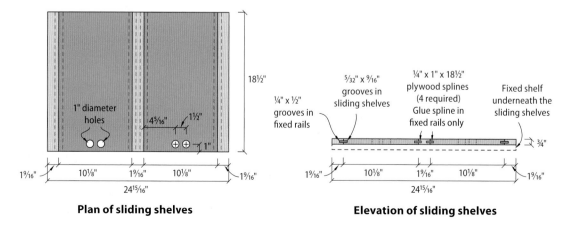

Plan of sliding shelves

18½"

1" diameter holes

4⁵⁄₁₆"

1½"

1"

1⁹⁄₁₆" 10⅛" 1⁹⁄₁₆" 10⅛" 1⁹⁄₁₆"

24¹⁵⁄₁₆"

Elevation of sliding shelves

⁵⁄₃₂" x ⁹⁄₁₆" grooves in sliding shelves

¼" x 1" x 18½" plywood splines (4 required) Glue spline in fixed rails only

Fixed shelf underneath the sliding shelves

¼" x ½" grooves in fixed rails

¾"

1⁹⁄₁₆" 10⅛" 1⁹⁄₁₆" 10⅛" 1⁹⁄₁₆"

24¹⁵⁄₁₆"

Arts & Crafts Mirror

by Glen D. Huey

Arts & Crafts furniture, sometimes known as craftsman or mission, is simple in style and solidly built. This style first appeared in the United States about the turn of the 20th century. Although Gustav Stickley, a New York furnituremaker, had conceived this design in his shop and is credited as the American inventor of the style, it was not until the manufacturers of Grand Rapids, Mich., picked up the ball and made this furniture available to the masses that the design picked up steam. This design boasts clean lines, great wood grain and strong joinery.

In building furniture there is no joint stronger than the mortise and tenon, which is used in the construction of our mirror. While the joints on our project are not through-mortise and tenons (where the end of the tenon shows on the outside of the stiles), as they are on many pieces in this style, they are classic examples of the joint. The chamfering on the edges of the top, along with the corbels (another often-seen element of this period), provide you with a great introduction to the Arts & Craft-style of our furniture history.

We could not leave well enough alone when it came to the mirror's design. We decided to add inlay – a common feature on some mission-style furniture – to kick it up a notch.

If you have tackled inlay in other projects this will be a walk in the

The inlay design of the raised ebony strips with the flush maple circle bounces off of the quartersawn white oak's mellow tones and adds to the overall look of the mirror.

Developing a routine to mark out mortise measurements keeps confusion at bay. Clamping two pieces together for layout saves time. The long lines indicate the inner edges of the rails; the short lines indicate the length of the mortises.

Plunge the first cut then skip an equal amount of waste material. Plunge again and repeat the steps until you move along the entire mortise. Next, return to remove the balance of the waste material. This extends the life of the chisel and bit set.

There is no need for a step-off block because we are not cutting completely through the rail. Adjusting for the edge cuts is simply a matter of raising the blade height from the previous step.

park. If this is your first foray into the world of inlay, rest assured that this is a simple introduction. You will have no trouble with this eye-popping addition. But, let's not get ahead of ourselves – the frame comes first!

Strength in Joints

Mirrors of the Arts & Craft style tend to have varying thicknesses of material that add an extra shadow line to the work. Be careful as you mill the pieces for this project – the stiles are thicker than the rails. This is important because we are going to cut the mortises in the stiles based on the thickness of the rails.

In order to have the back of the mirror fit flush to the wall, we need to keep the four parts of our frame flat at the back face, so we will position the mortises in those stiles off-center.

When I lay out the mortise measurements on the stiles, I begin by defining the width of the rails. Those lines are drawn across the entire edge of the stile. I then know not to extend my mortise cuts beyond that line or the mortise will show in the finished

Whether it is shop-made, as shown, or a commercially available jig, consistent thickness of your material is the secret to getting repeatable results in cutting the tenons.

project. In the mirror, the top rail is aligned with the top edge of the stiles while the bottom rail is held 1" above the bottom end of each stile.

Next, I define the mortise length with two short lines (see picture on the top left of this page). This measurement reflects the ⅝" shoulders of the tenon. It is between these lines that I will cut the 1¼"-deep mortises.

Finally, I mark the location of the mortise in relationship to the front and back. It is offset toward the back edge of the stiles. I then repeat these exact layout steps for each and every mortise that I cut.

Using hand pressure should be all that is necessary to fit a mortise-and-tenon joint. The primary gluing surface is the face grain of each piece, therefore it is not necessary to achieve a perfect fit over the width of the tenon.

There are a number of ways to create the mortise. You can use a drill press to remove a portion of the material and finish cleaning things up with a chisel, make the cut with a plunge router or use a dedicated mortise machine.

The mortise machine is my choice. To begin, you need to place the ¼" tooling into the machine while setting the back edge ¼" away from the mortiser's fence. This measurement makes the math easy. A tenon of that thickness in ¾" stock will result in two ¼" shoulders as well.

Position the stile with the back

Setting up the hole for the circle inlay is precise work. The edge of the inlay must fit tight to the circumference of the hole drilled and be able to be affixed to the bottom.

face against the machine's fence and cut the mortise using the step method (center top photo, previous page). As you cut the spaces you'll notice that there is always equal pressure on the opposing sides of the cut.

With the mortises complete we now need to make the matching tenons. I create the tenons at the table saw. First, set the blade height to ¼" then set the rip fence to cut the 1¼" length of the tenons (1¼" between the fence and the far side of the blade). Use the miter gauge to guide the cut on each face of the rails, while holding the piece tight to the saw's fence.

Next, raise the blade height to slightly above ⅝" in height without relocating the fence and make these cuts on the edges of the rails, forming the edge shoulders of the tenon.

The second phase is to cut the tenons' cheeks. I use a shop-made tenon jig. To begin, set the table saw's blade height to the top edge of the shoulder cut made in the previous step and adjust the fence to cut the cheeks of the tenon. This is where you need to be precise. The idea is to cut one face cheek, without trapping the waste between the blade and fence, then reverse each rail in the jig and make the second cheek cut with the balance of material resulting in a tenon of the correct thickness, as shown

in the photo at right. This ensures that the tenon will be located in the center of each rail. Test the fit of the tenon to the mortise, making any adjustments as needed. You need a snug fit that does not require the use of a mallet to assemble.

The last step to create the tenons is at the band saw. Set the fence to remove ¹¹⁄₁₆" of material at each edge cheek. I recommend cutting a bit more than the lay out measurement of ⅝" so that you can adjust the rail in the mortise at assembly time to achieve the correct final positioning without significant loss of joint

strength – remember, end grain does not have great holding power.

Inlay Makes it Pop

The inlay needs to be created prior to any assembly because it is easier to work with the individual pieces rather than an assembled frame. The inlay is fit and then removed prior to staining to achieve the desired results. If it were stained like the mirror frame, the inlay would lose its impact.

I suggest running through these steps on a piece of scrap wood first, then once perfected you can work on the frame.

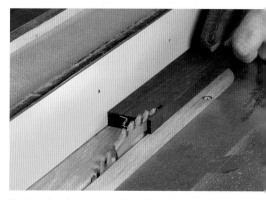

A fence guide with your router is required for cutting the grooves for the inlay. If you overshoot the exact entry point for the bit, carefully climb-cut back to the beginning of the groove before completing the pass.

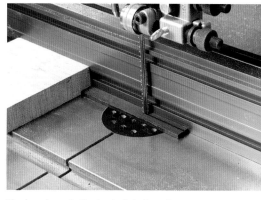

Cutting the ebony using the table saw wastes more material than the band saw, but the consistency of its cut makes it easier to fit the inlay.

The router bit will leave a rounded end on the grooves. The choice is to square the ends with a ⅛" chisel or round the inlay with a file. Either method proved successful in the shop.

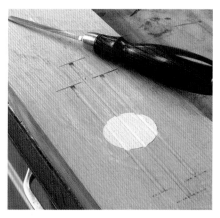

The band saw is the tool of choice when resawing the ebony to final size. The top edge of the string can be sanded and the pieces are small enough to rule out a table saw cut.

After fitting the inlay and stringing, remove the pieces and bundle them with blue painter's tape. This will ensure a proper fit after the finish is applied.

Arts & Crafts Mirror

No.	Item	Dimensions (inches)			Material	Comments
		T	W	L		
1	Top	¾	2	26½	QSWO*	
1	Top rail	¾	4	16	QSWO*	1¼ tenon on both ends
1	Bottom rail	¾	3	16	QSWO*	1¼ tenon on both ends
2	Stiles	1	4	60	QSWO*	
2	Corbels	¾	1¾	16	QSWO*	
2	String inlay	3⁄16	⅛	15	Ebony	
1	Circle inlay	½	1⅜		Maple	35mm hinge repair kit
1	Mirror backing	¼	14⅜	53	Plywood	
1	Mirror	¼	13⅞	52½		

*QSWO = Quartersawn White Oak

Beginning the inlay is as simple as drilling a hole. Chuck a 1⅜" Forstner bit into the drill press and drill a hole that is 13⁄32" deep. Why so precise? The circle inlay for this project is actually a 35mm hinge hole repair kit (see Supplies box at the end of the story). Because of the tapered sides of the inlay piece, it is necessary that the inlay not only be tightly fitted to the circumference of the hole but that it seats tight to the bottom as well.

Next, install a ¼" drill bit in your drill press and bore through the frame at the center of the larger hole. This smaller hole provides access for the maple disk to be removed by pushing a small dowel in from the back of the mirror.

Position the round portion of the inlay into the hole and use a low-angle block plane to flush the circle to the stile. Pop the disk out and then lay out the lines for the string inlay on the stile according to the plan and remember to establish start and stop limits for each string piece.

You need to secure the round inlay temporarily when routing the string inlay to keep it from spinning. I used a brad that I drove in from the backside of the stile. Find a non-

routed area to install a brad (I used a 4*d* finish nail that I trimmed to ¾" in length), drill a pilot hole, put the disk in place and set the brad in from the back.

String Inlay, Rout On

Now you're ready to rout the recesses for the string inlay, which will sit proud of the stile when you are done. The 5¼"-long center string extends 1" below the 3¾"-long flanking pieces. Install a ⅛"-diameter upcut spiral bit into a plunge router with an edge guide attachment and position the bit to cut at the exact center of the stile. Set the depth of cut by zeroing out

the bit against the face of the stile, then set the depth adjustment to the desired depth of cut on your plunge router. I set the depth of cut scientifically – with a good ol' American nickel (which is 5⁄64" thick).

Start the router with the fence of the edge guide tight against one edge of the stile and plunge the bit into the cut at one end of your layout lines. Carefully move the router forward until you reach the opposite end, all the while holding the fence tight to the stile's edge. Repeat these steps for the second stile.

Now prepare to rout the second set of recesses. Adjust the edge guide

Cutting the bevel on the front edge of the bottom of each stile is best completed at the miter saw. Make sure that you are cutting the face of the stile and that the piece is set flat on the saw's table.

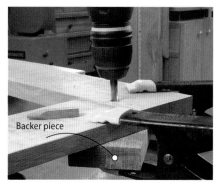

Backer piece

A backer piece of scrap material will keep the hole from blowing out of the frame back. Spring clamps will do the job. If you are feeling artsy, use different materials or turn the peg to a 45° angle in the hole so it appears diamond shaped.

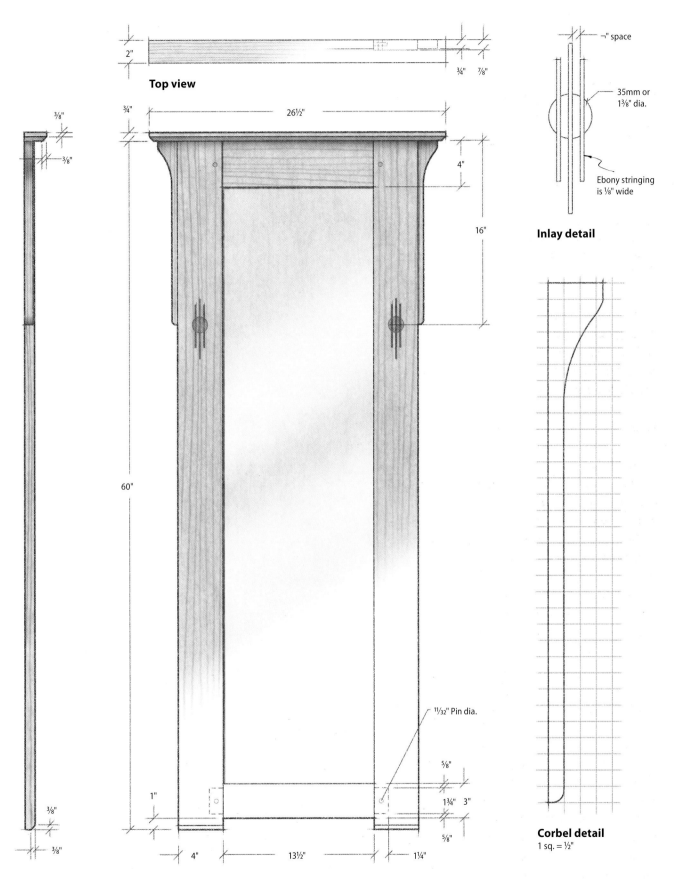

Top view

2"

¾" ⅞"

26½"

¾"

3/8"

3/8"

4"

16"

60"

1"

3/8"

3/8"

11/32" Pin dia.

5/8"

1¾" 3"

5/8"

4" 13½" 1¼"

Side view **Front view**

¬" space

35mm or
1⅜" dia.

Ebony stringing
is ⅛" wide

Inlay detail

Corbel detail
1 sq. = ½"

to leave a ¼" of material between the center recess and an outer recess. Run the grooves as before, first with the edge guide's fence against one edge of the stile, then again with the edge guide's fence against the other edge of the stile. The hard work is done!

Ebony is my wood of choice for the stringing. To cut the strips safely I make a first pass at the table saw to rip the edges of my stock parallel. Then I adjust the fence to have the off fall of the next cut be the piece that is used as inlay.

To do this, set the fence closer to the blade by ¼" – one ⅛" for the blade thickness and one ⅛" for the inlay. Set the thickness a bit on the strong side. It is easy to pare the string down to fit the groove with sandpaper or a cabinet scraper. Once the fit is complete it's time to cut the individual pieces to length.

First things first: You have a decision to make. You can either square the rounded ends of the recess left from routing with an ⅛" chisel or you can round the ends of the inlay to fit the rounded recesses. Whichever path you choose, fit one end of the inlay to the groove then mark the opposite end. Cut the pieces with a handsaw, keeping them long enough to trim to a snug fit. A disk sander, file or sandpaper will do the trick.

The string inlay is held proud of the face of the mirror. If you set the depth of cut as explained in the text, you need to resaw the ebony to 3⁄16" thick. Step away from the table saw! The band saw is the correct tool for this cut. Set the fence appropriately and slice the pieces making sure to use a push stick or block for safety.

Fit all the stringing pieces into the recesses, then remove each assembled inlay set. Make sure to keep track of the orientation of each piece so that the sets will go back in the correct orientation at the end of the project.

Some Assembly Required

A few additional steps should be completed before gluing the frame's rails and stiles. The bottom end of each stile needs to have a ⅜" x ⅜" chamfer created, the interior edges of the frame need to be sanded and the sharp corners need to be knocked down with sandpaper.

I elected to cut the chamfer using the miter saw. It is simple and effective. You could also use a chamfer router bit. Adjust the saw to a 45° cut and remove the front ⅜" of material. Make sure that you are cutting the front face of the stiles.

The different thicknesses of the pieces of the frame make it necessary to sand certain areas prior to assembly. The inside edge of each piece and the face of each rail need attention at this time. Also, because of the ⅛" setback above the rails, the thicker stiles need to have their corners lightly sanded or knocked down at this time.

The pieces of the frame are now ready for assembly. It is especially important to not get glue onto the faces of the frame. Over-application of glue in the mortises or on the

Start the rabbet by climb-cutting (cutting from right to left) will help to reduce tear-out from the router bit as you complete the cut in the standard left-to-right fashion. You should be able to make this cut with the project resting on the bench.

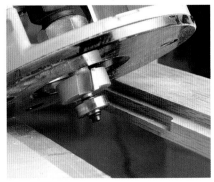

The second setup for the rabbeting is accomplished quickly after changing the bearing of the bit. Repeat the steps as before, making sure that the router's baseplate is resting on the work surface and that the tip of the bit is off of the bench.

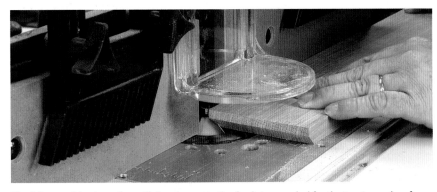

Moulding a wide piece that will then be cut to the final size needed for the top is much safer than working with narrow stock.

Cut the corbels from a larger piece of stock at the band saw. Cleaning the cut at a spindle sander makes short work of the task.

tenons will result in squeeze-out and considerable clean up. I apply glue into the mortises and move it around with an acid brush in order to coat all sides. Pull any excess out with the brush and paint it on the tenons.

Working with the rails is a bit more delicate. I add glue to the back-side face cheeks of the tenons rather liberally because squeeze-out here is not a big issue. But, for the fronts, I add a very thin coating – just enough to smear a layer into the grain of the wood and not starve the joint.

Slip the joints together and slide the pieces up or down in order to align the top of the stiles with the top edge of the rail (remember the heavy cut on the tenon at the band saw allows positioning of this piece). The bottom rail needs to be placed according to the plan. Add clamps and allow the glue to dry.

When the assembly has cured it is time to add the pocket-screw holes that are used to attach the top to the frame. Follow the instructions for your particular jig to create the holes. Place one screw location in the center of each stile and then evenly space two additional holes along the top rail.

A New Tool for the Shop?

The mortise-and-tenon joints of the mirror are reinforced with $11/32$" x $11/32$" pegs. First drill an $11/32$" hole through the frame so that the hole is centered on each rail and is $5/8$" into the stile from where the two parts meet.

Again, why so precise with the size of the hole and the peg stock? This time it has to do with one of my favorite tools in the shop. I don't like

to shave the corners off of my peg stock with a knife or chisel. I revert back to those early school days and the oversized, first-grade pencils. Remember the apparatus used to sharpen those bad boys? That style of pencil sharpener has for years created all the pegs I've used in my furniture. Dial in the largest hole on the sharpener, which happens to be $11/32$" in this case, and cut the tapered end on all your pegs.

Next, add a bit of glue to the peg, position it into the hole and tap the stock until the end of the peg is flush with the front of the frame. It is possible to be artistic with this process by choosing to use pegs of ebony to match the inlay, but I decided on a scrap of white oak.

To prepare the frame for the mirror and its backboard I elected to use a double rabbet cut: one rabbet for the glass and a second rabbet to house the plywood back. Creating this two-fisted cut on the back of the frame is a snap with an adjustable-bearing rabbet bit and router.

The first pass is set up to create a $1/4$"-deep cut that is $1/2$" wide. To prevent any tear-out of the wood I like to climb cut all around the frame to start, then follow up with a standard pass to clean the rabbet to size. Clamp the frame to the bench and

work all the interior edges. Climb-cutting requires a firm grip on the tool, so be careful.

For the second rabbet, change the bearing to make a $1/4$"-wide cut with the rabbet bit and lower the cutter to take another $1/4$" of material. Hang the frame off the edge of the bench to complete this cut because the depth of cut causes the bearing's screw to extend beyond the thickness of the frame. It's important to keep the base plate of the tool flat to the frame.

Cap it Off

Creating the top is straightforward. Mill a wide piece of stock to thickness and cut it to the correct length. Do not rip it to final width, however, until after you have chamfered the piece.

To chamfer three edges – the two end-grain edges and one long edge – I turn to the router table with a chamfering bit. Set the bit so it is $3/8$" above the table. Always rout the end grain prior to cutting the long

Supplies

Rockler
800-279-4441 or Rockler.com
1 35mm Hinge Hole Repair Kit,
#37977, $6.29
Prices correct at publication.

grain. This will minimize any chip out problems.

Once the edges are routed, rip the top from the wide stock at the table saw and sand the piece to #150 grit, making sure to sand the end grain.

To attach the top to the frame, position the top so it is centered on the frame and add a couple clamps to hold everything in place as you flip the mirror onto its front. Allow the top to extend past the edge of your bench and for the stiles to lay flat to the bench top. All that is left is to drive home the pocket-hole screws.

The corbels, present in a number of Arts & Crafts furniture designs, are the finishing touch. Transfer the pattern from the plan to your stock then cut the pieces at the band saw. A quick session at the spindle sander will have them ready in no time. Position the pieces against the frame for a quick check to ensure proper fit and make a light pencil mark at the bottom edge of each piece.

Now is the time to sand the edges of the stiles as well as the corbels and to knock off the sharp edges on each. Just as with the variations between the stiles and rails, the stepped thicknesses presented here mean that future sanding would be difficult at best.

Because the long grain of the corbels matches the long grain of the stiles, you can use glue to secure them in place. No additional fastening is required. Add a thin coating to both the corbel and the frame, right up to the pencil line, and then slide the pieces in place. No glue is needed on the end grain of the corbels. Clamps or small brads will work until the glue dries.

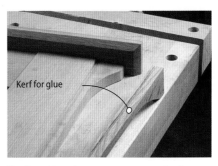

The last thing that you want to see is glue squeeze-out on the project. Before adding the glue for the corbels cut a kerf on the table saw to create a glue reservoir. Apply the glue to the wide area left after the cut.

Install the circle inlay in the correct orientation. Use a string inlay piece to fine-tune the setting. The grooves must be aligned.

Final-sand the mirror to #150 grit and fit painter's tape into the circle and string inlay areas to protect them from the finishing products. Keeping the oils off of the inlay is key to attaining a good glue bond when you are ready to install the pieces for the final time.

Now the mirror is ready for finish. Robert W. Lang, senior editor for *Woodworking Magazine* and author of "Shop Drawings for Greene & Greene Furniture" (Fox Chapel), has a finishing process that could not get any easier.

Before adding a topcoat to the mirror, remove the painter's tape from the recesses and, if necessary, scrape away any stain or oil that crept into those areas and glue the inlay into the frame.

The maple disk will fit into the holes without a problem, but you want to make sure that the grooves line up and that the stringing will glide into place. Unless you achieved perfection in routing the grooves, the alignment will fit in only one direction. Find that fit and apply glue into the recessed hole and onto the back of the disk. Apply glue sparingly; you need only attach the disk into the frame. You do not want any squeeze-out.

The string is set into the grooves with a small amount of glue as well. I used the nose of the glue bottle in the groove to lightly spread the glue. Position the appropriate piece to the groove and tap in place with a mallet. If any glue escaped from the recess you need to clean it with a dry cloth. Depending on the tightness of your fit of the inlay, you may need to apply pressure to the pieces with a clamp. Once the glue has dried, apply a final topcoat of finish.

Finally, have a mirror cut to fit into the first step of the rabbeted frame and a piece of ¼"-thick plywood that will fit the second step. Slide the two in place and attach the back.

It is your choice on how to affix the plywood back to the frame. You can use small brads and a nail gun or, as I have elected, add a number of ⅝" screws spaced along the back's edge. It helps to add a bit of wax to the screws to drive them more easily without pre-drilling into the frame.

Now attach a heavy-duty mirror hanger (kits are available at any hardware store), find a well-suited wall for hanging, and this classic Arts & Crafts designed mirror will last forever and look exquisite.

Hannah's Inlaid Chest

by Glen D. Huey

In 1746, at the age of four, Hannah Pyle stored her prized possessions in a small three-drawer chest with line and berry inlay. Lines of holly stringing on the front of that chest included her date of birth and initials – a common practice in southeastern Pennsylvania in the mid-1700s. The pale white numbers and letters stood out against the dark walnut background, as did the inlay on each of the three arched-top drawers.

Hannah's father, an accomplished Pennsylvania cabinetmaker named Moses Pyle, built the chest for his daughter. A second chest, also with inlaid initials and drawer fronts, was owned by Hannah Darlington, Pyle's sister-in-law. Her chest, built

a year later in 1747, is also attributed to Pyle. That chest is now part of the collection at the Winterthur museum. I left the date off my chest and chose to work with mahogany.

Scratch a Design

There are two natural starting points for this project. If you're new to dovetails, build your box then do the inlay work – it would be disheartening to complete the inlay work only to trash the piece as you dovetail. If, on the other hand, you are dovetail-savvy, begin with the inlay.

Grooves for stringing can be created using a router setup, scratched by hand or with some combination of the two. For the straight lines of

the box front, I suggest a trim router and a $\frac{1}{16}$"-diameter bit. For all other grooves, a radius cutter and .062" blade (available from Lie-Nielsen Toolworks) works great.

To begin, cut your box front to length and width then mark its center. Work off the centerlines to layout the sides of the $2\frac{5}{8}$" x 5" rectangle at the center of the design. Use a router with a guide fence to cut the top and bottom lines then use a router and a shop-made dado jig to complete the shape. (Details of my jig are available online.)

The remaining lines – all arcs scratched into the chest front– rely on layout accuracy. Measure and draw lines at each step to keep your four quadrants identical.

Draw a line $1\frac{7}{16}$" beyond the ends of the rectangle. Set your radius cutter at $2\frac{5}{8}$" (equal to the rectangle's side length), position the pivot point of the radius cutter at a corner then swing your groove out to the line. Repeat the steps at all four corners.

To create the second groove – the longest – slide out another $4\frac{1}{2}$" and draw a vertical line across the front. Mark a line $1\frac{7}{8}$" from the horizontal centerline. Set the radius cutter to cut at $2\frac{3}{4}$", then find a pivot point that allows the tool to reach both the end of the first groove and the point marked on the outermost line.

The third groove begins at the intersection of the first two arcs then moves out $2\frac{1}{8}$". The tool is set at a $2\frac{1}{8}$" radius, which indicates that the pivot point is aligned with the intersection.

The S-shaped line begins at the corner of the rectangle and arcs out toward the end $\frac{1}{2}$". The second

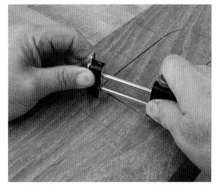

Begin radius work. Use a back-and-forth action as you scratch the pattern and be mindful to keep the pivot point planted.

The key. A successful inlay design is accomplished only with a smooth transition from arc to arc.

Two arcs, one radius. The short S-shaped line is a double arc made with the cutter set at a 1" radius.

Get the point? The design pattern repeats over the four quadrants of the front. The only connection of the arcs is the arrow near the ends.

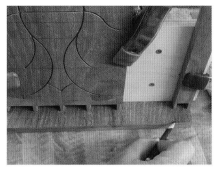

An easier choice. Because the base moulding completely covers the lower-front rail dovetails, you could use an easier joinery method for the case in that location, such as a nailed or pegged butt joint.

Smaller than usual. With the front's thickness at $^9/_{16}$", a standard $^1/_4$" mortise would leave mortise walls too weak. Cut a $^3/_{16}$"-thick mortise here instead.

section of groove transitions from the end of the first and continues out another $^1/_2$" as seen in the photo above left.

The last grooves in the design form an arrow that connects the quadrants. From the outermost vertical line, move back toward the center $^3/_8$" then draw a vertical line. Draw a second line in another $^3/_4$" then, with your tool set at a $1^3/_4$" radius, work between the two points.

Case Construction

The four corners of this chest are dovetailed together. As with most chests of this design, the pins are in the front and back panels with tails in the ends or side panels. The size and number of pins and tails is left

to your discretion. There are a couple tricky spots to bear in mind as you layout your joinery.

When working on the front panel, it's best to begin the layout with a small half-tail at the bottom edge – this keeps you from making one 90° cut in your tail board when cutting your dovetails.

A second tricky area is the lower front rail. The rail has a single tail socket with half-pins on each side. Aesthetically, I would prefer this piece also begin with small half-tails, but its narrow width makes this impractical.

Before any case assembly, cut the mortises for the two vertical dividers into the bottom edge of the front panel and the top edge of the lower

front rail.

Because the rail thickness is $^9/_{16}$", keep your mortise at $^3/_{16}$" in width for stronger mortise walls. I went with an "old school" power and hand approach to make the mortises; use a drill press to remove most of the waste then chisels to complete the $^1/_2$"-deep mortise.

Two dividers are cut to width and length, including the $^1/_2$"-long tenons. Rough-cut the tenons at a table saw, but leave them oversized. Use a shoulder plane to trim them to a snug fit.

Holly-lujah

Before you assemble the case, cut and fit stringing into the grooves. An easy way to thickness stringing is to rip a couple pieces at a table saw with the fence set at a strong $^1/_{16}$", then sand the pieces between a shop-made fence and a spindle sander drum. Dial in a perfect fit by adjusting the fence's position.

For string material, I use what's in my shop, which is generally maple. For this piece, however, I chose holly. I found it easier to use. Grooves in this chest do not have a tight radius, but if maple is your

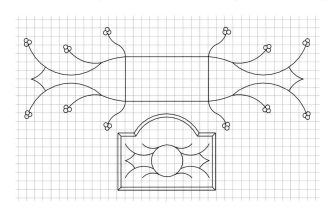

Line & Berry Pattern
Grid = $^1/_2$" squares

Supplies

Londonderry Brasses
londonderry-brasses.com or 610-593-6239
3 William & Mary drop pulls, #WM11
1 William & Mary escutcheon, #WM37
Horton Brasses
horton-brasses.com or 800-754-9127
1 pair butt hinges, #CP-11, semi-bright
Call for prices

string material, you may need to heat-bend a few pieces. Holly, at least in my experience with this project, does not require any heat-assisted bends; moist holly easily bends to fit these grooves.

Cut your pieces to length, but don't worry about hitting the groove ends exactly. Berry placement covers a multitude of sins.

Berries are made using a ¼" plug cutter at a drill press, and need to be ⅛" thick. There are 36 berries on the front panel, but always cut a few extra plugs. My piece of holly had a bad end that provided an otherwise unusable area from which to make berries. Cut your plugs, then use a screwdriver to pop them free.

To plant your berries, drill ¼"-diameter holes about ³⁄₃₂" deep at the ends of your string. For a realistic look, I find it best to drill and install the berries one at a time so they can overlap. After the glue dries on the first one, add a second berry to start to form a bunch. When the second installation is dry, drill and install the third and last berry. This process is time-consuming, but results in the best appearance.

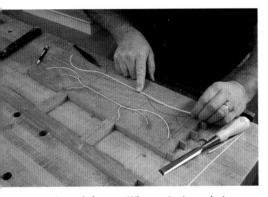

Long is better. When stringing a design, begin with the longest piece of inlay; you can then work to the shortest.

Grown by the bunch. As you install your berries, it's better to arrange the plugs to replicate how berries grow in the wild. Nature forms bunches, not straight lines.

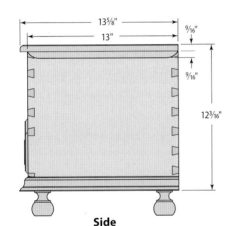

Side

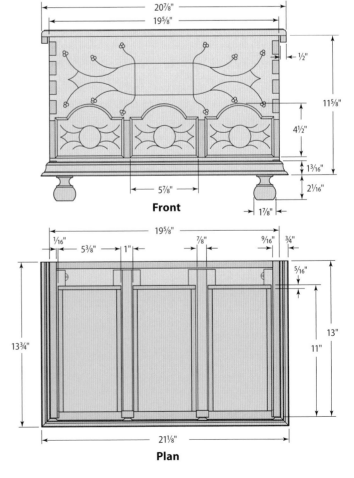

Front

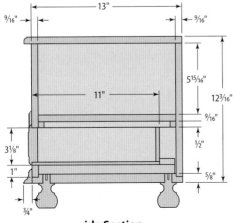

side Section

Plan

After the glue for the berries is dry, apply glue to the pins and tails then assemble the case. Add clamps if necessary and make sure the case is square.

A Firm Foundation

Before you fit the interior parts, you'll need to turn the bun feet. As turning goes, this is a simple task. Turn a design to your liking, or download the full-size drawing for my foot (see Online Extras). It's best to make an extra foot if you're not a talented turner so you can select the four feet that most closely match – but don't sweat it if they are not identical. It's impossible to see all four feet at the same time.

The chest bottom is milled to match the case and has a ⅛" x ⁹⁄₁₆" rabbet cut along the outer edge. This allows the bottom to fit an ⅛" up into the case making ¾"-thick material ideal for drawer runners. The thinner edge also minimizes the overall height of the base moulding.

The feet, after turning, are installed into holes drilled in the case bottom. Adjust the foot's grain to run perpendicular to the bottom's grain. Make a saw kerf across the foot tenon, add glue to a small wedge then tap it into the cuts to secure the feet.

As the glued wedges dry, mill and install the ½"-square chest cleats that support the false bottom. The chest cleats are flush and level with the front panel's bottom edge. Glue and

Hannah's Inlaid Chest

No.	Item	Dimensions (inches)			Material	Comments
		t	w	l		
Chest						
1	Front panel	⁹⁄₁₆	7	19⅝	Mahogany	
1	Front rail	⁹⁄₁₆	1	19⅝	Mahogany	
1	Side	⁹⁄₁₆	11⅛	13	Mahogany	
1	Back	⁹⁄₁₆	11⅛	19⅝	Mahogany	
1	Lid	⁹⁄₁₆	13⅝	20⅞	Mahogany	
2	Lid cleats	⁹⁄₁₆	⁹⁄₁₆	13	Mahogany	
2	Vertical dividers	⁹⁄₁₆	1	4⅛	Mahogany	½" TBE*
2	Cleats - long	½	½	17½	Poplar	
2	Cleats - short	½	½	11⅞	Poplar	
1	Chest - bottom	⅝	13	19⅝	Poplar	
1	Foot blank	1⅞	1⅞	16	Mahogany	Material for 4 feet
2	Base moulding	¾	1¼	28	Mahogany	
1	False bottom	⁹⁄₁₆	18½	11⅞	Poplar	
Drawers						
3	Fronts	¾	4½	5⅞	Mahogany	
2	Runners - outside	¾	¾	11¾	Poplar	
2	Runners - middle	¾	1¾	11¾	Poplar	
2	Guides	⅝	⅞	11¾	Poplar	

*TBE = Tenon both ends

Simple lathe work. Lay out the major transitions for the feet, including the top and bottom of the ball and the top edge just below the tenon that fits into the chest bottom. Use a parting tool to set the proper diameters then shape the ball and cut the cove.

A strong hold. Foot tenons slip into holes drilled into the bottom after each tenon is sawn with the grain to accept glued wedges.

Primarily for looks. Because these nails will be seen throughout time, the bottom is the perfect place to use period-correct reproduction nails. But don't forget to drill pilot holes.

Incremental increases. I used a French Provincial Classical bit to begin my moulding profile. As planned, small increases in the bit height trimmed away the full-bead leaving only the cove-and-bead portion used.

Lying flat. With your workpiece flat to your router table, extend a ¼"-roundover bit to the cut area. Set your fence flush with the router bit bearing.

Also, because the router bit cut is so high, it's important that you make your moulding on a wide board.

Begin with a cove-and-bead router bit set up in your router table. Set your fence flush with your router bearing. To get the extended flat portion of the moulding as shown in the photo at right above, make a number of passes, raising the bit height with each pass.

Complete the two-step moulding profile by adding the roundover detail at the top edge. Use a ¼"-roundover bit, and leave a small fillet for an additional shadow line. After completing this profile, trim your moulding from the edge of the wider stock.

Fit the moulding around the front and ends of your chest, then miter the corners. Apply glue to the entire front piece, but only along the front half of the side pieces. Brads finish the work and hold the moulding in place as the glue sets.

Mill the lid and lid cleats according to the cutlist. Profile the front and ends of the lid using a ½"-roundover router bit set to leave a small

brads hold them in place.

With the case inverted, add a bead of glue along the front edge and halfway back the sides. Position the bottom assembly to the case then nail along all four sides.

Mill the drawer runners and guides to size. The two outside runners fit tight to the sides and butt to the front rail. Middle runners split the vertical dividers and are squared to the front rail. Add a thin bead of glue to the front half of the runners, position them to the case then

secure with brads. Drawer guides fit on top of the middle runners and are attached with glue and brads.

The false bottom above the drawers floats as it rests on the cleats. Mill the panel so the grain runs front to back in the chest to increase rigidity.

Mouldings & Top

The moulding on the case is a bit of a troublemaker in that it is 1¼" tall, but only ¾" thick. This dictates that you stretch the profile more than most router bits allow, so be creative.

Bring to a point. Rounded corners need to be squared. Continue the reveal to a sharp corner, then use a sharp chisel to trim both shoulders to transition the thumbnail.

Plane is better. Material behind the arch is nibbled away at the table saw, but final clean-up is best done using a shoulder plane.

Pattern tweak. String patterns are pushed above the center of the drawer front. Make sure you have ample room for the radius tool's pivot point. It is tight.

fillet. Cleats at the ends help hold the lid flat. Glue the front half of each cleat then screw them to the lid. Place the screws toward the inside edge of the cleats to keep them from poking through the top's moulded edge.

Arched-top Drawers

The chest drawers are built with through dovetails at the back and half-blind dovetails at the front. The ¼"-thick bottoms fit into rabbets cut in the drawer fronts and are nailed to the drawer box. Most of the work, including the string inlay, focuses on the fronts.

The arch of the three drawers is a centered 2⅛" radius with the compass point set at that distance from the top edge. Draw the arch then mark a line 3⅜" up from the bottom edge to locate the shoulders. After the shape is cut, form the thumbnail edges with a roundover bit. The inside corner at both ends of the arch needs to be squared as shown in the photo above.

Each drawer front is rabbeted as if it were a rectangle. The ends and bottom have a ¼"-wide x ½"-deep rabbet. The entire arch, including a ¼" at the shoulders, is also rabbeted. Make the cut at your table saw, then nibble away the area behind the arch.

The stringing pattern on the drawer fronts is offset toward the top of the drawer front. Position your pattern 1⅝" from the thumbnail edge. Also, take the time to lay out the pattern to ensure you have adequate space for the pivot point of the radius tool.

Begin with the ⅞"-radius center circle. Remaining arcs transition from the circle and extend to the layout lines. This exercise is like that used on the case front. The one difference is that there are no berries used on the drawer fronts to mask the string ends.

Fit & Finish

The finish on my chest begins with a coat of boiled linseed oil to highlight the grain. After a coat of shellac, apply a layer of Van Dyke brown glaze to darken the project without

discoloring the inlay. Follow that with multiple coats of shellac until a sufficient build is reached. Buff with #0000 steel wool to reduce the shine of the shellac.

With the finish complete, install an escutcheon with the area behind the keyhole drilled out and painted black – unless you choose to install a lock. The drop-pendant pulls are mounted using a snipe, and the lid is attached with small butt hinges.

I think this is a perfect project. Material costs are low and construction techniques are not over the top. As an introduction to string inlay, this design is easy and the work can be by hand or power. Just have fun with it.

Square ends. The grooves on the drawer front need to stop at your layout lines and the cut has to be at full depth to the very end. A nice trick is to use a screwdriver, sized to fit your lines, to crush fibers at the end of the lines.

Line & Berry
Chest of Drawers

by Glen D. Huey

In southeastern Pennsylvania, just northwest of Philadelphia, is Chester County. It was one of the original three counties formed by William Penn in 1682, under a charter signed by King Charles II. In 1729, a large portion of the western county was split off to become Lancaster County, and in 1789, the southeastern townships closest to Philadelphia were organized as Delaware County. That left Chester County as we find it today.

Throughout the 1700s, Chester County furniture makers produced pieces with unique surface decoration, such as the line and berry inlay shown on this chest. Furniture makers of the period scribed inter-connected half-circles into the surface. The design was scratched using a compass, which is why the process is often referred to as "compass inlay." Sometimes, at the termination of those circles, small groupings of round berries completed the design. This decoration reached a popularity peak in the 1740s.

Where to Begin?

The striking feature on this chest is the inlay on the drawer fronts – but the chest, on its own, has attributes not often seen in furniture construction.

Inlay gets noticed. This arresting, seemingly complex inlay is accomplished using a router and series of patterns.

Begin by prepping the panels for the case sides and bottom. Notice that there is a difference in the widths of these components. The ⁵⁄₁₆" offset allows for the added double-bead moulding on the case sides and drawer blades, a common feature during the William & Mary period. That offset is at the front of the chest, so when transferring your dovetail layout, work with the rear edges of the panels aligned.

There is quite a bit of work needed on the case sides. Dovetails join the sides to the case bottom and single sockets hold the support rails, both front and back. From a pins-first point of view, set your marking gauge to ⁵⁄₈" and scribe the two case sides along the bottom edge. Why ⁵⁄₈" when the thickness of the bottom is ¾"? It's to hide the dovetail joints when the base pieces wrap the chest. Lay out and cut the pins in the case sides.

With the pins complete, mark the case bottom where the front edge of each side ends. Chuck a straight bit into your router, set the depth of cut for a shallow rabbet that leaves ⁵⁄₈" of material and clamp a fence even with the inside layout line. Now make the cut from that mark to the back edge of the bottom on both sides. The rabbets help register the sides to the bottom and provide a more accurate transfer of the pin layout. Cut the tails at both ends of the bottom and fit the joints. Tweak the fit as necessary.

After the dovetail joints are fit, lay out and cut four sockets at the top of the sides, along the front and rear edges. The tails for the support rails slip into the sockets from the top

Disappearing joinery. Form the tails in the case bottom after you cut a rabbet ⅛" below the inside surface. This allows the base moulding to cover the dovetail joint.

Mortise both ends of lower drawer blades

Strong connections. The top and rear blades are mortised for the housed and center runners. The lower drawer blades have a single mortise cut at each end to hold the runners in position.

down. The front support rail fits ⁷⁄₁₆" behind the front edge of the sides; the rear support rail is set flush to the backboard rabbet, or ¾" in from the rear.

Slide-in Blades

The drawer blades attach to the case sides with sliding dovetails. Lay out the sockets along the front edge of each case side and on the back edge for the one rear blade, making sure that each location matches its counterpart in the opposite side –

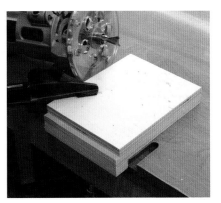

Best router setup. A platform jig, ¾"-dovetail router bit and a ¾"-outside-diameter guide bushing are used to create the sliding dovetails that attach the drawer blades to the case. It's simple.

Want to make it easy? All the joinery work on the center divider is hidden – covered by the mouldings or the top. To make quick work of the divider, attach the piece to the blade and support rail with screws.

you want the blades to be level across the front of your chest. Slide a ¾" dovetail bit through a ¾"-outside-diameter guide bushing, then chuck these in your router. Position the platform to the left of the socket area as shown in the top right photo, then cut the ½"-deep x 2¼"-long sockets.

For the backboards, cut a ⁷⁄₁₆"-deep by ¾"-wide rabbet along the rear edge of the case sides. Now the

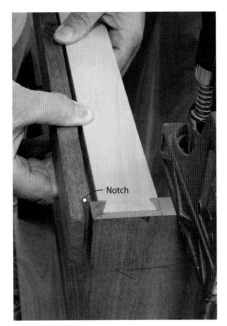

Notch

Built out to match. Here you can see exactly how the front top rail fits with the support rail to bring the front edge equal with the case bottom. The notches at the ends of the rail are nibbled away at the table saw.

Set for change. The bottom drawer runs on the case bottom and the top bank of drawers rides on housed runners. The middle runners, to allow for seasonal changes, are attached to the case side with cut nails.

Left-hand stop. The magnetic stop set to the left of the material is used to precisely align the moulding profile with the saw blade. Push the stock tight to the auxiliary stop then pull the table saw fence tight to the stock before ripping.

work on the sides is complete.

Next, mill your drawer blades, front top rail, support rails, vertical divider and drawer runner stock to thickness and size. To get exact lengths, measure off of your assembled case. The blades' lengths includes the two dovetails, as do the support rails. The top front rail runs from outside edge to outside edge.

Dry-fit the sides and bottom, position the support rails to the sockets cut in the sides, then transfer the layout onto the rails. Trim the ends then fit the rails to the case – be sure to mark front or rear. The drawer blades get the tail portion cut into both ends. Do this with the same dovetail router bit used to create the sockets. Install the bit in your router table and adjust the cut height first, then set the fence to cut the sliding tail to fill the socket. (It's best to test the setup using a scrap of the proper thickness of stock.) To complete the work on the blades, lay out and cut mortises for the runners.

A Runner to Ride On

The next step is to assemble the case. Apply glue to the bottom, sides and dovetails, and slip the joints together. For the front blades (leave the rear blade floating), apply a dollop of glue at the front of each dovetail slot then add a thin coat on the tail before slipping the blade into position. A light touch with a mallet should set the blade flush with the front edge of the case sides – that's a correct fit.

In the center of the front support rail, cut a through-mortise that's ¼" wide and 1¼" long (oriented front-to-back) for the center divider. Take a look at the photo above. The divider has a unique shape because the top notches around the front top rail as the tenon fits through the support rail. The divider is joined at the bottom with a ¼"-thick dovetail that slips into the top blade. That's a lot of work. If you want to simplify the process, a couple screws through the rail and blade make this quick.

With the center divider ready to install, add glue to the joinery, including the sockets in the case sides and the dovetails on the support rails, then slide it all together. The front top rail fits tight to and is glued to the support rail and wraps over the case sides, building out the ⁵⁄₁₆" to match the case bottom. The

Accuracy is important. A sharp chisel marks the beaded moulding exactly at the place the V-shape is to be cut.

Back up that cut. The V-shaped notches that accepts the drawer blade bead moulding need to be perfectly cut, as do the mouldings. Use a backer with a 45° opening cut made at the table saw to pare them.

Form the foot. Use a 1³/₄" Forstner bit to clean out the rounded portion of each design that forms the spur. Then at your band saw, cut away the remaining waste.

Work on your bench. Use scrap 8/4 to raise the chest off your bench and make fitting the base that much easier. One piece at each corner does the job.

notches are cut at the table saw.

Cut tenons where needed on the ends of the runners. The housed and center tenons each get a ¼" tenon at the front and a 1" tenon at the back. Glue the tenons in position (the rear tenon is not glued, which allows for seasonal movement) square the runners, then nail them to the case side.

Keep Your Bevels Sharp

Except for the bottom and front top rail, the front face of the chest is covered with a double-beaded moulding. Use a traditional beading bit to form the twin beads. The setup for the beaded moulding requires accurate

adjustment to get the beads evenly spaced without the second pass cutting into the first bead. Once set up, create the profile on a wide board that's milled to the proper thickness. Slice the moulding from the board then produce another set of mouldings until you have the pieces needed.

Use blue tape to hold the moulding pieces to the case sides then use a chisel to mark the exact location where the blades meet the sides. From those marks, draw lines along the back of the moulding at a 45° angle to show the waste area that's removed to accept the end of the

blade mouldings.

Saw as much of the waste out as you can without working past the lines then pare exactly to the lines. To keep the edges square and the angle correct so the perpendicular moulding fit is tight, use a simple

Supplies
Ball & Ball
ballandball.com or 610-363-7330
8 A69 backplate with A72 drop on post, #A000-000, $26.47 each
5 1¾ x 1¾ Wm & Mary chased, cast escutcheon, #L61-002, $17.12 each
Prices correct at time of publication.

V-shaped guide block. Pare the V-shape until the chisel rides the guide block.

The bead mouldings that cover the blades have pointed ends to fit the V-shaped cutouts. Form the ends just as you did on the side mouldings. That's easy. The trick is to get an accurate cut length. It's best to cut it long then pare to a good fit. The center-divider moulding is cut square, to fit against the front top rail.

To attach all the mouldings, add a thin bead of glue to the back of each then secure the pieces to the case with blue tape. Add a few inconspicuous 23-gauge pins to help keep pieces from moving.

Simple & Solid Base

The base for this chest is as simple as it gets. Mill the pieces to thickness and size before adding your favorite profile along the top edge. Next, miter the pieces to length using the chest as your guide. The top edge of the base is flush with the top edge of the case bottom. After the pieces are fit, trace the cutout profile at each end of the three pieces and draw a line connecting the profiles.

The base pieces have a thin bead of glue along the top edge and are attached to the case using cut nails. To keep glue squeeze-out to a minimum, cut a shallow groove on the back face of the base approximately ¼" down from the top. Align the front piece to the chest then add a couple clamps to hold it in place and tight to the chest. Add glue along the

Proper layout. The design of the drawer fronts is dependent on getting your layout right. Space the lines off each drawer's center to keep the designs aligned.

Keep it straight. The jigs used in this project are all held square to the drawer front. Proper placement is essential to the task.

That's step one. These are the first set of lines in the design. The depth should be a strong ¹⁄₁₆" for a secure fit that's easily trimmed after installation.

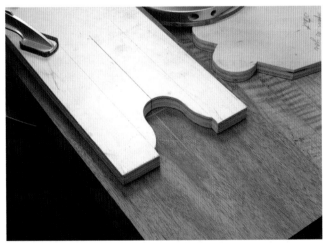

Accurate placement. After the jig is properly placed, the two flat steps at the top of the tulip are where the router guide bushing begins and ends. The bushing snaps into the corner.

front 6" of the base side, position that piece to the front piece and tack it in place with a 23-gauge pin. Work the second side, too.

Next, remove the front piece, add glue along the top edge and on the miters, then clamp it back in place. Pin the mitered corners to keep them aligned until the glue sets. For an authentic look, drill pilot holes and install cut nails in the base, with the nails set just below the surface.

To complete the base, slip the rear feet in position and reinforce the corners with glue blocks. The chest actually stands on the blocks, which extend slightly beyond the base. Glue blocks should also be installed along the base/bottom intersections behind the feet.

The top is attached to the chest with #8 x 1¼" wood screws through the support rails (screws in the rear rail should be in oversized holes) and two wooden clips per end that are evenly spaced between the rails. I cut the ¼" slots for the clips with a plate joiner; screws hold the clips in place.

The underhung moulding is made at a router table with the lower portion of a specialty moulding router bit (Rockler # 91881). With a wide board stood on its edge, create two profiles then rip the mouldings at your table saw. The moulding is attached to the chest just as the base is – glue and square-head nails.

Patterns Make Repeating Easy

With the chest assembled, mill and size the drawer fronts to fit the openings – these are flush-fit drawers so

Step two. The completed tulip design faces away from the drawer center and is spaced just outside the bump design.

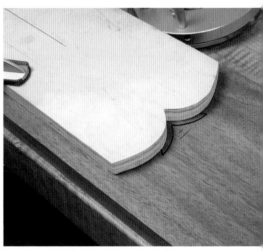

Plunge to begin. The tulip top string groove is the first of two grooves that require that you see the bit as you work – or develop a feel for when to stop at the line.

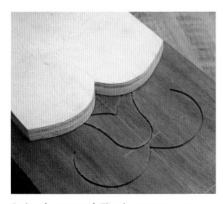

A simple reversal. Flip the wave pattern then set the distance between the pattern and the previous groove at 1" for the two top drawers and 1¼" for the lower drawers.

It's all in the base plate. The arcs around the center of the design are cut using the router base plate as a circle-cutting jig. Place a dowel into the drawer front's centered hole, slip the router plate over the pin then cut the groove from bump to bump.

Sized right. Clamp a fence at your spindle sander to perfectly size the stringing thickness. Run a sample. If the fit is too tight, adjust the fence and try the setup again.

Line & Berry Chest of Drawers

No.	item	T	W	L	Material	Comments
		Dimensions (inches)				
1	Case bottom	¾	20¹³⁄₁₆	39½	Poplar/Walnut	
2	Case sides	¾	20½	35¾	Walnut	
3	Drawer blades	¾	2	39	Walnut	
1	Rear blade	¾	2	39	Poplar	
2	Support rails	¾	1¾	39	Poplar	
1	Front top rail	¾	1¾	39½	Walnut	
1	Center divider	¾	2	9⅛	Walnut	¾" TBE*
1	Center runner	¾	2¾	16⅞	Poplar	¼" TOE**, 1" TOE
1	Drawer guide	⅝	¾	15	Poplar	
2	Housed runners	¾	1	16⅞	Poplar	¼" TOE, 1" TOE
4	Runners	¾	1	18¼	Poplar	¼" TOE
2	Kickers	¾	1	9⅜	Poplar	
1	Top	¾	21¹¹⁄₁₆	4¹¹⁄₁₆	Walnut	
Mouldings & Base						
2	Side beads	⁵⁄₁₆	¾	33¼	Walnut	
3	Blade beads	⁵⁄₁₆	¾	39	Walnut	
1	Divider bead	⁵⁄₁₆	¾	6⅞	Walnut	
2	Underhung mouldings	⅝	1¼	44	Walnut	
1	Base front	¾	6¼	41	Walnut	
2	Base sides	¾	6¼	21⁹⁄₁₆	Walnut	
2	Rear feet	¾	5½	6⅛	Poplar	
Drawers						
2	Top fronts	¾	6⅝	18⅝	Walnut	
1	#2 front	3/4	7⅜	38	Walnut	
1	#3 front	3/4	8⅛	38	Walnut	
1	Bottom front	¾	8⅞	38	Walnut	

*TBE = tenon both ends, **TOE = tenon one end

keep the reveals at a minimum (¹⁄₁₆" or less). Depending on your preference, at this time either build the drawers or work on the inlay for the drawer fronts.

The drawers are built using 18th-century construction techniques – half-blind dovetails at the front and through-dovetails at the rear. The drawer backs are sized so the drawer bottoms slide under the backs. The bottoms are beveled to fit into ¼" grooves in the drawer sides and front – the tops of those grooves are cut ¾" above the edge. Cut a slot in the drawer bottoms even with the inside edge of the drawer back. Nails driven through the slot and into the drawer back secure the bottoms and allow for seasonal movement.

Patterns for the string grooves can be created from a design you already have in mind – or use the plans included here on page 177. To make your own patterns, create a design in a full-size drawing (Google SketchUp is great for this step). Next, select a guide bushing size (for this piece, I used a ⅜"-outside-diameter bushing) and offset the lines to compensate for the bushing. Transfer your new lines to ¼" plywood then cut out the patterns. Plywood thicker than ¼" causes problems with the bit length when cutting the grooves.

For this project, three patterns were developed. The included patterns are sized for the top drawers. Because the drawers are graduated, make a second set of patterns (20 percent larger) for the lower three drawers.

Each of the inlay designs is created around a center point. That point is established using one of the

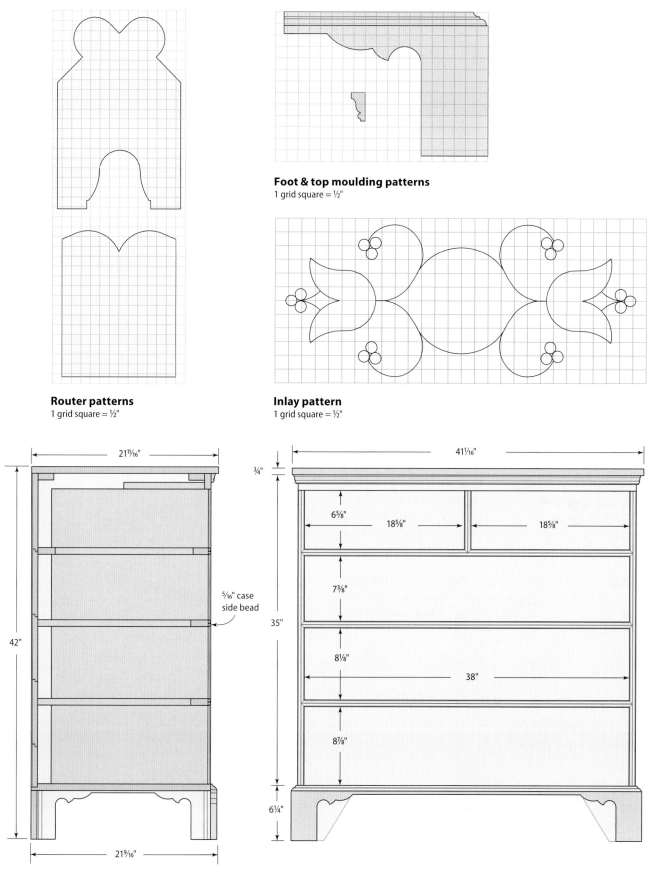

Router patterns
1 grid square = ½"

Foot & top moulding patterns
1 grid square = ½"

Inlay pattern
1 grid square = ½"

⁵⁄₁₆" case
side bead

21¹¹⁄₁₆"

42"

21⁹⁄₁₆"

Section

41¹⁄₁₆"

¾"

6⅝"

18⅝"   18⅝"

35"

7⅜"

8⅛"

38"

8⅞"

6¼"

Elevation

top drawers. Find the exact center of the drawer front then measure from the edge of the drawer front to that center point. Each drawer inlay design, whether on the right or left of the drawer, is set to that measurement – all the designs line up vertically on the chest.

For the top drawer, draw vertical lines that are equally spaced 2⁵⁄₁₆" off the center point (the line spacing for the larger drawers is 2¹¹⁄₁₆"). Also draw a line horizontally as shown in the photo below.

Begin with the twin-bump-shaped pattern. Set the pattern square to the drawer front with the valley of the bumps set at the intersection of the horizontal centerline and one of the 2⁵⁄₁₆" lines. Point the bumps toward the drawer center.

With the guide bushing and a ¹⁄₁₆" straight bit chucked in the router, and the bit set to cut a strong ¹⁄₁₆" into the fronts, locate the bushing at the top end of the pattern, plunge the bit into the drawer front then rout the design. Stop when the bushing hits against the pattern's flat step, completing the pattern. Repeat the steps with the pattern set to the opposite lines, again facing the center.

The second pattern is the tulip design. Place this pattern squared to the drawer front with its top-to-bottom center aligned with the drawer front's centerline. The pattern is also aligned with the outer edge of the twin-bump routed line as shown in the bottom right photo on the opposite page. Begin with the bushing located at one of the corners. Plunge

WORKING WITH INLAY BITS

A ¹⁄₁₆" router bit is used to create the grooves in the line and berry design found on Chester County furniture and elsewhere. Bits available through most suppliers have ¼" shanks and the cutting length is a short ¼" at most.

Two potential problems arise when using these bits in string inlay work. First, the cutting length is too short so as not to allow ample depth of cut for your stringing if you push through a guide bushing and beyond a plywood pattern, as we're doing with this project.

Second, the ¼" shank, when extended enough to reach through the above-described scenario, requires that you use a larger guide bushing than the ³⁄₈" bushing used for the chest – the inside diameter of the bushing is only slightly larger than the shank diameter, so without spot-on setup, the bit has the potential to rub the bushing. What to do?

The first and most simple fix is to use a larger-diameter guide bushing. Working with a larger-diameter bushing reduces the crispness of the design, but allows the bit's shank to easily pass through the guide bushing as the router bit tip reaches your drawer front.

You can also use thin pattern material. With less thickness to pass by, your bit doesn't have to extend as far to cut the grooves. (Remember, it's OK to shorten the length of the guide bushing to make everything work.)

Another option is to use a ¹⁄₈"-diameter router bit in conjunction with a collet reducer. This setup (as shown in the photo) allows you to extend the collet reducer beyond the router's collet and if you pull the ¹⁄₈" router bit out of the reducer to its fullest extent, the bit's reach is enough to create the grooves without adjustments to either the bushing or your pattern.

One source for the ¹⁄₁₆" straight bit is inlaybandings.com; collet reducers can be found at IMService (cadcamcadcam.com).

Stretching the point. Collet reducers, chucked into regular collets, can help to lengthen a router bit's reach.

Hot pipes. The heat from the torched galvanized pipe steams the water and dries the string at the shape needed to fit into the grooves. It's always good to have pipes of various sizes on hand.

Take your time. With the stringing bent to closely match the grooves, begin at one end of the run then work to the opposite end. String left in the groove tends to hold its shape better. As you glue the pieces in place, work again from end to end of the groove.

Berry nice. The placement of the berries is left to your discretion. I think it's best to have the berries overlap and appear like clusters of grapes on the vine.

into the wood then rout through the tulip shape until the bushing nestles into the opposing corner.

The next two steps of string routing are the most difficult. To locate the wave pattern, you need to lay out a couple lines as shown in the top right photo below. The first line is squared off the drawer front and aligned with the ends of the tulip design. The next line toward the center is half the width of the guide bushing being used. It's used to set the wave pattern square to the drawer front and just at that inside line.

This time, fully plunge the router off the pattern then place the router bit to drop into the tulip line, right at the end. Hold the bit out of the wood and the bushing against your pattern as you start the router then allow the bit to settle into the tulip line. Rout to the center of the pattern then back out toward the second end of the tulip design. When you get to that second line, stop your movement and release the plunge on your router. As you repeat this process for each inlay design, you'll develop a feel and ear

for it – you'll hear a different sound as you break into the second line. But on the first couple passes, watch the router bit as you move.

The last bit of pattern work is to reverse the wave pattern and cut in the pointed end. To locate the pattern, measure along the drawer centerline out from the valley of the wave line and place a mark at 1" for the top drawers and 1¼" for the other drawers. Again, the valley of the wave sits at the intersection. Routing the line is a repeat performance, but on a smaller scale.

The center grooves are cut with a circle-cutting setup. Drill an ⅛" hole at the center of the inlay design. Due to the diameter of the circle being so tight, I simply drilled a ⅛" hole in the router's base plate, set to cut from pattern to pattern. For the top drawers, the radius is 1¹¹⁄₁₆" and on the other drawers the radius is 1¹⁵⁄₁₆". Rest the bit in one of the routed grooves, start the router and rotate it to cut the arced groove. Stop the cut as you reach the opposite string groove. Repeat the steps for the second arc.

Finally, String & Berries

There are straight grooves for inlay, too. The small section between the bumps and the tulip can be routed or you can use a regular screwdriver to punch the surface just deep enough for stringing. The other straight grooves are around the entire perimeter of each drawer. This line is routed using a fence attached to your router. Space the grooves ⅞" from the outside edge of the drawers.

Traditionally, string used in Chester County furniture was made of holly for its white appearance, but I have oodles of scrap maple lying around my shop. That's what I chose for my string. (You can also purchase string material.)

String inlay needs to be sized to fit your grooves. Mill a piece of scrap that's about 3" wide into pieces that are a strong ¹⁄₁₆" thick then rip thin strips from the wider stock – a cutting gauge is ideal for this work.

After the string is made, it's necessary to size each piece. The best method for sizing the string to an exact fit is at your spindle sander. Fit the string between the fence and the drum while pushing into the rotation of the drum. Test the fit. If it's good, you're good. If not, adjust the fence and try it again.

Straight pieces are ready to fit. Miter the corners and, unless your stock is plenty long, use scarf joints to hide additions. The curved pieces are another story. I've tried a variety of methods to bend stringing, but the best I've found is to heat-bend the pieces on a pipe that's heated with a torch. For the larger-diameter curves created with the bump pattern, a 2"-diameter piece of galvanized pipe works perfectly; 1¼" pipe is ideal for the tulip area.

Heat the pipe until it's hot but not scorching hot – a couple test pieces should clue you to what temperature is best. Lightly wet the string then, using a backer strip such as a piece of pallet banding, bend the string around the heated pipe.

Fit the string to the grooves and don't sweat the areas where the string ends. Those spots get berries to cover the raw ends. The place to work meticulously is where two pieces of string meet. The tighter the

fit, the nicer the look. However, as with dovetails, a few imperfections says "handmade."

A few small dabs of glue along the groove keep the string in place. As you tap in the string, the glue chases around the groove. Wipe off any excess when all the string is placed.

The berries are where you become the artist. On the original, each berry cluster – most likely made from red and white cedar – was set with the two berries that touched the vine perfectly aligned with the length of the drawers. A third berry was placed directly at the center while just touching the other two berries. The symmetrical look was very regimented.

My take is to lighten up. I randomly located the berries that touched the vine, and made sure the two lapped, as did the third when it was installed. To do this, you have to install a single berry at a time. Drill an ⅛"-deep x ⅜"-diameter hole at each berry location.

The berries themselves are face-grain plugs, either shop-made or store-bought. Dab glue in the hole

then tap in the berry. Use a chisel to flush the berry to the drawer front prior to drilling and installing the second and third berries. I used two cherry berries and a single maple berry for each of my clusters. The choice is yours.

At the Finish Line

With the drawers and drawer front inlay complete, the only wood-working left is the chest back. The backboards run from side to side and fit one another with a tongue-and-groove joint. Each board is nailed with a single nail at each end; the top board has two nails per end.

As for the finish on the chest, stain or dye would reduce the contrast of the string against the walnut background. So, to achieve a deeper color in the walnut while highlighting the string, apply a coat of boiled linseed oil. Follow that with a layer of clear shellac once the oil is dry. From there, I sanded the clear shellac then added multiple layers of amber shellac – the amber color warms the walnut, but also colors the other woods – sanding between coats to smooth the walnut grain. Once I achieved the color I wanted, I returned to clear shellac in order to build a smoothed surface. I thoroughly sanded the shellac before spraying a layer of dull-rubbed-effect pre-catalyzed lacquer to dull and further protect the surface.

After the hardware is added to the drawers (I ordered post-and-nut equipped pulls instead of snipe pins), the chest is ready for use. Mine is going into my bedroom, but you might just want this piece in a high-visibility area. It commands attention.

It's a perfect match. The face-grain plugs that become berries are fit into holes drilled with a ⅜" drill bit. Because of the flat-grain to flat-grain gluing surfaces, the berries will stay put.

Voysey Mantel Clock

by Robert W. Lang

Charles Francis Annesley Voysey (1857-1941) was one of the eminent architects and designers of the British Arts & Crafts movement of the late 19th and early 20th centuries. Voysey designed complete environments, including textile and wallpaper patterns. His work influenced American designers such as Harvey Ellis, who is also known for the use of architectural details in furniture designs.

The original drawings for this clock are dated 1895, and examples exist in various materials. The best-known of these clocks features a painted bucolic landscape, and a gilded dome and spire. There are also examples in wood, including ebony with ivory inlay and dark oak. There is even a version from 1903 made from aluminum.

For my version, I decided to use contrasting woods, with exotic materials for the inlay. The four legs, dome and spire are tiger maple and the panels and foot mouldings are ebonized walnut. The dots and ring on the face are mother-of-pearl, and the horizontal stripes on the legs are ebony.

Despite the sophisticated appearance of the clock, the case is simple construction: panels fit in stopped grooves in the legs. Where things get tricky is under the top, where the moulding steps in and out around the perimeter. The challenge is one

Right-side up. Making the grooves first makes it difficult to mix up the inside and outside of the legs.

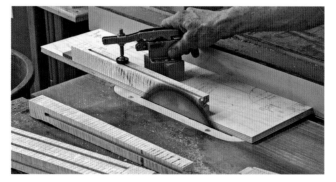

Keep it simple. This jig takes only a few minutes to assemble, and provides a safe method to taper the legs at the table saw.

Smooth sailing. A handplane quickly removes the machine marks from the columns and it leaves a flat, smooth surface.

of scale, and finding ways to make the process as simple as possible.

Thin Panels, Tapered Legs

I worked to the original 1895 drawing, and resawed the panels from 4/4 stock. I first made the panels ¹⁄₁₆" thicker than finished size and let them sit for a few days. I piled some scrap lumber on top to help keep them flat, then milled the front, back and sides to ¼" thick and the top to ⁷⁄₃₂" thick. I made the back panel ¼" wider than the finished size to allow for two rips for the back door.

While the panels acclimated, I went to work on the legs, feet and moulding. The legs were milled to 1¼" square, and after deciding which piece of wood looked best in which position, I marked the tops with a cabinetmaker's triangle.

The sequence of tasks on the way from rough blank to finished leg isn't critical. I milled the grooves and

cut the stub tenons on the bottoms before cutting the tapers on the outside faces. That – along with the cabinetmaker's triangle – made it easy for me to keep the parts properly oriented.

I set up a ¼" straight bit in the router table, then set the fence and stop-block to make the ¼"-deep grooves that are ⁹⁄₁₆" from the inside faces and stop 13⁵⁄₁₆" down from the top. That setting works for only one

First on edge. The first cut of the cornice moulding is made with the wood on edge.

groove on the four legs, so I reset the fence to make the second set of grooves.

With a ⅜"-wide dado stack in the table saw, I set a stop on the miter gauge to make the tenons. After cutting the tenons, I used a simple table saw jig to taper the legs to 1" square at the top, then planed away the saw marks. To complete the legs, use a chisel to square off the ends of the grooves.

Second on face. The final cut leaves the narrow edge at a uniform thickness.

Mouldings in Miniature

There are two mouldings used in this piece: a simple ¼"-radius cove on the feet and a more complex profile used as a cornice under the top. Both of these are rather small, so I carefully ripped the rough material then brought the pieces to finished size with the planer. I made plenty of blanks about 24" long.

When thin mouldings are mentioned, someone will offer the advice to run the profile on wide pieces then rip the parts to their finished size. Sometimes this makes sense, but with this project it made more sense to me to be careful with the router table setup rather than stop after every pass to move to the table saw and jointer.

That gave me more control over the final size, and took far less time. The key to milling small parts is to use a setup that holds the parts in position as they are cut and keeps fingers out of harm's way.

The foot moulding is made with one pass and a ¼"-radius cove bit, but the ogee moulding requires two setups with different cutters. The ogee is flattened out, so there isn't a standard cutter available that matches the profile. The first cut is made with the moulding on edge, using a portion of a vertical raised-panel bit (Lee Valley #16J63.54). For the second cut, the material is laid flat to pass below a rounded-end grooving bit with a ⅛" radius (Lee Valley #16J42.01).

Make the Cut

There are lots of mitered corners in this project. See "Small Miter Setup" (above) for the two fixtures that

SMALL MITER SETUP

One of the challenges of this project is making small miters accurately and efficiently. I made a small miter block to speed the process. Using a table saw or powered miter saw with pieces this small would be insane, but I did use a powered saw to cut a piece of scrap at 45°.

After gluing the three pieces of the miter block together, I clamped the 45° piece to the back fence of the fixture and used it to position my backsaw to make kerfs in the fence to guide the saw through the rest of the project.

I also built a small shooting board to use with my block plane. One piece of plywood serves as a base, and the smaller rectangular piece raises the work into the plane iron. The two narrow fences are aligned at 45° to the front edge and are held in place with glue and brads.

Shooting removes a very thin slice from the end of the workpiece. With a sharp plane iron and a bit of wax on the shooting board's base, it doesn't take long to get a feel for how to hold the wood against the plane and how to adjust the cuts for a good fit.

Simple solution. This shop-made miter cutting block (raised to a comfortable height) makes quick work of cutting the numerous miters for this project.

Shoot to fit. This fixture holds the workpiece at the correct angle and guides the block plane to perfect the ends of the mitered pieces.

I used. I began with the feet, and placed a leg tenon-side up in my vise for reference. I cut one piece of the moulding and when I was satisfied with the length, I made a pencil mark on the base of the miter block and proceeded to cut all 16 pieces of the foot moulding.

After cutting a few pieces, I glued them together in pairs, rubbed the joints and set the pairs aside to dry. With eight pairs completed, I checked the fit of two pairs against the tenon. To adjust the fit, I used my shooting board or, to remove just a tiny bit, rubbed both ends at once against sandpaper glued to scrap plywood. When I was happy with

Two easier than four. Each half of a foot is put together, then two pairs are assembled to fit the tenons on the ends of the legs.

the fit, I glued each foot together. If the assembled foot mortise is a little small, the tenon or the inside of the assembled foot can be filed down.

A Little Off the Top

The top has indented notches, 3" in from each outside corner. It's a nice touch, but the detail that looks simple from above gets complicated down below. There really isn't a way to avoid running the cornice moulding as separate pieces that

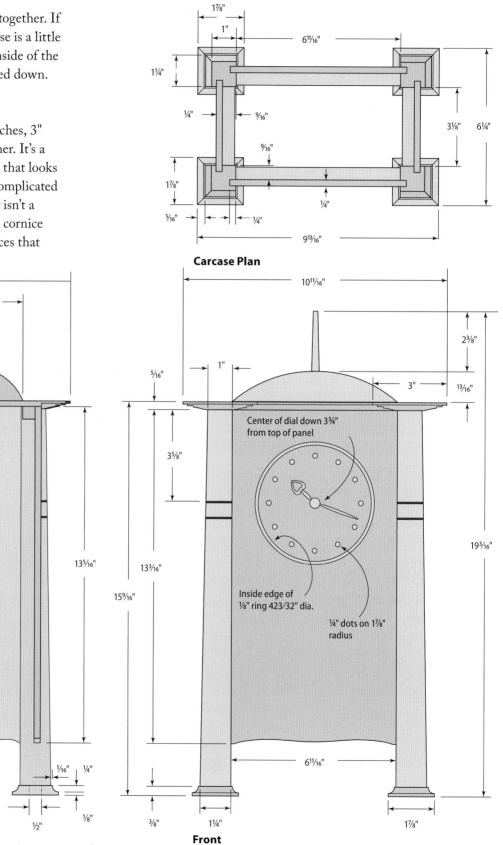

Carcase Plan

Center of dial down 3¾" from top of panel

Inside edge of ⅛" ring 423/32" dia.

¼" dots on 1⅞" radius

Section

Front

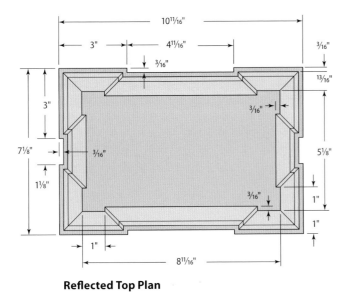

Reflected Top Plan

are mitered at the corners. I used a method that makes it relatively simple, albeit tedious.

The completed top is ⁵⁄₁₆" thick, but Voysey's drawings don't detail how the top attaches to the case, or where the moulding ends and the top begins. It makes sense to run the legs and panels past the bottom edge of the moulding to allow them to cover the transition, yet reduce the thickness of the top.

The top is only ³⁄₃₂" thick at the edge – too thin to be practical for the entire part. I realized that a wide rabbet around the perimeter of a thicker top would provide an edge to butt the moulding to as I fit and assembled.

I cut a piece of ½" plywood 2" smaller than the top, and cut a ³⁄₁₆"-deep notch 1" in from each corner. Then I cut a second plywood rectangle ⅜" smaller than the first and attached it to the first piece, aligned with the ends of the ³⁄₁₆" notches. I ran a router with a flush-trim bit between the notches to make a pattern the shape of the top, but offset in 1".

I planed the top to ⁷⁄₃₂" thick and cut it to size, then cut a ³⁄₁₆"-deep notch 3" in from each outside corner, and made a straight rip from notch to notch at the band saw. Using double-sided tape, I attached the pattern to the bottom of the top then headed to the router table. I installed a straight bit with a bearing above the cutter and set the height to leave ³⁄₃₂" at the edge of the top.

It took several passes to cut the rabbet because the bit diameter is smaller than the width of the rabbet. I made the first pass as a climb-cut to create a nice edge without tear-out, bracing the piece against the router table fence to keep it under control. The last pass was with the bearing against the template.

Multitude of Miters

With the top bottom-side up near my miter block, I began to fit the moulding to the inner notches. The rabbet made it easy to set one end against the inside corner so I could mark the other. With the four inside

Follow me. The pattern is made to the exact size of the perimeter rabbet. The bearing on the bit follows the pattern to make the cut.

Start inside. The rabbet provides exact locations for the cornice moulding. The first piece fits within the notch.

Slight return. The outside corners are used to mark the length of the moulding returns after the first miter is fit.

Handle it. The smallest pieces are glued to longer ones to make it possible to hold them for trimming the ends to the exact length.

Happy ending. The outer corners are the last to be fit (and are the easiest to adjust) to complete the cornice moulding.

pieces cut, it was time to deal with the small return pieces.

I shot one end of each return piece, cut it to rough length and glued it to a long piece; by the time the last piece was cut and glued the first was dry. I then used the shooting board and block plane to trim to my pencil marks.

For each outside corner, I cut and assembled two pieces. The final assembly of the top's moulding was made easier by dealing with eight sub-assemblies instead of 20 individual pieces.

For Appearance's Sake

The inlays on the face are mother-of-pearl, available pre-cut from online suppliers to luthiers. The ⅛"-wide ring is made for the sound hole of a guitar, and the ¼"-diameter dots are fingerboard markers. The location of the inlays is based on the clock face.

The inner diameter of the ring is 120mm, or slightly more than 4²³⁄₃₂". I made a disc from ½" plywood, ½" smaller than that size, and attached it to the front panel with double-sided tape and a screw through the center and into my bench. With a ⅛"-diameter straight bit in a small plunge router with a ⅝"-diameter guide collar, I routed the recess for the ring.

The dots are laid out on a 3¾"-diameter circle. I drew vertical and horizontal centerlines, then drew the circle with my compass. That radius equals one-sixth of the circumference so I stepped off the location of half the dots from the intersection of the vertical centerline and the circle, and the other half from the horizontal centerline.

The shallow holes for the pre-cut dots are made with a Forstner bit at the drill press. I aimed to set the mother-of-pearl slightly below the surface of the wood. That is ideal, but it's not critical because the inlay can be sanded with common woodwork-

Voysey Mantel Clock

No.	Item	Dimensions (inches)			Material
		t	w	l	
4	Legs	1¼	1¼	15¼	Tiger maple
1	Front panel	¼	7³⁄₁₆	13⁵⁄₁₆	Ebonized walnut
2	Side panels	¼	3⅝	13⁵⁄₁₆	Ebonized walnut
1	Back panel	¼	7⁷⁄₁₆*	13⁹⁄₁₆	Ebonized walnut
1	Foot moulding	⅜	⁹⁄₁₆	48	Ebonized walnut
1	Top panel	⁷⁄₃₂	7⅛	10¹¹⁄₁₆	Ebonized walnut
1	Top moulding	⁷⁄₃₂	¹³⁄₁₆	72	Ebonized walnut
1	Dome	¹³⁄₁₆	3⅛	6¹¹⁄₁₆	Tiger maple**
1	Spire	⁵⁄₁₆	⁵⁄₁₆	2⅝	Tiger maple†
16	Column inlays	⅛	⅜	1⁹⁄₁₆	Ebony
1	Hour hand	¹⁄₁₆	⁹⁄₁₆	1⁹⁄₁₆	Tiger maple**
1	Minute hand	¹⁄₁₆	⁹⁄₁₆	2¼	Tiger maple**

*Larger than front panel to allow back door cutout; **Cut to pattern;
†Tenon one end (¼" long)

ing abrasives. Duco cement holds the inlays in place.

Around the Back

A small door on the back panel on the original accesses the clockworks; a small knob and wooden keeper hold it shut. I marked the location of the door, drew reference marks across the panel then made two rip cuts at the table saw to create the stiles. That was followed by two crosscuts to form the rails.

I installed the hinges on the door and the right-hand stile before gluing the panel back together. The hinges are tiny, so I made the gains for them by slicing the ends with a knife and "routing" the depth with my marking gauge.

At this point I made a test assembly, fitting each panel between two legs and testing the fit on the inside of the top panel. I made a couple of adjustments as needed by planing the edges of the panels or scraping away the back of the moulding. When each panel fit individually, I assembled all four with the legs

and made sure everything fit neatly within the moulding.

Four ½"-square cleats were cut from scrap to fit in between the legs; I simply glued them to the top, taking care not to get any glue on the panels. I then took the case apart to make the dome and spire, and to inlay the horizontal bands on the legs.

The slots for the dark bands are made at the table saw. I raised the blade to match the distance from the outer edge of the groove to the face of the leg at the top band and made a cut across each of the tapered faces. The slot for the lower band needs to be slightly deeper, so I used the edge of a file to adjust the slot. The goal is to leave the bands barely proud of the show surface and trim them flush later.

These inlays are genuine ebony, as opposed to the ebonized walnut for the panels and moulding. The ebonizing solution reacts with the maple, so these inlays can't be stained after they are in place. I milled some ebony to match the width of the

slots, and ripped them slightly wider than necessary. I mitered the outer corners and glued them in place, then trimmed them flush with my block plane after the glue was dry.

A Dome of Your Own

After printing a full-size drawing of the front and side arcs for the dome, I used spray adhesive to attach the paper to the dome blank. There is a small flat square at the top of the dome to mate with the bottom of the spire. I cut a ³⁄₁₆"-square mortise with a drill bit and a square punch, about ¼" deep.

Because the curves go entirely to the bottom edge of the dome, I temporarily attached a 1½"-square block to the blank with double-sided tape. I made the vertical cut first, then used blue painter's tape to put the scraps back on the blank. Then I made the cuts in the other direction. The bulk of the saw marks were removed with rasps before finish-sanding the dome.

The spire starts as a ⁵⁄₁₆"-square piece, and I used the full-size draw-

Take a turn. A plywood circle is used as a template for the router guide collar to follow when making the groove for the inlaid ring.

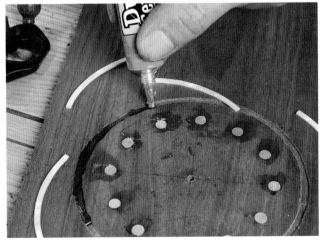

Drop in. The inlay materials were purchased as pre-cut parts from a luthier's supply store. These parts could also be fabricated from wood or other materials.

Perfect match. The back door is cut with four straight cuts from a single panel; the hinges are installed before reassembly.

One at a time. Each panel is fit to the top before attempting to fit the entire carcase. That makes it easy to find the troublemakers.

ing to lay out the tapers and the teeny tenon. The shoulders of the tenon were cut with a backsaw, then I used a chisel to pare down the cheeks. The taper was made with a block plane.

Time on my Hands

The inexpensive quartz movement mounts to the clock at the center of the face. These movements are nice, but the metal hands that come with them are not – so I decided to make $\frac{1}{16}$"-thick wood hands, and attach those to the standard-issue metal ones. Using the metal hands as a backing allowed me to easily mount the wooden ones.

My first attempt at cutting hands with the scrollsaw failed; the wood split at the heart-shaped cutout of the hour hand. I tried again, this time using three thicknesses glued in a stack with contact cement. This survived the session at the scrollsaw, and after shaping the hands with a

file, I separated the strips by pouring a little lacquer thinner on the edge of the stack.

After trimming the metal hands to size and roughing the surface with sandpaper, I epoxied the metal hands to the back of the wood ones, let the epoxy cure, then pared the circular end of the minute hand with a chisel

Hold on there. Square cleats glued to the bottom of the top capture the panels. Final assembly comes after the panels are ebonized and the columns are oiled.

to provide room for the nut to thread securely.

Color with Chemistry

Good old American walnut can be colored to a dramatic black with a home-brew solution. I put a pint of vinegar in a plastic cup, tossed in a ripped-up pad of steel wool and let that soak for a few days. (Gas forms as the acid in the vinegar works on the metal, so leave the container open; if you cap it, it can explode.) The liquid remains clear, but the metal starts to dissolve and scum forms on the surface. Before using the solution, strain it through a coffee filter into another container.

When you brush the liquid on the walnut, nothing happens at first. A chemical reaction between the tannins in the wood and the solution changes the color, and that takes a few minutes.

When the wood dries out, there may be some residue on the surface.

One, two, three. Rasps remove the band saw marks, refine the shape and smooth the surface of the dome.

Nothing yet. The ebonizing solution won't change the color immediately. The chemical reaction between the rusty vinegar and the tannic acid in the wood takes a few minutes.

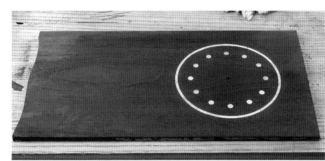

Inlay-safe. The solution has no effect on the mother-of-pearl inlay. Residue from coloring is removed with a non-woven abrasive pad, then the panel is ready for assembly.

The rusty vinegar doesn't react with the mother-of-pearl, so I only needed to wipe off the sludge after coloring. I buffed the surfaces of the panels with a nylon abrasive pad to remove the residue and to smooth the surfaces.

The walnut may look more blue than black, but the application of clear shellac (or other clear finish) delivers a nice dark color. The figured maple on the legs is accented with a coat of clear Danish oil applied before final assembly.

My last step before putting the clock together permanently was to locate and drill two holes through the underside of the top and into the dome.

Together at Last

With the top upside down on the bench, I ran a bead of liquid hide glue down each groove, then put the panels in the grooves. I then ran a bead of glue in the corner where the cleats meet the top and set the assembled legs and panels in place.

After making sure that everything was in the right position and after gluing the spire into the dome, I left the parts to dry overnight. The following day, I flipped the assembly over and permanently attached the dome by reaching in through the back door to drive the two screws.

The assembled clock was sprayed with four coats of clear shellac (on a small project such as this, you can use the stuff in the spray cans). After allowing the shellac to dry completely, I sanded the surface with #320-grit sandpaper, followed by an abrasive pad. A coat of satin lacquer, also from a spray can, completed the finish.

Supplies

Klockit

klockit.com or 800-556-2548

1 Q-80 quartz clock movement, #10082, $5.00

1 flat hand, #66943, $.50

1 sweep second hand, #68047, $.40

Duke Luthier

dukeluthier.com

1 120mm guitar rosette, #MOP 3mm rosette, $9.95

Stewart-MacDonald

stewmac.com or 800-848-2273

12 ¼" pearl dots, #0011, $.65 each

Lee Valley

leevalley.com or 800-871-8158

1 pair 20mm x 13mm hinges, #00D30.04, $1.40

Prices correct at time of publication.

READ THIS IMPORTANT SAFETY NOTICE

To prevent accidents, keep safety in mind while you work. Use the safety guards installed on power equipment; they are for your protection.

When working on power equipment, keep fingers away from saw blades, wear safety goggles to prevent injuries from flying wood chips and sawdust, wear hearing protection and consider installing a dust vacuum to reduce the amount of airborne sawdust in your woodshop.

Don't wear loose clothing, such as neckties or shirts with loose sleeves, or jewelry, such as rings, necklaces or bracelets, when working on power equipment. Tie back long hair to prevent it from getting caught in your equipment.

People who are sensitive to certain chemicals should check the chemical content of any product before using it.

Due to the variability of local conditions, construction materials, skill levels, etc., neither the author nor Popular Woodworking Books assumes any responsibility for any accidents, injuries, damages or other losses incurred resulting from the material presented in this book.

The authors and editors who compiled this book have tried to make the contents as accurate and correct as possible. Plans, illustrations, photographs and text have been carefully checked. All instructions, plans and projects should be carefully read, studied and understood before beginning construction.

Prices listed for supplies and equipment were current at the time of publication and are subject to change.

Metric Conversion Chart

to convert	to	multiply by
Inches	Centimeters	2.54
Centimeters	Inches	0.4
Feet	Centimeters	30.5
Centimeters	Feet	0.03
Yards	Meters	0.9
Meters	Yards	1.1

The Ultimate Router Guide. Copyright © 2014 by Popular Woodworking. Printed and bound in China. All rights reserved. No part of this book may be reproduced in any form or by any electronic or mechanical means including information storage and retrieval systems without permission in writing from the publisher, except by a reviewer, who may quote brief passages in a review. Published by Popular Woodworking Books, an imprint of F+W, A Content + eCommerce Company, 10151 Carver Rd. Blue Ash, Ohio, 45236. (800) 289-0963 First edition.

Distributed in Canada by Fraser Direct
100 Armstrong Avenue
Georgetown, Ontario L7G 5S4
Canada

Distributed in the U.K. and Europe by F+W Media International, LTD
Brunel House, Ford Close
Newton Abbot
TQ12 4PU, UK
Tel: (+44) 1626 323200
Fax: (+44) 1626 323319
E-mail: enquiries@fwmedia.com

Distributed in Australia by Capricorn Link
P.O. Box 704
Windsor, NSW 2756
Australia

Visit our Web site at www.popularwoodworking.com
or our consumer website at www.shopwoodworking.com
for more woodworking information or projects.

Other fine Popular Woodworking Books are available from your local bookstore or direct from the publisher.

18   17   16   15   14   5   4   3   2   1

Acquisitions editor: David Thiel
Designer: Daniel T. Pessell
Production coordinator: Debbie Thomas

fw
a content + ecommerce company

ABOUT THE AUTHORS

Nick Engler

Nick Engler is the author of dozens of books and articles on woodworking, including one of the longest selling titles *Woodworking Wisdom*. He continues as president of Bookworks, a company specializing in woodworking and how-to books, and is also the director of the Wright Brothers Aeroplane Company, an educational institution teaching and inspiring young people about science, technology, engineering and mathematics.

Glen D. Huey

Glen Huey has been associated with *Popular Woodworking Magazine* for 13 years and now serves as managing editor. In addition to his work as an editor, author, video host and woodworking teacher, Glen is a long-time professional woodworker, who specializes in period reproductions.

Bill Hylton

Bill Hylton is the author of countless articles on woodworking in general, and routers in particular. He is also the author of some of the most respected books on routers including, *Router Magic, Woodworking with the Router*, and the *Ultimate Guide to the Router Table*.

Robert W. Lang

Robert W. Lang is executive editor of *Popular Woodworking Magazine* and was a contributor to *Woodworking Magazine*. A lifetime professional woodworker and noted author of books on Arts & Crafts-style furniture, he also is considered a foremost authority on Google SketchUp and a power user who Google consults regularly.

Gary Rogowski

Gary Rogowski is the author of numerous articles on woodworking, and is the author of *The Complete Illustrated Guide to Joiner* and appears in DVDs and video on woodworking. He is currently the director of, and teaches at the Northwest Woodworking Studio in Portland, Oregon.

Jim Stuard

Jim Stuard is a former editor with *Popular Woodworking Magazine*, and now spends the majority of his time focusing on his new passion of fly-fishing.

Charles Bender

Chuck Bender began his woodworking career making pieces for family and friends in his basement. He studied under Master Werner Duerr and later worked for a number of high-end cabinet shops before starting his own custom furniture business, and later, the woodworking school Acanthus Workshop. He is currently senior editor for *Popular Woodworking Magazine*.

Steve Shanesy

Steve Shanesy was one of the founders of *Woodworking Magazine* and part of *Popular Woodworking Magazine*'s staff for 19 years, serving as editor and publisher during that time. Steve is an avid woodturner and also likes to make contemporary furniture. In his retirement, he's spending as much time as possible in the shop with his son.

Troy Sexton

Troy Sexton wrote numerous articles for *Popular Woodworking Magazine* showcasing his no-nonsense approach to building. If if could be done faster with a power tool, Troy would make it work.

David Thiel

David Thiel was a senior editor with *Popular Woodworking Magazine* for 12 years before moving to our book division. He new serves as editor for the woodworking books and is also responsible for our woodworking video products.

IDEAS · INSTRUCTION · INSPIRATION

These are other great Popular Woodworking products are available at your local bookstore, woodworking store or online supplier.

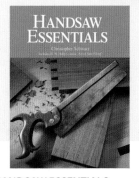

HANDSAW ESSENTIALS
By Christopher Schwarz, plus the editors and contributors to Popular Woodworking

Many woodworkers – from beginners to professionals – are intimidated handsaws, yet once you master their use, there is no other tool in the hand-tool woodworker's kit that is as powerful. In this book you'll learn how to choose the right saw for your budget and project, use it successfully and keep it cutting like new.

Hardcover · 312 pages

BUILDING CLASSIC ARTS & CRAFTS FURNITURE
By Michael Crow

Charles Limbert was one of the leading figures in the Arts & Crafts furniture movement, and also one of the most unique. Now, for the first time, author Michael Crow has carefully detailed 33 of Charles Limbert's finest designs in measured shop drawings so you can build this beautiful furniture yourself.

Paperback · 176 pages

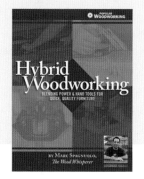

HYBRID WOODWORKING
By Marc Spagnuolo

Known online as The Wood Whisperer, Marc Spaguolo presents a fresh approach to woodworking and furniture making by showing the most efficient ways to utilize both power tools and hand tools in the furniture building process. Not only will you learn which tools are best for which tasks, but you will also find tips for how to use, maintain, and fine tune them.

Paperback · 192 pages

ULTIMATE WORKSHOP SOLUTIONS
By Popular Woodworking Editors

From better clamp storage, to the perfect miter saw stand to benches and beyond, you'll find 35 projects specifically designed to improve and organize your favorite space. These projects have been created by the editors of Popular Woodworking Magazine for your shop, and now we're pleased to share them with you.

Paperback · 192 pages

SUPER-TUNE A HAND PLANE
By Christopher Schwarz

Many woodworkers are looking for a handplane that can be brought back to working life with just a little time and effort — and at a great bargain. This DVD from Christopher Schwarz shows you how to rehab a flea-market find (or soup up a new tool) into a perfectly tuned plane that can handle any task.

Available at Shopwoodworking.com DVD & instant download

BUYING & RESTORING HAND TOOLS
By Ron Herman

Learn how to bring a fine old woodworking tool back to life. Traditional hand-tool expert Ron Herman will help you assess individual tools and shop for the best deal to ensure you're making a smart purchase. Once you have what you know is a quality tool, he'll show you how to restore it to working condition and tune it for maximum performance.

Available at Shopwoodworking.com DVD & instant download

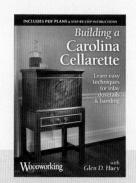

BUILDING A CAROLINA CELLARETTE
By Glen D. Huey

Watch as Glen Huey walks you through the steps to build this elegant, walnut, maple and pine cabinet using a router, a table saw and a few choice hand tools. You;ll learn tips and techniques you can use to speed your work on this and every new project

Available at Shopwoodworking.com DVD & instant download

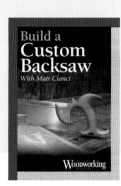

BUILD A CUSTOM BACKSAW
By Matt Cianci

Backsaws should be very personal tools, so building your own custom backsaw will ensure that it fits you and your woodworking needs. By starting with a simple kit including the blade, back and hardware, Matt Cianci walks you through the steps to customize your own saw.

Available at Shopwoodworking.com DVD & instant download

Visit **popularwoodworking.com** to see more woodworking information by the experts, learn about our digital subscription and sign up to receive our free newsletter or blog posts.